D1759148

BANKS, CONSUMERS AND REGUI

Recent developments in law, public policy, and regulation have ensured that questions regarding the relationship between banks and their customers have seldom been out of the spotlight. This important book provides a timely, original, and critical examination of the role of the law in regulating banks in the interests of the consumer. The work examines the social and economic rationales for, and the objectives of banking regulation. In so doing, it focuses on the crucial role of regulation in the protection of the consumer. The book then provides a critical appraisal of the principal techniques by which regulation is delivered and protection ensured. Such techniques include prior approval by licensing, continued supervision, and information remedies such as disclosure. The work also looks at how the law protects depositors of insolvent banks through financial compensation schemes, and how it provides consumer redress through mechanisms for ensuring access to justice, in particular ombudsmen. Finally, the book looks at the topical question of consumer access to banking services, and considers the extent to which the law can justify placing social obligations on banks in the consumer interest. This is the first monograph to examine these important topics in this way.

Banks, Consumers and Regulation

Peter Cartwright
The University of Nottingham

·HART·
PUBLISHING

OXFORD AND PORTLAND OREGON
2004

Published in North America (US and Canada) by
Hart Publishing
c/o International Specialized Book Services
5804 NE Hassalo Street
Portland, Oregon
97213-3644
USA

Hart Publishing is a specialist legal publisher based in Oxford,
England. To order further copies of this book or to request a list of
other publications please write to:

Hart Publishing, Salters Boatyard, Folly Bridge, Abingdon Rd, Oxford, OX1 4LB
Telephone: +44 (0)1865 245533 Fax: +44 (0)1865 794882
email: mail@hartpub.co.uk
WEBSITE: http//:www.hartpub.co.uk

British Library Cataloguing in Publication Data
Data Available

ISBN 1-84113-483-X (paperback)

Typeset by Olympus Infotech Pvt Ltd, India, in Palatino 10/12 pt
Printed and bound in Great Britain by
Lightning Source, UK, Ltd

Contents

Acknowledgements

I have benefited enormously from the help, advice and encouragement of my friends and colleagues in the academic community. First of all I would like to express my deepest thanks to Joanna Gray and Andy Campbell, both of whom read large parts of the manuscript in draft form, and made characteristically helpful and pertinent comments. I would also like to thank others who read draft chapters, namely Jim Devlin, Geraint Howells, Rhoda James, Andrew Leyshon, Eva Lomnicka and Karen Scott. Thanks are also due to all those, too numerous to mention, who answered specific questions that emerged during the writing of the book. I would also like to express my gratitude to the Arts and Humanities Research Board, who provided replacement funding for me as part of its research leave scheme, and the School of Law at the University of Nottingham who provided me with sabbatical leave to work on the project. I delivered a number of conference papers related to aspects of the book, and am particularly grateful to members of the Consumer Law Section of the Society of Legal Scholars, and the Regulation Section of the Socio-Legal Studies Association for their input. The University of Nottingham has proved to be a helpful place in which to pursue research on this topic. I would like, in particular, to thank Christine Ennew of the University's Financial Services Forum, and Andrew Leyshon of the Cultures of Money Research Colloquium, for helping me to broaden my law-based scholarly horizons. Thanks are also due to Richard Hart for his assistance and encouragement, in particular during the latter stages of the work, and to Juliette Challenger for research assistance.

Finally, and as always, I would like to thank Sue, Emma and Joe for all their love, support and encouragement.

1

Banks, Consumers and Regulation: An Introduction

INTRODUCTION

T HE PURPOSE OF this book is to examine the role of the law in regulating banks in the interests of the consumer. This is a subject of enormous importance. The vast majority of households have dealings with banks, and access to banking services is increasingly seen as necessary to participate appropriately in society. It can be argued that there is something 'special' about banking—something that sets it apart from other services. From an economic point of view, this might be located in the nature of fractional reserve banking. As banks do not maintain enough liquid assets to meet their liabilities as they fall due, it is possible for banks to become illiquid very quickly, and this can rapidly turn to insolvency.[1] Provided there is widespread confidence in the banking market, this is unlikely to present major difficulties for those external to the bank. But where that confidence diminishes, the risk of bank failure increases. This may have widespread implications, affecting the continuance of even well-run and well-capitalised institutions. Banks may fail 'not because they are weak but because some depositors think that other depositors think that a collapse is possible'.[2] As part of the financial services industry, banks may also be special from an economic perspective because of the extent to which there is information asymmetry between supplier and consumer. As will be seen shortly, these factors, which can be described as examples of 'market failure', may provide a justification for the regulation considered in this book.

Banks and banking may also be special because of the expectations of the consumer. It is plausible to argue that consumers' relationships with their banks are based upon a degree of trust that is unlikely to exist between consumers and many other suppliers. This may have a number

---

[1] See C Goodhart, *The Central Bank and the Financial System* (Basingstoke, MacMillan, 1995) ch 17.
[2] C Ford and J Kay, 'Why Regulate Financial Services?' in F Oditah (ed), *The Future of the Global Securities Market* (Oxford, Clarendon Press, 1996) 145 at 147.

of implications. First, it may demonstrate that consumers have high expectations of how banks will deal with them, and that where such expectations are not met, consumer detriment is likely to occur. Secondly, it might suggest that it is justifiable to impose high standards upon banks because of those expectations. This might operate in a number of ways, from how bank communications are interpreted by the courts, to whether banks can be expected to provide services on a non-economic basis in the interests of some concept of social justice. But consumer expectations may not only apply to the relationship between bank and consumer, but also to that between bank, consumer and the state, particularly the regulator. There is an increasing recognition of the mismatch between what the law requires of, and what the consumer expects of, the regulatory system. These points, which are developed further below and throughout this book, demonstrate the difficult relationship between banks, consumers and regulation.

BANKS AND BANKING

There is no universally accepted definition of the term 'bank', and the common law has recognised that a comprehensive definition may be impossible to find. In *Woods v Martins Bank Ltd*, Salmon J recognised that the answer to the question 'what is a bank?' will be answered differently at different times and places.[3] Wadsley and Penn conclude that even within the UK 'any general definition would probably be inflexible, or so general as to be meaningless'.[4]

An alternative approach is to try to define what constitutes banking business. Here, the common law provides some guidance. In *United Dominions Trust v Kirkwood*, Lord Denning argued that there were two characteristics found in bankers. The first is that they accept money from, and collect cheques for, their customers and place them to their credit. The second is that they honour cheques or orders drawn on them by their customers when presented for payment and debit their customers accordingly.[5] However, this seems inadequate, with its emphasis on making payments by cheque. Cranston offers some support to the approach of Isaacs J in *Commissioners of the State Savings Bank of Victoria v Permewan, Wright and Co Ltd* Isaacs J argued that the essential characteristics of banking business were: 'the collection of money by receiving deposits upon loan, repayable when and as expressly or impliedly agreed upon, and the

---

[3] [1959] 1 QB 55 at 56.
[4] J Wadsley and G Penn, *The Law Relating to Domestic Banking*, 2nd edn (London, Sweet and Maxwell, 2000) at 92.
[5] [1966] 2 QB 431 at 447.

utilization of the money so collected by lending it again in such sums as are required.'[6] But this could also be seen as unduly restrictive. Cranston argues that where multifunctional banks are concerned, the scope of banking business is elastic.[7] Accepting that a comprehensive definition may be impossible, it is still possible to consider what the 'core' of banking is, and accepting deposits and making loans appear to be at this core. Furthermore, given that the focus of this book is on banks and consumers, it seems appropriate to focus primarily upon this. This is not to suggest that banks do not engage in a variety of other financial services activities when dealing with consumers, for it is clear that they do. Indeed, it will be appropriate at times to make reference to such activities, which raise important issues for our discussion. It should also be noted that building societies should be regarded as falling within the scope of this book. As the Jack Committee recognised, 'the definition of bank today embraces building societies', and since that time the distinction between the two has, perhaps, become even less stark.[8]

CONSUMERS, CUSTOMERS AND INVESTORS

The term 'consumer' can be defined in many different ways. Here, statute does offer some guidance. For example, s 20(6) of the Consumer Protection Act 1987, states that in relation to services or facilities, the term consumer means 'any person who might wish to be provided with the services or facilities otherwise than for the purposes of any business of his'. Furthermore, regulation 2 of the Unfair Terms in Consumer Contracts Regulations 1999 describes a consumer as 'a natural person who, in making a contract to which these Regulations apply, is acting for purposes which are outside his business'. The Distance Marketing Directive applies to contracts with 'consumers', and article 2 of that Directive defines the consumer as 'any natural person who, in distance contracts covered by this Directive is acting for purposes which are outside his trade, business or profession'.[9] These definitions suggest that the consumer is a private individual acting in a private capacity. The party with whom 'the consumer' is dealing must also generally act in the course of a trade

---

[6] (1915) 19 Commonwealth Law Reports 457 at 470. R Cranston, *Principles of Banking Law*, 2nd edn (Oxford, Oxford University Press, 2002) at 4–5. This also reflects the definition of credit institution in Art 1 of the Credit Institutions Directive.
[7] Cranston, *ibid.*
[8] *Banking Services Law and Practice: Report by the Review Committee* (the Jack Report) Cm 622, (1989) para 2.04. The Committee was set up to examine the law relating to the provision of banking services within the UK to personal and business customers.
[9] Directive 2002/65/EC.

or business.[10] This book takes a similar approach, regarding consumers as private individuals, acting in a private capacity in their dealings with banks.

It is possible to envisage a very wide concept of the consumer, which draws on the idea of consumer as citizen.[11] We could even go as far as Ralph Nader, and equate the word 'consumer' with 'citizen'. This has the benefit of enabling us to look beyond the narrow economic function of the consumer, and to consider the individual's wider role in society.[12] There will be some discussion of the respective roles of banks, the state and the consumer in relation to the access debate in chapter eight, and this might be seen primarily to involve questions of citizenship. However, it is submitted that the interpretation of consumer explained above is more fitting for the purposes of this book.

Private bank customers may be viewed as a paradigm of the consumer. However, where individuals are investors (rather than say depositors or borrowers), it could be argued that they play a different role in the economic process from consumers. More particularly, one might argue that investment involves different legal relationships from consumption.[13] It has been stated, for example, that although there are similarities between investors and consumers, investors are part of the apparatus of producers rather than consumers.[14] However, it is submitted that this is too narrow an interpretation of the concept of the consumer. The analogies between investor and consumer have long been recognised. In its 1992 Report, Justice observed that: 'the small investor in the contemporary financial world is not unlike a consumer in the domestic appliance market'.[15] Page and Ferguson go even further by arguing that private investors 'are also consumers – of financial services, namely the services of advisors, brokers, dealers, managers etc'.[16] It is submitted that for our purposes, investors are aptly described as consumers. It should be remembered that the focus of this book is not on 'investment business', as that term is generally understood. However, it is also important to note that where financial services are concerned, the concept of the consumer should not be restricted to its economic definition.

---

[10] For discussion of the meaning of this see R Bragg, *Trade Descriptions* (Oxford, Clarendon Press, 1991) ch 2.

[11] For discussion see I Ramsay, *Consumer Protection: Text and Materials* (London, Weidenfeld and Nicolson, 1989) ch 1 and C Scott and J Black, *Cranston's Consumers and the Law*, 3rd edn, (London, Butterworths, 2000) at 8–11.

[12] See P Cartwright, *Consumer Protection and the Criminal Law* (Cambridge, Cambridge University Press, 2001) at 3–4.

[13] See A Page and R Ferguson, *Investor Protection* (London, Weidenfeld and Nicolson, 1992) at 11.

[14] B Harvey and D Parry, *The Law of Consumer Protection and Fair Trading*, 6th edn (London, Butterworths, 2000) at 8.

[15] Justice, *The Protection of the Small Investor* (London, Justice 1992) at 9.

[16] Page and Ferguson, above n 13 at 14.

REGULATION AND SUPERVISION

The next question is what is meant by 'regulation'? It should first be noted that it is not a term of art and has 'acquired a bewildering variety of meanings'.[17] In the area of financial services we find terms such as 'regulation', 'supervision' and 'monitoring' used almost interchangeably. But it can be argued that their meanings differ. Evans argues that it is convenient to use the term supervision 'for all the work of overseeing financial institutions' and regulation 'for the narrower process of setting rules'.[18] Hadjiemmanuil uses the term regulation to cover 'governmental interventions of a coercive character, regardless of their aims, which determine the outcome or control the operation of a private activity, restricting the free operation of markets'. By contrast, he uses 'supervision' to refer to 'the associated or complementary process of monitoring the behaviour or private parties, especially for the purpose of monitoring compliance with the regulatory requirements'.[19] This book uses the term 'regulation' in a broad sense to refer to intervention in the marketplace to control the activities of banks in the public interest. We are concerned with all the methods by which the banking sector is controlled in the interests of the consumer.[20] As explained below, it therefore looks at a variety of regulatory tools or techniques.

TYPES OF REGULATION

Where regulation which is directed at protecting the consumer is concerned, a distinction can be made between prudential regulation and conduct of business regulation. Prudential regulation is concerned with the solvency, safety and soundness of banks. It can be distinguished from systemic regulation (although similar) in that systemic regulation addresses safety and soundness for the purposes of avoiding systemic risk.[21] Prudential regulation is concerned with safety and soundness in relation to consumer protection, and so can apply even if there is no question of systemic risk.[22] Conduct of business regulation focuses on

---

[17] A Ogus, *Regulation: Legal Form and Economic Theory* (Oxford, Clarendon Press, 1994) at 1. For discussion see eg R Baldwin, C Scott and C Hood, *A Reader on Regulation* (Oxford, Oxford University Press, 1998) introduction; R Baldwin and M Cave, *Understanding Regulation: Theory Strategy and Practice* (Oxford, Oxford University Press, 1999) ch 1.
[18] H Evans, *Plumbers and Architects* (FSA Occasional Paper 4, January 2000) at 10.
[19] C Hadjiemmanuil, *Banking Regulation and the Bank of England* (London, Lloyds of London Press, 1996) at xii.
[20] See the discussion of the techniques of regulation below.
[21] C Goodhart *et al*, *Financial Regulation: Why, How and Where Now?* (London, Routledge, 1998) at 5. See also below and ch 2.
[22] *Ibid.*

how banks conduct business with their customers.[23] Both are relevant to this book.

From an economic point of view, the case for prudential regulation is based upon the idea of information asymmetry. Although the safety and soundness of a bank are important issues for many consumers when deciding whether to deal with the bank, they are unable effectively to ascertain such matters. Consumers lack the knowledge and expertise to make such judgements because they are at a significant informational disadvantage in relation to the bank at the time of entering the contract. Furthermore, the bank's safety and soundness depend upon decisions taken by the bank subsequent to entering the contract, and consumers are unable successfully to monitor the bank's subsequent performance. As Llewellyn puts it, 'no amount of information at the time contracts are signed and purchases made protects against subsequent behaviour of the firm'.[24] Those who fund any deposit protection scheme will also have an interest in prudential regulation, and this is especially so where premiums are not related to the risk posed to the scheme by the bank in question.[25] It is also possible to justify prudential regulation on social grounds. The effect of bank failure is likely to be particularly harmful to less affluent consumers who are likely to have a large proportion of their assets in banks. Distributive justice may therefore demand that we pay attention to the prudential regulation of banks.[26]

As conduct of business regulation is concerned with how banks deal with their customers, it may be seen as the most obvious type of regulation for the protection of the consumer. It is 'designed to establish rules and guidelines about appropriate behaviour and business practices in dealing with customers'.[27] This can be achieved in a variety of ways, such as by imposing disclosure requirements, or requiring advisors to be qualified. The FSA's *Principles for Businesses* require firms (not just banks) to pay due regard to the interests of their customers and to treat them fairly. This is concerned largely with conduct of business. The Financial Services Authority (hereafter FSA) has given indications about what fair treatment might involve, and has mentioned matters such as: refraining from exploiting customers; disclosing material information; honesty openness and transparency; acting in good faith and with integrity, competence and diligence; and meeting legitimate expectations.[28] As chapter five explains,

---

[23] D Llewellyn, *The Economic Rationale for Financial Regulation* (FSA Occasional Paper 1, April 1999) at 10.

[24] *Ibid* at 10.

[25] Goodhart *et al*, above n 21 at 5. See also ch 7.

[26] See chs 2 and 7.

[27] Llewellyn, above n 23 at 11.

[28] See the discussion in A Bradley's 'Speech to the Building Societies' Association Conference' (8 May 2003), available at <http://www:fsa.gov.uk/pubs/speeches/sp130.html> (17/05/04).

a good deal of conduct of business regulation in relation to retail banking is contained in the self-regulatory *Banking Code*.

It is important to note that there is a connection between conduct of business and prudential regulation. Briault argues that in most cases there is no conflict between conduct of business and prudential regulation: 'to a large extent, both seek to mitigate the problems arising from the asymmetry of information between consumers and the providers of financial services'.[29] However, he envisages some circumstances where these conflicts will be apparent, such as where treating consumers fairly and providing them with useful information might threaten a bank's financial soundness. Examples might be where compensating some consumers damages the overall soundness of the firm, or where disclosing adverse information causes consumers to take their business elsewhere.[30] As he concludes, such conflicts are difficult to resolve and, in each case 'a balance has to be struck between the interests of particular groups of consumers'.[31]

REGULATORY OBJECTIVES AND RATIONALES

In chapter two, the book draws a distinction between the rationales for regulation (why we need to regulate), and the objectives of regulation (what we are trying to achieve by regulating). In relation to the former, it considers both economic rationales (such as the need to correct market failure in the form of information asymmetry and systemic risk) and social rationales (in particular distributive justice). The chapter concludes that while an economic approach to regulation which concentrates on correcting market failure is helpful, it is important to recognise that regulation may also be justified on non-economic grounds. In particular, it is suggested that it is reasonable to expect governments, in some cases through the regulatory system, to ensure some degree of social justice. With regard to the objectives of regulation, these are set out in the Financial Services and Markets Act 2000 (hereafter FSMA), those of most relevance to this book being the consumer protection and public awareness objectives. These objectives make it clear that the FSA is charged with securing the appropriate degree of protection for consumers, and that this can be achieved in a variety of ways. The links between consumer protection and public awareness are obvious. For example, the consumer protection

---

[29] C Briault, *Revisiting the Rationale for a Single Financial Services Regulator* (FSA Occasional Paper 16, February 2002) at 18. His discussion should be viewed in the context of arguments about the appropriate form of institutional structure.
[30] *Ibid* at 18–19.
[31] *Ibid*.

objective recognises the needs that consumers have for information and advice, and the public awareness objective involves the provision of appropriate information and advice. There is some concern that FSMA may place too much emphasis on correcting information deficits which, although important, will not necessarily ensure the appropriate degree of protection.[32] It is important to encourage consumers to take responsibility for their actions where they can, and s 5(2)(d) of FSMA requires the FSA to have regard to 'the general principle that consumers should take responsibility for their decisions'. However, it could be argued that this might lead the FSA to pay too little regard to the interests of those consumers who are unable to reach the heights expected of them by economic theory.

TECHNIQUES OF REGULATION

The structure of this book enables us to assess the different techniques by which banking is controlled in the interests of the consumer. Scholarship in the areas of regulation generally, and consumer protection in particular, have emphasised the role of regulation in addressing information deficits, in particular information asymmetry.[33] Indeed, the existence of information asymmetry is one of the principal justifications for intervention in the marketplace.[34] Chapter three examines the role of information in protecting the consumer of banking services. The chapter looks at why unregulated markets may not provide the information that consumers need. It also argues that the provision of information plays a vital role in helping the consumer and, in particular, in helping the consumer to help him or herself. However, it is important to think carefully about two matters: first, what types of information do consumers need, and secondly how can those types of information be provided? In many areas, the response to information deficits has been primarily one of mandatory disclosure, and while this is important, the chapter argues that attention is paid to other ways of correcting information deficits, in particular through improving financial education and public awareness.

The principal regulatory technique that has been used to control banks is prior approval. This involves giving the regulator the power to screen out institutions that fail to meet minimum standards.[35] The FSA has

---

[32] See the discussion of this in ch 3.
[33] See H Davies, '*Why Regulate?*', Henry Thornton Lecture (City University Business School, 4 November 1998); D Llewellyn, above n 23.
[34] See I Ramsay, *Rationales for Intervention in the Consumer Marketplace* (London, OFT, 1984) paras 4.3–4.35.
[35] See Ogus, above n 17, ch 10.

argued that 'vetting at entry aims to allow only firms and individuals who satisfy the necessary criteria (including honesty, competence, and financial soundness) to engage in the regulated activity'. It continues by stating that 'experience in the UK and elsewhere shows that regulatory objectives are more likely to be achieved by setting and enforcing standards for entry, rather than having to deal with major problems later'.[36] Largely because of its position as the most interventionist form of regulation, prior approval has its critics, but it has become a central part of the regulatory landscape for banks. One criticism sometimes levelled at prior approval regimes in general is that they focus upon whether a firm meets the minimum criteria at the time authorisation is granted, but pay little attention to whether those standards continue to be observed.[37] Where banks are concerned, however, a system of continued supervision is in place, ensuring that minimum criteria continue to be observed. The roles of prior approval and continued supervision are fundamental to the regulation of banks in the UK and are examined in chapter four. This chapter examines the regime under FSMA in some detail, and combines this with a critical examination of the use of prior approval.

Although we tend to think of regulation being underpinned by statute, banking is an area where self-regulation has played an important role. Before the establishment of the Financial Ombudsman Service (hereafter, FOS) by FSMA, the banking ombudsman played a central role in providing access to justice for consumers, as well as some role in raising standards within the industry.[38] Now that the ombudsman has been placed on a statutory footing, the principal example of self-regulation is that of the *Banking Code*. The *Code* sets standards of good banking practice for banks to follow when dealing with consumers in the UK. Chapter five looks at the *Code*'s provisions in some detail and provides a critical appraisal both of the *Code* itself, and of self-regulation more generally. The chapter argues that self-regulation suffers from certain inherent characteristics that will always limit its effectiveness as a regulatory technique. However, there is no doubt that the *Banking Code* has brought benefits for consumers, and it is submitted that with some development it can continue to play a significant role in regulating banks in the interests of the consumer.

COMPENSATION AND REDRESS

The previous section has looked at some of the techniques that might be used to regulate banks in the interest of consumers. It is important

---

[36] *Ibid* at 29.
[37] Ogus, above n 17 at 223.
[38] As explained in ch 6, there is some debate about the extent to which ombudsmen should play a part in raising industry standards.

too to think about ways in which consumers might be able to achieve some form of compensation or redress. Chapter six looks at the mechanisms in place to ensure redress when consumers complain about the treatment they receive from their bank. This involves consideration of the role of the private law, and the limitations inherent in obtaining redress through litigation. As the chapter explains, the existence of transaction costs, in particular enforcement costs, means that, if left to regulation through the private law, many wrongs will go uncorrected. One response to this has been the creation of mechanisms for alternative dispute resolution. The most significant of these in the area of banking is the Financial Ombudsman Service (FOS), and chapter six looks closely at the role of the FOS in providing redress for consumers. The chapter supports the view, put forward by a number of commentators, that financial ombudsmen are increasingly seen as the only effective means of redress for consumers when dealing with financial services firms.[39]

Another aspect of redress concerns compensation for consumers where the bank with which they deal becomes insolvent, and this is examined in chapter seven. Deposit protection schemes have become important in protecting consumers from the effects of bank insolvency. From the perspective of consumer protection, they can be justified both on an economic and social basis. It has already been noted that consumers suffer from information asymmetry when dealing with banks, and an important element of this is that they are unable to judge the safety and soundness of a bank, both at the time they enter a contract, and throughout its duration. This can be tackled in number of ways, including through prior approval and supervision, and through disclosure.[40] However, the most appropriate response may be to ensure that should the bank fail, the consumer will receive a degree of compensation. In social terms, deposit protection can be justified on the basis of the significant social harm that consumers would suffer should the bank with which they deal be unable to meet its liabilities to them. This justification is particularly convincing when it is considered that the least affluent and least sophisticated consumers may have placed a particularly high proportion of their assets with banks. The chapter also considers the particular problems raised by moral hazard for deposit protection schemes, and the initiatives taken to limit this.

---

[39] See, eg, E Ferran, 'Dispute Resolution Mechanisms in the UK Financial Sector' (2002) 21 *Civil Justice Quarterly* 135; R James, 'The Application of EC Recommendations on the Principles Applicable to Out of Court Procedures to the New Arrangements for the Settlement of Consumer Complaints in the UK Financial Sector' (1999) *Consumer Law Journal* 443.
[40] See above.

ACCESS, EXCLUSION AND THE LIMITS OF REGULATION

Recent years have seen considerable interest in the topic of financial exclusion, and a large body of literature has charted the rise of such exclusion and the reasons for it.[41] Chapter eight considers the extent to which its is appropriate to place obligations upon banks to address financial exclusion by supplying products that they would not provide under market forces. In 2000 the former Economic Secretary to the Treasury suggested that banks have 'a responsibility to ensure that everyone has access to their services', and there have been calls from other commentators for more attention to be paid to placing social responsibilities on corporations, including banks.[42] Before the details of FSMA were finalised, there were also calls from the House of Commons Treasury Select Committee and the National Consumer Council for more explicit social policy objectives to be included in the FSA's statutory objectives. The latter suggested that reference be made to 'the need for reasonable access to financial services for those who have difficulty in getting access to products appropriate to their needs'.[43] This was rejected, and the FSA's consumer protection objective focuses largely on helping consumers to play the economic role of the utility maximising consumer.[44] The chapter suggests that there have been efforts to address issues of access and exclusion, and that these have taken a wide variety of forms, including encouraging the supply of appropriate products such as basic bank accounts, and encouraging new providers such as credit unions.

[41] For an excellent summary of the literature see Financial Services Authority, *In or Out? Financial Exclusion: A Literature and Research Review* (FSA Consumer Research 3, July 2000).
[42] M Johnson, 'Speech by the Economic Secretary to the Treasury to the Conference on Tackling Financial Exclusion' 12 April 2000, available at <http:www.hmtreasury.gov.uk/newsroom_and_speeches/soeeches/econsecspeeches/speech_est_index.cfm> (17 May 2004). See also T Wilhelmsson 'Services of General Interest and European Private Law' in C Rickett and T Telfer (eds) *International Perspectives on Consumers' Access to Justice* (Cambridge, Cambridge University Press, 2003) 149.
[43] Cited in M Taylor, 'Accountability and Objectives of the FSA' in M Blair *et al, Blackstone's Guide to the Financial Services and Markets Act 2000* (London, Blackstone Press, 2001) 17 at 33.
[44] See ch 3.

2

Banking Regulation:
Rationales and Objectives

INTRODUCTION

T HE FINANCIAL SERVICES industry is one of the most important sectors of the UK economy.[1] It is also one of the economy's most closely regulated areas.[2] Around the globe, the financial services industry, and in particular the banking sector, is seen as somehow special—as different from other industries. It can be argued that these differences justify, at least in part, the extent to which the industry is regulated. The purpose of this chapter is to examine the rationales for, and the objectives of, financial regulation, with particular reference to the regulation of banks. A distinction can be drawn between rationales and objectives.[3] The objectives are the ultimate aims or targets of regulation. The rationales are the reasons why regulation is necessary to achieve the objectives.[4] Rationales can be divided into two principal categories: economic and non-economic/social.[5] The Financial Services and Markets Act 2000 (hereafter FSMA) identifies four objectives of regulation which are examined below.[6] First, it is helpful to say something about the rationales for regulation.[7]

---

[1] Financial services account for around 5.3 per cent of UK GDP, employ around one million people and, in 2002, generated exports of £17.8 billion. (International Financial Services London, see <http://www.ifsl.org.uk/research>).

[2] It has been suggested that it is the most regulated industry in the UK. See G Wood, 'Too Much Regulation?' (2001) 9(4) *Journal of Financial Regulation and Compliance* 350 at 350.

[3] Discussed in D Llewellyn, *The Economic Rationale for Financial Regulation* (FSA Occasional Paper 1, April 1999). Llewellyn suggests a separate category, the reasons for regulation, which are why in practice regulation takes place (at 8).

[4] *Ibid.*

[5] Although, as will become apparent, the distinction is not perfect.

[6] It is possible to identify objectives of regulation in addition to those identified in FSMA, in particular the encouraging of competition.

[7] See Llewellyn, above n 3; H Davies 'Why Regulate?', 'Henry Thornton Lecture (City University Business School, 4 November 1998); C Ford and J Kay, 'Why Regulate Financial Services?' in F Oditah (ed), *The Future of the Global Securities Market* (Oxford, Clarendon Press, 1996) 145; G Benston, *Regulating Financial Markets* (London, Institute of Economic Affairs, 1998).

RATIONALES FOR FINANCIAL REGULATION: ECONOMIC

Economic theory suggests that were the market for banking services to operate perfectly there would be no need for intervention by the state.[8] The perfect market is viewed as an effective method for maximising the welfare of economic actors because of its role in allocating resources efficiently. This 'free market approach' makes certain assumptions about the ways that markets operate. First, it assumes that individuals are rational maximisers of their own utility. This means that individuals (such as consumers) are the best judges of what is in their best interests and can be expected to act rationally, in the sense of acting consistently on the basis of what they believe to be in their best interests.[9] Secondly, it assumes that decisions made in the marketplace, for example purchasing decisions by consumers, influence suppliers. Consumers send signals to the supplier by those purchasing decisions, and a supplier who does not respond to these signals will be forced out of the market. In other words, consumers are seen as sovereign.

The free market approach can be justified on grounds both of efficiency and ideology. In terms of efficiency, traders are under an incentive to compete with each other in order to win custom. In so doing they will improve standards and lower prices. With respect to ideology the free market approach can be supported as championing the rights of individuals to make their own decisions about what is in their best interests, safe in the knowledge that these decisions will be respected. Many of those who support the free market do so on grounds of ideology as much as efficiency.[10]

Although it is widely recognised that markets are frequently imperfect in practice, the theoretical arguments put forward by some free market economists lead them to conclude that regulation is frequently both unnecessary and harmful.[11] In the area of banking, some commentators have championed a system of free, or laissez-faire banking.[12] Free banking can

---

[8] This does not mean that there is no role for the state and law. Laws are necessary to define and protect property rights, and enforce contracts for example. See A Hutchinson, 'Life After Shopping: From Consumers to Citizens' in I Ramsay (ed), *Consumer Law in the Global Economy* (Aldershot, Dartmouth, 1997) 25 at 31; and C Sunstein, *Free Markets and Social Justice* (New York, Oxford University Press, 1997) at 5.

[9] The meaning of rationality in this context has been the subject of fierce debate in recent literature. See, eg, C Jolls, C Sunstein and R Thaler, 'A Behavioural Approach to Law and Economics' (1998) 50 *Stanford Law Review* 1471; and R Posner, 'Rational Choice, Behavioural Economics and the Law' (1998) 50 *Stanford Law Review* 1551.

[10] See C Fried, *Contract as Promise: A Theory of Contractual Obligation* (Cambridge MA, Harvard University Press, 1981); P Atiyah, 'The Liberal Theory of Contract' in P Atiyah, *Essays on Contract* (Oxford, Clarendon Press, 1990) at 121.

[11] G Benston, one of the leading critics of financial regulation argued that 'with the exception of deposit insurance, most regulations [relating to financial services] are not useful except for those who benefit from constraints on competition' (1987) *Economic Affairs* at 8–9.

[12] See K Dowd, *Laissez-faire Banking* (London, Routledge, 1993); Benston, above n 7.

be used to describe a system where banks enter the market without having to obtain prior authorisation, and operate with few governmental restrictions. Such a system was present in Scotland from 1716 to 1844, and is sometimes held up as a model of efficiency and innovation.[13] Some present day commentators support free banking, challenging the prevalent orthodoxy about the need for regulation to protect consumers and avoid systemic risk.[14] However, as will become apparent, the fear of the potential consequences of free banking has led to the creation of systems of financial regulation in all major economies.

In the perfect market certain factors are present.[15] First, there are numerous suppliers and consumers, such that no one can influence the price of goods and services. Although there is fierce competition in some areas of banking provision, the lack of competition in other areas is apparent.[16] Secondly, there is free entry into, and free exit from the market. Neither of these is present in the case of banking. Barriers to entry are erected in the form of prior approval requirements under statutes such as FSMA, which provide that to be authorised, firms must meet certain minimum criteria.[17] Although such regulation can have an anti-competitive effect, and runs counter to free market theory, there are strong arguments in its favour.[18]

Barriers to exit are also present in the form of lender of last resort provision. Central banks frequently operate a lender of last resort facility where they provide emergency lending to banks facing illiquidity, or even insolvency.[19] Deposit protection schemes provide a guaranteed payout to depositors in the event of a bank becoming insolvent. Although in the case of explicit deposit protection schemes the firm still exits the market, it does not bear fully the cost of that exit. Furthermore, governments may decide to step in to bail out a failing bank for social or political reasons, or to maintain confidence in the financial system.[20] This raises the spectre

---

[13] R Cameron (ed) *Banking and Economic Development: Some Lessons of History* (New York, Oxford University Press, 1972).

[14] See for example, Dowd, above n 12; Benston above n 7.

[15] See I Ramsay, *Rationales for Intervention in the Consumer Marketplace* (London, OFT, 1984) at 15–16.

[16] See HM Treasury, *Competition in UK Banking: A Report to the Chancellor of the Exchequer* (the Cruickshank Report) (20 March 2000), which drew particular attention to the lack of competition in the provision of services for small businesses.

[17] See ch 4.

[18] Financial Services Authority, *A New Regulator for the New Millennium* (FSA, January 2000) para 50. See also the discussion in ch 4.

[19] In the classical model of lender of last resort, loans should only be made to illiquid and not insolvent banks. However, it has been pointed out that the distinction is frequently difficult to make. See C Goodhart, 'Bank Insolvency and Deposit Insurance: A Proposal' in C Goodhart, *The Central Bank and the Financial System* (Basingstoke, MacMillan Press, 1995) at 80–82.

[20] Although the FSA has made it clear that failing banks should not expect to be bailed out, the need to maintain confidence in the financial system will mean that this will sometimes occur. See Financial Services Authority, *Reasonable Expectations: Regulation in a Non-Zero Failure World* (FSA, September 2003).

that large banks are 'too big to fail', and will always be saved should they face severe financial difficulties.[21] Thirdly in the perfect market there is product homogeneity. This means that in each market essentially the same product is sold, thus avoiding monopolies. In reality, there is product differentiation, and while this is to be welcomed as an appropriate response by banks to the demands of consumers, there is a risk of artificial product differentiation. Here, the consumer may be persuaded through advertising to concentrate on apparent differences between products to the detriment of making an informed choice.[22] Next, in the perfect market there is perfect information about the nature and values of commodities traded, and finally, there are no third party effects, or externalities. The chief ways in which markets for banking, and financial services in general, fall short of the ideal are through information asymmetries and externalities. These will now be examined in more detail.[23]

Imperfect and Asymmetrical Information

A distinction can be drawn between imperfect information (knowing less than the ideal) and information asymmetry (knowing less than another person). Scholarship on financial regulation has tended to emphasise information asymmetry as a key economic rationale for regulation.[24] Davies, for example, identifies two elements of information asymmetry in financial markets: complexity of contracts and difficulties in judging the financial soundness of firms.[25]

In relation to the first point, it is frequently difficult for consumers to obtain the information they need to make informed choices in the marketplace. These issues are examined in more detail in chapter three, but it is helpful to outline them here. These difficulties are particularly apparent where some financial products are concerned.[26] First, some financial products are credence goods, which means that some of their essential characteristics, such as the effects of their use, will only be known far in the future.[27] Disclosure at the time the contract is entered into can do little

---

[21] Some regulators have explicitly accepted this. See Goodhart, above n 19 at 76.
[22] I Ramsay, *Advertising, Culture and the Law: Beyond Lies, Ignorance and Manipulation* (London, Sweet and Maxwell, 1996) at 31–32.
[23] For a helpful description see Davies, 'Why Regulate?' above n 7.
[24] See also Goodhart, above n 19 at 454.
[25] Davies, 'Why Regulate?' above n 7.
[26] But see Benston who argues that information asymmetry is greater in many other sectors of the economy. Benston, above n 7 at 56–63.
[27] MR Darby and E Karni, 'Free Competition and the Optimal Amount of Fraud' (1973) 16 *Journal of Law and Economics* 67. See also D Simpson, *Regulating Pensions: Too Many Rules, Too Little Competition* (Institute of Economic Affairs, 1996). This is perhaps more true of products such as pensions and other long-term investments than more traditional banking products.

about the subsequent behaviour of firms and the long-term performance of a financial product. Secondly, there may be incentives upon suppliers not to give the customer a full picture of the characteristics of a product. This may be because the consumer is dealing with a seller acting on commission, because the information is seen as too complex or too vague to influence the consumer, or even because an honest appraisal would put the supplier's product in an unfavourable light.[28] Competitors might appear to be under an incentive to draw the shortcomings of a product to the attention of a potential customer, but may choose not to for fear of reprisals or even fear of reducing the overall demand for that category of product.[29] In markets such as financial services where consumer confidence is so important, the fear of putting consumers off a type of product altogether may be particularly strong. Although one might expect third parties to emerge who meet consumers' demands for objective information, and to an extent this has happened, they may be under insufficient incentives to fulfil this role. This is largely because information has the characteristics of public goods, and so it is possible to benefit from its supply without having to pay the full cost of that supply.[30] A further difficulty is that consumers may not know which questions to ask in order to find information which would benefit them. Even where accurate information is supplied to consumers there is the problem that consumers suffer from bounded rationality. This means that their ability to deal with complex information is limited.[31] Many financial products are complex, and need a degree of expertise to be fully understood. As suppliers are aware of consumers' cognitive limitations this will influence their decision about what information to supply. In particular, they may choose to focus on particular characteristics, eg price, at the expense of equally valuable but less quantifiable characteristics such as quality.[32] Where a market begins to focus on a particular characteristic, in other words where there is focal point competition, consumers may get a misleading picture of the product in question.[33]

The second element of information asymmetry identified by Davies is the difficulty in assessing the financial soundness of firms. Consumers are interested not only in the characteristics of the product on offer, but also

---

[28] Office of Fair Trading, *Consumer Detriment Under Conditions of Imperfect Information* (OFT Research Paper 11, prepared by London Economics, August 1997) at 39.

[29] *Ibid* at 38.

[30] A Ogus, *Regulation: Legal Form and Economic Theory* (Oxford, Clarendon Press, 1994) at 33–35.

[31] H Simon, *Administrative Behaviour: A Study of Decision-making Processes in Administrative Organization* (New York, MacMillan 1957).

[32] See G Akerlof, 'The Market for Lemons: Qualitative Uncertainty and the Market Mechanism' (1970) 84 *Quarterly Journal of Economics* 488.

[33] See Office of Fair Trading, above n 28. These issues are examined in more detail in Ch 3.

in the soundness of the institution offering that product. However, consumers have neither the time nor the expertise to judge the soundness of the institution with which they are proposing to contract.[34] To do so they would need access to qualitative and quantitative information which, even if they could obtain it, they would be unlikely to be able to process and act upon in any appropriate manner. Although some regulatory regimes, such as that in New Zealand, have attempted to encourage consumers to make judgements about the safety of financial institutions the success of such initiatives seems likely to be limited.[35] As Cranston observes, unsophisticated depositors in particular cannot be expected to be vigilant.[36] In short, the inadequacy of the market in providing perfect information is one of the prime justifications for regulating financial services.

Externalities

The main externality, or third party effect, presented by financial markets is that of systemic risk.[37] Systemic risk is the risk that the failure of a financial institution will lead to the domino-like failure of other institutions and even the collapse of the financial system itself. Banks are generally said to be particularly susceptible to systemic risk for a number of reasons.[38] However, it is far from clear that other financial intermediaries present the same levels of systemic risk, or indeed any risk at all. This is examined in more detail below under the market confidence objective.

The existence of market failure should not automatically lead to the conclusion that regulation is necessary. Regulation is costly—in some cases more costly than the failure it seeks to correct.[39] It is customary now to undertake some form of cost–benefit analysis before the introduction of new regulation.[40] On a purely economic basis, it could be argued that

---

[34] See D Llewellyn, *The Economic Rationale for Financial Regulation* (FSA Occasional Paper 1, April 1999) at 18.

[35] See D Mayes, *A More Market Based Approach to Maintaining Systemic Stability* (FSA Occasional Paper 10, August 2000) at 36.

[36] R Cranston, *Principles of Banking Law*, 2nd edn (Oxford, Oxford University Press, 2002) at 78–79.

[37] See EP Davis, *Debt Financial Fragility and Systemic Risk* (Oxford, Clarendon Press, 1992); many leading economic works are collected in C Goodhart and G Illing, *Financial Crises, Contagion and the Lender of Last Resort* (Oxford, Oxford University Press, 2002). Externalities are also sometimes known as spillovers.

[38] See below.

[39] See Goodhart, above n 19 at 440.

[40] In discharging its functions, the FSA is obliged, under s 2(3) of FSMA to use its resources in the most efficient and economic way, and to ensure that any burdens or restrictions are proportionate to the benefits that result from them.

regulation is appropriate where it is addresses market failure cost effectively.[41] However, this assumes that there are only economic rationales for regulation. There may, in addition, be non-economic, or social rationales for financial regulation. These are now considered.

RATIONALES FOR FINANCIAL REGULATION: SOCIAL

There are rationales for intervening in financial markets which are not primarily justified on economic grounds, although in some cases their effect may be to improve the functioning of the market.[42] These may be described as ethical, non-economic, social or public interest rationales.[43] The prime examples of such rationales for regulation are paternalism, distributive justice and community values.[44] Although as rationales they may be contextually distinct, in practice many regulatory provisions can be explained and justified on more than one basis.[45]

Paternalism

First, regulation can be justified on paternalistic grounds. In its strictest sense, paternalism concerns intervention on behalf of a person, in the interests of, but regardless of the wishes of, that person.[46] This is at odds with market-based regulation, which is concerned to reflect the wishes of individuals and enable them to give effect to those wishes. Paternalism in this strict sense removes choice from the individual and replaces it with the choice of the state. This is anathema to those who believe that individual decision-making should be at the heart of the supplier–consumer relationship.

[41] See the discussion in Ramsay, above n 15 paras 3.17–3.24.
[42] See I Ramsay and T Williams, 'Racial and Gender Equality in Markets for Financial Services' in P Cartwright (ed), *Consumer Protection in Financial Services* (London, Kluwer, 1999). Indeed, it should be recognised that the distinction between economic and social rationales is imperfect. See I Ramsay, 'Consumer Credit Law, Distributive Justice and the Welfare State' (1995) 15 *Oxford Journal of Legal Studies* 177.
[43] Ramsay refers to 'ethical goals', in I Ramsay, *Consumer Protection: Text and Materials* (London, Weidenfeld and Nicolson, 1989) at 47, Prosser to 'public interest' rationales T Prosser, 'Regulation, Markets and Legitimacy' in J Jowell and D Oliver (eds) *The Changing Constitution* 4th edn, (Oxford, Oxford University Press, 2000) at 229, and Ogus to 'non-economic justifications for intervention' (above n 30 at 46). The term 'social rationales' will be used here.
[44] See Ogus, above n 30; also ch 3.
[45] For example, consumer compensation schemes, in particular depositor protection schemes, can be seen as paternalistic, distributive, based upon community values, a response to information asymmetry or a response to systemic risk. See ch 5.
[46] G Dworkin, 'Paternalism' in R Wasserstrom (ed), *Morality and the Law* (Belmont, Wadsworth, 1971) at 108.

A principal difficulty with describing a provision as paternalistic is that most apparently paternalistic laws can be justified on other grounds. For example, the deposit protection sub-scheme of the Financial Services Compensation Scheme may be described as paternalistic to the extent that it provides a payout to depositors in the event of a bank becoming insolvent, regardless of the wishes of the depositor.[47] However, such schemes can also be justified as a way of avoiding externalities (namely systemic risk), and addressing information asymmetry (banks are far better placed than consumers to identify the risk that they might become insolvent). Viewed in this way, the scheme has an important role in correcting market failure. It may be that the prime justification of such schemes is paternalistic, but there are additional justifications for this form of regulation. Such schemes are examined in more detail in chapter seven.

Another difficulty with the notion of paternalism is that the strict interpretation of the doctrine concerns decisions made *regardless* of the wishes of the individual. However, it is possible to argue that individuals may want to be protected from their own mistakes. If consumers consent to others' making decisions on their behalf because they realise their own limitations, then decisions taken by those others may be consistent with free choice. This 'rational paternalism' has attractions, not least because it seeks to match the pragmatism of public decision-making with the ideology of private choice.[48] Howells has some sympathy for this approach, calling for 'a certain humility about one's own abilities to look after one's own interests'.[49] In practice, it seems reasonable to assume that many consumers are willing to forego the right to make decisions in all aspects of their lives in order for experts to make judgements about what level of choice and/or protection they should have. Goldring argues that consumers must 'surrender a degree of their power to make decisions and choices—a power which in this context is often meaningless—to the state'.[50] Indeed, it seems likely that if consumers were asked about the level of protection they would like, they would frequently demand more regulation rather than less.[51] As Ramsay has recently noted:

> it is often very difficult to distinguish between situations where governments are responding to problems that prevent individuals from reaching a

---

[47] They are classified as paternalistic by A Page and R Ferguson. See *Investor Protection* (London, Butterworths, 2002) at 38.
[48] B Barry, *Political Argument* (New York, Humanities Press, 1965) at 226–27.
[49] G Howells, *Consumer Product Safety* (Aldershot, Ashgate, 1998) at 17.
[50] J Goldring, 'Consumer Law and Legal Theory: Reflections of a Common Lawyer' (1990) 13 *Journal of Consumer Policy* 113 at 129.
[51] This may be based on the mistaken assumption that regulation is free. See Benston, above n 7 at 62, and the discussion in ch 4 of this book.

rational judgment and those where government is overruling preferences and substituting its own judgment.[52]

In some cases there will be a conflict between the wishes of the majority (for example, for regulation) and the minority (for no regulation). In the perfect market, those consumers who want extra protection will be willing and able to pay for it, and there will be a choice of products to reflect consumers' various wishes. In practice it may be better to have a single standard that reflects the wishes of the majority. Consumers may find it difficult to judge the protection offered by different products, and the transaction costs of having different schemes might be prohibitive. In the words of Ogus: 'paternalist regulation ... has to proceed by applying *uniform* controls on certain activities where it is assumed that many individuals make unwise decisions'.[53] Although this may result in those consumers who are able to make an informed choice being denied that choice, it can be justified on the basis of the need to protect those who are not so able, and also on grounds of efficiency.

A further point is that it is far from clear that paternalism is an improper ground for intervention. Perhaps individual choice should not always be at the heart of decision-making. The notion of choice within the free market model is based on the idea of the rational consumer, and, even allowing that there are different conceptions of what rationality means in this context, there is ample evidence that consumers make choices that they are liable to consider inappropriate shortly afterwards. Jackson claims, for example, that decision-making is systematically biased in favour of present consumption.[54] Sunstein argues that people's choices are 'a function of the distinctive social role in which they find themselves', and that they frequently act irrationally or 'quasi-rationally'.[55] Rather than consider only the consumer's wishes at the time of the transaction, perhaps the law should allow some flexibility, for example by providing a mandatory cooling-off period. This allows a consumer a period in which to cancel a contract that would otherwise have been binding. This guards against pressure selling, and allows consumers to gather more information about a transaction.[56] Alternatively, we might argue that consumers are simply liable to make irrational decisions in certain

---

[52] I Ramsay, 'Consumer Redress and Access to Justice' in C Rickett and T Telfer (eds), *International Perspectives on Consumers' Access to Justice* (Cambridge, Cambridge University Press, 2003) 21.
[53] Ogus, above n 30 at 53.
[54] TH Jackson, 'The Fresh Start Policy in Bankruptcy Law' (1984–85) *Harvard Law Review* 1393 at 1405, cited in Ramsay, above n 43 at 54.
[55] C Sunstein, *Free Markets and Social Justice* (New York, Oxford University Press, 1997) at 7.
[56] Ramsay, above n 43 at 337–40.

contexts and remove from them the capacity to make those decisions.[57] Although we might not wish to go this far in most areas of economic activity, it may be justified where the result of an incorrect decision can be particularly harmful.[58] In some cases, the experts may simply know better.

Distributive Justice

The free market emphasises the importance of corrective justice. Under corrective justice, where there is breach of a specific legal wrong, such as breach of contract, there will be a remedy to rectify that.[59] Distributive justice concerns the idea of distributing resources (including rights) on the basis of what is fair rather than what is merely economically efficient.[60] The simplest example of distributive justice is the tax and benefits system.[61] However, regulation can also be used to achieve distributive ends. If we seek to justify regulation on the grounds of distributive justice we are doing so because we believe it appropriate that the regulatory system should seek to provide particular benefits to particular groups, such as consumers in general, the poor, or the vulnerable.[62]

There is a close relationship between measures that can be described as distributive, and those that can be described as paternalistic. When provisions are introduced to help a particular group, it is doubtful to what extent the instigator of such provisions will have rationalised the reason for them as paternalistic, distributive, or indeed, market-correcting. It is far more likely that the provisions will have been introduced with some vague notion of providing appropriate protection.[63] It is, therefore, important not to think of specific laws as *merely* paternalistic, distributive, market-correcting etc. Frequently they can be explained on a number of

---

[57] The Crowther Committee argued that 'there is a level of cost above which it becomes socially harmful to make loans available at all, even if the cost is not disproportionate to the risk and expense incurred by the lender' (*Report of the Committee on Consumer Credit*, Cmnd 4596, 1971) para 6.6.6.

[58] Goodhart, above n 19 at 455; Ogus, above n 30 at 51–53.

[59] P Cartwright, *Consumer Protection and the Criminal Law* (Cambridge, Cambridge University Press, 2001) p 28; Ramsay, above n 43 at 57.

[60] See Ramsay, 'Consumer Credit Law' above n 42, and T Wilhelmsson, 'Consumer Law and Social Justice' in I Ramsay (ed), *Consumer Law in the Global Economy* (Aldershot, Dartmouth, 1992); Ogus, above n 30, ch 3.

[61] Some commentators see this as the most effective method of securing appropriate redistribution. See J Rawls, *A Theory of Justice* (Oxford, Oxford University Press, 1971).

[62] See Ogus, above n 30 at 47–52. In practice, most ideological positions recognise that free markets may not lead to fair outcomes. But see also R Nozick, *Anarchy, State and Utopia* (Oxford, Blackwell, 1974).

[63] Ramsay notes the lack of rigour with which legislative action is sometimes taken in the consumer protection area. See Ramsay, above n 43 at 274.

different bases. This is an important point, and one that will be returned to later.

Distributive justice appears relatively easy to justify on ideological grounds. It concerns making decisions on the basis of fairness, recognising that it is appropriate and desirable to help those who need it most. It may be helpful to think of ways in which provisions can be described as distributive, and to consider practical examples of laws that have these characters. However, a couple of points need to be emphasised. First, as already stated, the provisions considered below can be explained on other grounds as well as on the basis of distributive justice. Secondly, the discussion below is intended to contain an illustrative, rather than an exhaustive list of types of distributive measure, with attention being focused on measures aimed at protecting the consumer in the context of banking business.

First, a provision might be described as distributive if it gives consumers a right to have a contract set aside on the grounds of its being in some way substantively unfair. For example, a law which allows a consumer to have a contract set aside on the basis that its terms are extortionate can be seen as premised on distributive justice.[64] Secondly, a provision may be distributive because it gives protection to certain consumers on the basis of a change of circumstances. For example, social *force majeure* clauses in Nordic law provide protection for those consumers who, through not fault of their own, find themselves unable to meet their liabilities.[65] Thirdly, there are provisions such as credit ceilings, which regulate terms such as prices in advance in order to protect certain consumers. Fourthly, there are provisions that allow consumers to extricate themselves from a contract that they decide, in retrospect, that they should not have signed. An example would be a cooling-off period in s 68 of the Consumer Credit Act 1974 (hereafter CCA).

In addition to the examples given above, there may be provisions that prevent banks from making business decisions that are deemed to have a damaging social impact. An example would be a provision forbidding a bank from closing a branch in a poor area. Although such laws do not exist in the UK there is evidence that some governmental pressure has been applied to banks not to close branches.[66] Finally, there are provisions that require banks to offer products which are believed to have a positive distributive effect, for example basic bank accounts. The last two examples

---

[64] See for example ss 137–40 of the Consumer Credit Act 1974. Other examples are the good faith provision of the Unfair Terms in Consumer Contracts Regulations 1999 and the law of unconscionability.
[65] See T Wilhelmsson, '"Social Force Majeure"—A New Concept in Nordic Consumer Law' (1990) 13 *Journal of Consumer Policy* 1.
[66] See ch 8.

are unlikely to be enshrined in legislation, but are included as they can be seen as useful illustrations of how the government may seek to achieve distributive results without resorting to the law.

There are several difficulties with those provisions that might be categorised as distributive. It seems reasonable to assume that a rationale for the above measures is to ensure a desirable redistribution from one group to another, principally from trader to consumer. However, if we examine the provisions more closely, we can see that the distributive effects of such measures may be more complex than that. This results largely from the response to such measures that are likely to come from the supplier. First, the extortionate credit bargain provisions in the CCA allow the court to re-open a credit agreement so as to do justice between the parties on the basis of that agreement's being extortionate.[67] If the court does that, there is an immediate redistribution from trader to consumer. Although this provides a socially desirable outcome from the perspective of the individual consumer, the trader's loss will fall somewhere, presumably largely on other consumers. In the cases of those lending at a rate found to be extortionate, that is likely to mean other poor consumers. This is liable to raise the trader's prices yet further. In the case of a trader lending at an unquestionably extortionate rate, one should have little sympathy for the trader. Indeed, one would hope that such traders would be obliged to refine their terms or exit the market. However, it is possible to argue that the courts will not be well placed to judge the bigger picture and take account of all the facts of the case.[68]

In the case of suppliers who are subject to social *force majeure* one is likely to have more sympathy, as there is no prior fault on their part. In practice of course, one can expect the existence of social *force majeure* clauses to be factored into the cost of credit, with those borrowers who stay healthy and in employment subsidising those who do not. The provision acts as a kind of insurance policy in the event of misfortune. There may be good social reasons for this, but it is important to appreciate the effect it has.[69]

If we examine the third category of distributive justice we will see that further difficulties may emerge. Credit ceilings limit the level of interest that a lender may charge a borrower. At first glance, they may appear a simple and effective method of combating exorbitant interest rates: it is easy to identify when a trader is in breach, and they are relatively easy to enforce. Indeed, they have some prominent supporters. Howells has argued in

---

[67] See further ch 6.
[68] See Ramsay, above n 43 at 348.
[69] It could be judged, for example, against private insurance, where a judgment could be made about the risk of an individual defaulting and premiums charged accordingly.

favour of a presumptive ceiling, and Ziegel has also championed their use.[70] In Ziegel's opinion, 'a ceiling serves a double function: it protects the unsophisticated and vulnerable borrower against exploitation and it encourages the lender to adopt more prudent credit standards'.[71] However, it has been argued that credit ceilings are both ineffective and degenerative. In a seminal article on the topic, Cayne and Trebilcock identify the following problems.[72] First, if the ceiling is set above the market rate, rates will be set by the market and not the ceiling. Secondly, if the ceiling is set below market rates credit will be removed from the market place. Thirdly, even if the ceiling is set at the market rate, that rate might become inappropriate very quickly. In addition, as the market may be made up of different types of creditor dealing with different types of consumer, it might be necessary to set a variety of limits depending on the nature of the business.[73] Furthermore, in a perfectly competitive market it could be argued that the ceiling would be unnecessary. Sunstein has similar reservations about distributive measures, and argues that 'the group particularly disadvantaged by the regulation will typically consist of those who are already most disadvantaged'.[74] In practice, it could be argued, the effect of credit ceilings will be to remove credit from those who are least likely to have a choice of lender, and to replace it with a black market for credit.

There are undoubtedly strengths to the arguments of Cayne and Trebilcock. If lenders cannot charge a rate which truly reflects the degree of risk posed by the borrower because it is above the limit allowed, they will not charge an amount below the limit; they will simply refuse to lend.[75] There is an argument that this is the very outcome that the law should support. The Crowther Committee, for example, argued that 'there is a level of cost above which it becomes socially harmful to make loans available at all, even if the cost is not disproportionate to the risk and expense incurred by the lender'.[76] To the extent that this is the rationale for intervention, it is submitted that it is perhaps more paternalistic

[70] G Howells, 'Seeking Social Justice for Poor Consumers in Credit Markets' in I Ramsay (ed), *Consumer Law in the Global Economy* above n 60 at 257.

[71] J Ziegel's brief to the Canadian Senate Committee on Poverty, cited in D Cayne and M Trebilcock, 'Market Considerations in the Formulation of Consumer Protection Policy' (1973) *University of Toronto Law Review* 396 at 411.

[72] Cayne and Trebilcock, *ibid*. Ramsay classifies credit ceilings as distributive, above n 43 at 51.

[73] *Ibid* at 414–18.

[74] Sunstein, above n 55 at 283.

[75] The same logic can be applied in other areas where terms are mandatory. See for example A Schwartz, 'A Re-examination of Non-substantive Unconscionability' (1977) 63 *Virginia Law Review* 1053.

[76] *Report of the Committee on Consumer Credit* (the Crowther Committee) (Cmnd 4596, 1971) para 6.6.6. The Committee concluded the interest rate ceilings were too problematic and did not recommend their inclusion in the Consumer Credit Act 1974.

than distributive. Credit ceilings do not involve redistribution to the borrower, except to the extent that loans made above the ceiling will be unenforceable. Perhaps the main weakness to the arguments of Cayne and Trebilcock is in the confidence they place in the potential to create workable competition. The authors argue that 'disclosure laws can be an effective means of protecting the poor...because they enhance the operation of free market forces'.[77] However, they recognise the limitations of disclosure. In particular 'they can only be of value if the consumer is intellectually and psychologically equipped to apply the information which disclosure regulation entitles him to have'.[78] The authors therefore recognise the limitations in relying on individual choice effected through the market mechanism. This demonstrates again the difficulty in relying upon the ability of consumers to act rationally and control markets accordingly.[79] It is submitted that credit ceilings may be useful as a method of controlling extortionate credit, alongside other discretionary controls.

The fourth type of distributive provision identified is one that allows the consumer to get out of a contract within a given time. An example is found in s 68 of the Consumer Credit Act 1974, under which consumers receive a cooling off period where oral representations are made in the presence of the debtor and the agreement is signed off trade premises. Here, a significant theoretical benefit is provided to the consumer. It has been argued that '[a]s a matter of policy it is desirable to allow consumers some time for reflection with major credit agreements because of their onerous and complex nature'.[80] However, it is unclear in practice to what extent consumers avail themselves of this. Again, the distributive nature of the provision is apparent. The trader bears the loss if the contract is avoided, the cost of course being passed on. It is likely to be the most vulnerable consumers who are in need of such a remedy, but such consumers would appear unlikely to take advantage of the provision. Cooling-off periods can be justified on the basis of the risk of consumers' making rash purchases, perhaps because of high-pressure sales techniques or inadequate information. However, there is no need to prove either of these before the remedy can be utilised.

One criticism of distributive measures is that they may bring uncertainty and therefore make it harder to construct markets.[81] This will be particularly so in relation to 'open texture' rules such as the extortionate credit bargain provisions considered above, because of the wide discretion

---

[77] Cayne and Trebilcock, above n 71 at 424
[78] *Ibid.* See also ch 3.
[79] See the discussion in Ramsay, above n 43 at 346–48.
[80] Cranston, above n 36 at 247–48.
[81] See H Collins, *Regulating Contracts* (Oxford, Oxford University Press, 1999) ch 11.

that they give the courts to interfere with the original contract. However, although there may be a risk of indeterminacy in some cases, there is widespread support for allowing the courts to challenge substantive unfairness, particularly where the applicant is a member of a vulnerable group. Kennedy suggests that there is 'real value, as well as an element of real nobility in the judicial decision to throw out, every time the opportunity arises, consumer contracts designed to perpetuate the exploitation of the poorest class of buyers on credit.'[82] It is by no means clear that the business community would expect the law to honour the terms of a contract no matter how unfair. Indeed, Collins goes as far as to argue that businesses would expect the law to allow contracts to be challenged on grounds of fairness, at least to some extent:

> general clauses such as good faith and reasonableness enable regulation to achieve results in accordance with expectations regarding the validity of clauses in contracts. A rigid rule that prevents such interventions would in fact come as a surprise to most commercial parties, who would expect the legal system to decline to enforce terms in the planning documents that impose extremely harsh bargains.[83]

The final examples in which distributive justice is seen in relation to the banking industry are closely related. Banks can either be forbidden from removing services from certain groups because of the distributive consequences, or required to supply services to groups because of the distributive benefits. What links these is that the bank is unable to act upon its commercial judgement about which services or products to offer. In the UK, there is currently no legal restriction on a bank's ability to close branches, nor is there any legal obligation to provide cheap products such as basic bank accounts. Indeed, when the Treasury Task Force on Access to Financial Services reported, it stated that its vision of financial inclusion was subjected to three broad principles: non-compulsion, going with the grain of markets, and cost-effective use of public funds. An important element of this is that 'banks' selection of which sections of the market to serve should be left to their commercial judgement'.[84] However, it has been argued that there is a divergence of views between some of the Government's other rhetoric about banks' social responsibilities, and the views of many within the banking industry.[85] Certainly there seems to be

---

[82] D Kennedy, 'Form and Substance in Private Law Adjudication' (1976) 89 *Harvard Law Review* 1685 at 1777.

[83] Collins, above n 81 at 271.

[84] HM Treasury Policy Action Team 14 (16 November 1999) para 4.2.

[85] In April 2000 Melanie Johnson referred to the banks having a responsibility to ensure that 'everyone has access to their services'. See M Johnson, 'Speech by the Economic Secretary to the Treasury to the Conference on Tackling Financial Exclusion' 12 April 2000, available at

evidence that the Government is prepared to put pressure upon banks to ensure a degree of distributive justice by making products and services available which they would frequently not offer on purely economic grounds.[86] Whether this is appropriate depends on the view taken of the appropriate division of responsibility between the State and private industry. It has long been recognised that the notion of laissez-faire, where the State keeps out of transactions between individuals, is a myth. Sunstein describes the notion of laissez-faire as 'a grotesque misdescription of what free markets actually require and entail'.[87] The market operates within the restrictions imposed by law, and any idea that there is some sort of natural state of the market where law and state are absent is fanciful.[88] The question of the appropriate division between business and state of powers and responsibilities is, however, highly relevant. These issues are considered in more detail in chapter eight.

When discussions were taking place about the scope of consumer protection in the statutory objectives in FSMA, there was some support for more explicit social objectives to be included. In particular, the House of Commons Treasury Select Committee felt that some reference should be made to social justice matters, and the National Consumer Council suggested that reference be made to 'the need for reasonable access to financial services for those who have difficulty in getting access to products appropriate to their needs'.[89] Certainly, there has been a lively debate about the extent to which it is appropriate for financial institutions, in particular banks, to act for social rather than profit-maximising purposes.

Distributive Justice, Public Awareness and Information Deficits

One way in which the FSA has to have regard to matters of distributive justice is through the public awareness objective. The FSA has stated that a key element of the public awareness objective is promoting a higher level of general financial literacy. There is an economic element to this, in that consumers will be better able to play the part of the utility-maximising consumer if they are more financially literate. The Cruickshank Report

---

<http:www.hm-treasury.gov.uk/newsroom_and_speeches/speeches/econsecspeeches/speech_est_index.cfm> (17 May 2004). A former Director General of the British Bankers' Association complained at the time that there was 'no shared language or shared view of the world' between the Government and the banks. T Sweeney, 'The Death of Banking' (26 March 2001) available at <http://www.bba.org.uk>. This is discussed in more detail in ch 8.

[86] *Ibid*.
[87] Sunstein, above n 55 at 5.
[88] See eg Ramsay, above n 60.
[89] Cited in M Taylor 'Accountability and Objectives of the FSA' in M Blair *et al*, *Blackstone's Guide to the Financial Services and Markets Act 2000* (London, Blackstone Press, 2001) 17 at 33.

recommended that the FSA should 'rebalance the resources it devotes to consumer awareness, to give more attention to the information problems experienced by people on low incomes, especially those currently excluded from banking services'.[90] The FSA has emphasised that it is keen to improve the financial literacy of those who are vulnerable or inexperienced in using financial services. However, its focus appears to be on retail consumers of investment products, where information asymmetry problems are most serious, and where the chance of consumer detriment is greatest.[91] Information remedies and the role of financial education are examined in chapter three.

Community Values

The third element of the social rationales for regulation is that of community values. It can be argued that there are certain values that we hold as a society which we want to see protected by regulation. Applying this logic to banking we could say that we want to preserve branches in rural areas, or impoverished urban areas because we believe that it is right to do so. The values we wish to preserve and promote may also include factors such as trust, fair dealing and honesty. We want these to be maintained, not merely because markets work more efficiently where they are present, but because as a society we think they should prevail. Ramsay identifies trust and confidence as necessary for markets to flourish, and they are of particular importance to financial markets. He suggests that consumer protection provisions, such as those contained in the Consumer Credit Act 1974 and the Financial Services Act 1986 were both intended to stimulate consumer confidence in financial markets.[92] Indeed, one of FSMA's statutory objectives is that of maintaining confidence in the financial system, and an important element in this confidence will be trust.[93] As will be seen below, such confidence is important for a number of reasons, and it is doubtful that financial markets could function effectively without it.

The close relationship between the social rationales for regulation is obvious, and it has already been argued that specific laws or other initiatives can frequently be explained and justified on different grounds. Regulation can both recognise and (to some extent) correct, market failure. The social rationales for regulation tell us that there may be other

---

[90] HM Treasury, *Competition in UK Banking: A Report to the Chancellor of the Exchequer* (the Cruickshank Report) (20 March 2000) para 4.126.
[91] Financial Services Authority, *Response by the Financial Services Authority to the Cruickshank Report on Competition in UK Banking* (July 2000) para 4.24.
[92] I Ramsay, above n 43 at 53.
[93] See O O'Neill, *A Question of Trust* BBC Reith Lectures 2002 (Cambridge, Cambridge University Press, 2002).

justifications for intervention. An additional point to bear in mind is that it is possible to argue that the assumptions upon which market-based thinking are founded are misconceived. It was argued above that perfect markets could be argued to work on the assumption that consumers are sovereign rational maximisers of their own utility. It has already been suggested that consumers may not be as rational as is sometimes argued. Behavioural studies reveal the plethora of bases upon which purchasing decisions are made. Although consumers might be theoretically sovereign, in the sense that suppliers cannot survive without at least some consumer demand for their products, it is important to consider the role that suppliers play in generating that demand. As Mishan argues:

> Unless the wants of consumers exist independently of the products created by industrial concerns it is not correct to speak of the market as acting to adapt the given resources of the economy to meet the material requirements of society …Therefore to continue to regard the market … as primarily a 'want satisfying' mechanism is to close one's eyes to the more important fact, that it has become a want-creating mechanism.[94]

The extent to which the producer is the creator of wants is a topic of great debate. It is perhaps venturing too far to suggest, as Gabriel and Lang do, that consumers can only be sovereign if they have 'a wide range of options, an unlimited amount of information and unlimited amount of money' and are 'immune from temptation.'[95] However, it is important to realise that wants do not exist in a vacuum, somehow irrespective of advertising push.

OBJECTIVES OF FINANCIAL REGULATION

Section 2(2) of the Financial Services and Markets Act 2000 (FSMA) sets out four regulatory objectives, which play a central role in ensuring that the Financial Services Authority (FSA) is accountable for its actions. In the words of one FSA publication '[t]he existence of such a set of objectives, and the bench mark they set against which others may judge our performance, will act as a crucial discipline on the Authority.'[96] However, some doubt the extent to which these objectives will allow the FSA to be

---

[94] EJ Mishan, *The Costs of Economic Growth* (New York, Penguin, 1967) pp 147–48.
[95] Y Gabriel and T Lang, *The Unmanageable Consumer: Contemporary Consumption and its Fragmentations* (London, Sage Publications, 1995) at 37.
[96] Financial Services Authority, *Meeting our Responsibilities* (FSA, August, 1998). It should be remembered that the FSA is responsible for regulating the majority of the financial sector in the UK, and not just banking.

held to account because they apply at a high level of generality rather than to the assessment of individual decisions. As a result, Lastra and Shams conclude that:

> while the statutory objectives could offer a helpful benchmark for the discharge of general political or public accountability, they will not be very useful for the enforcement of judicial accountability or public accountability for specific decisions and actions.[97]

In addition to the objectives, FSMA contains a set of regulatory principles which the FSA must follow, and also makes various provisions for institutional accountability.[98]

Although FSMA does not purport to prioritise among the statutory objectives, and so there is no formal hierarchy among them, the maintaining of market confidence could be viewed as the most fundamental of the FSA's objectives. In the words of Whittaker 'maintaining confidence in the financial system ... is, in one sense, an overarching objective, under which all others can be subsumed'.[99] Others emphasise consumer, or investor protection as the primary aim of financial regulation.[100] It is therefore perhaps wise not to make too much of any underlying hierarchy.

Market Confidence and Systemic Risk

Section 3(1) of FSMA describes the market confidence objective as maintaining confidence in the UK financial system. This includes financial markets and exchanges, regulated activities and other activities connected with financial markets and exchanges. A collapse in market confidence can arise from a wide variety of factors. The FSA has identified these as financial crime or market abuse on a major scale; widespread misconduct by, or mismanagement of, institutions; the financial collapse of significant participants in the financial system; significant market malfunction; and lack of understanding of what the regulator can and cannot do. It is clear

---

[97] RM Lastra and H Shams, 'Public Accountability in the Financial Sector' in E Ferran and C Goodhart (eds), *Regulating Financial Services in the 21st Century* (Oxford, Hart Publishing, 2001) 165 at 185–86. The FSA does set out some other ways of assessing whether its regulatory decisions are reasonable. See Financial Services Authority, *A New Regulator for the New Millennium* (FSA, January 2000) Appendix 3.

[98] For discussion see C Briault, *Revisiting the Rationale for a Single Financial Services Regulator* (FSA Occasional Paper 16, February 2002) para 3.2.

[99] A Whittaker, 'Architecture for the New Single Regulator' lecture at IALS, 1999, cited in Lastra and Shams above n 97 at 195.

[100] C Mayer, 'Regulatory Principles and the Financial Services and Markets Act 2000' in Ferran and Goodhart (eds), *Regulating Financial Services and Markets*, above n 97 at 26.

that the FSA has a wide range of regulatory tools to deal with these various causes of a fall in market confidence.[101]

Confidence is of supreme importance in financial markets, chiefly because of the threat of systemic risk. Systemic risk is the major externality, or spillover, to which financial markets are susceptible. It involves the risk that the failure of one financial institution will lead to the collapse of other institutions in a domino-like manner. This may ultimately lead to the collapse of the financial system at large, with devastating effects for the domestic and global economy. Perhaps the main reason that banks are thought of as being able to create, and be susceptible to, systemic risk, is because of the nature of fractional reserve banking. The role of banks is to transform assets from and into liabilities. Bank assets are generally in the form of loans, which are highly illiquid.[102] Their liabilities, generally in the form of deposits, are, by contrast, repayable on demand and highly liquid. Banks will only have a limited proportion of their assets in a liquid form, and this will generally be sufficient to meet their liabilities. However, where an unexpectedly large number of depositors demand their deposits in a short period of time, the bank can quickly become illiquid and then insolvent. The insolvency of one bank can have systemic consequences for a number of reasons. First, the inability of one bank to meet its obligations to another can have a knock-on effect by making the second bank unable to meet its obligations and so on. Banks are joined together by complex chains of transactions, and also manage the payments system, and these factors contribute to the likelihood of, and seriousness of, contagion. Secondly, because of information asymmetry, it is difficult for a depositor to identify whether a bank is likely to become insolvent. A seminal paper by Diamond and Dybvig argues that bank runs are self-fulfilling: if depositors believe that other depositors will withdraw their money it is rational for them to do the same.[103] As a result, a perfectly well-managed and well-capitalised bank can become insolvent quickly following a run on the bank.[104] As Ford and Kay nicely put it: 'banks could collapse not because they are weak but because some depositors think that other depositors think that a collapse is possible.'[105]

---

[101] See Financial Services Authority, *A New Regulator for the New Millennium*, above n 97. See further chs 3 and 4 of this work.
[102] Although their value to the originating bank may be high, it will be difficult to sell them for a similar amount. A bank's assets may therefore be more valuable on a going concern basis than on liquidation. See C Goodhart *et al*, *Financial Regulation: Why, How and Where Now?* (London, Routledge, 1998) at 9.
[103] D Diamond and P Dybvig, 'Bank Runs, Deposit Insurance and Liquidity' (1983) 91(3) *Journal of Political Economy* 401.
[104] For an alternative view see K Dowd, *Laissez-faire Banking*, above n 12; ch 6.
[105] Ford and Kay, above n 7 at 147.

The collapse of a bank may have implications for the wider economy as well as for the health of other banks. Banks are a vital source of credit for many businesses, as well as managing the payments system. Therefore, the collapse of major parts of the banking system is liable to have a damaging effect on the economy at large. This provides a particularly strong incentive for states to do what they can to maintain confidence in the banking system.

Financial institutions differ in the extent to which they are susceptible to systemic risk. Although banks are generally thought to be susceptible to systemic risk, it is less clear whether such risk exists to any great extent in relation to other financial institutions. Dale argues that it is the potential for systemic crisis that distinguishes the insolvency of banks from the insolvency of other firms.[106] However, it could be argued that in some circumstances, securities firms pose a systemic threat, particularly where they form part of a banking group.[107] The failure of insurance firms, on the other hand, appears not to have major systemic implications. There are still sound reasons for regulating insurance companies, but not on the basis of systemic risk.[108]

An important point to emphasise, albeit briefly at this stage, is that it is important that the regulator does not give the impression that failing banks will be bailed out as a matter of course. There has been criticism that a regulatory contract has been created, which amounts to 'something close to a general decree that banks should not be allowed to fail'.[109] In particular, a feeling has emerged that some banks are too big and too influential to be allowed to fail.[110] The too big to fail (TBTF) doctrine states that the authorities will not allow a bank to fail where that failure might lead to further failures and, potentially, the collapse of the banking system. There is certainly a widespread feeling that states will not allow their national banks to be liquidated. This might explain the action taken to save Continental Illinois and Crédit Lyonnais to name but two.[111] If the doctrine is correct, it means that smaller banks are at a competitive disadvantage as, unlike their larger competitors, they are not subject to an implicit guarantee that they will be bailed out should the need arise.

The FSA has always emphasised that a zero failure regime would be both impossible and undesirable. In its September 2003 Paper

---

[106] R Dale, *The Regulation of International Banking* (Cambridge, Woodhead-Faulkner, 1984).
[107] Goodhart, above n 102 at 13; Organisation for Economic Cooperation and Development, *Systemic Risks in Securities Markets* (Paris, OECD, 1993).
[108] Unless, of course, the insurance company forms part of a banking group.
[109] Cruickshank, above n 90, para 2.10.
[110] See M Wolgast, 'Too Big to Fail: Effects on Competition and Implications for Banking Supervision' (2001) 9(4) *Journal of Financial Regulation and Compliance* 361.
[111] Indeed, the Federal Deposit Insurance Corporation (FDIC) in the USA has explicitly recognised that large banks will not be allowed to fail. See Goodhart, above n 19 at 76.

Reasonable Expectations, it stated again that it is concerned to run what it calls a 'non-zero failure' regime.[112] However, this does not mean that steps will not be taken to save failing banks. If a bank is so influential in the markets that its failure is likely to lead to a collapse in market confidence then the regulator is likely to step in. As is discussed below, the FSA adopts a risk-based approach to regulation, where it makes decisions on the basis of the risks posed to its regulatory objectives. As the failure of larger banks is more likely to adversely affect confidence than that of smaller banks, it can be assumed that some large banks will not be allowed to fail.[113] Although the FSA has recently stated that 'we do not say that firms in higher [impact] categories will never fail' it seems inconceivable that a large retail bank would be allowed to fail because of the likely impact of such failure on the FSA's market confidence objective.[114] One risk with such intervention is that it may create a moral hazard, where bank officers engage in risky lending on the assumption that they will be bailed out in the event of their banks finding themselves in difficulty. Another risk is that there will be an uneven playing field, with smaller banks being unable to compete.[115] There is an obvious consumer protection angle to the market confidence objective too. The systemic risk that follows from a fall in confidence and resulting bank failure has an immediate impact upon consumers. This is dealt with below.

Consumer Protection and Public Awareness

The focus of this book is upon the role of the law in regulating banks in the interests of the consumer. The consumer protection objective in FSMA is, of course, central to this role. FSMA identifies consumer protection and public awareness as separate regulatory objectives. However, they are so closely connected that it is proposed to deal with them together.[116] Indeed, although few financial regulators are given public awareness as a statutory objective, it seems likely that many will treat public awareness as an element of any consumer protection objective. The FSA itself recently stated that it had increasingly come to see the interdependence

---

[112] Financial Services Authority, *Reasonable Expectations: Regulation in a Non-Zero Failure World* (FSA, September 2003).
[113] I use the phrase 'large banks' in a slightly loose way. The FSA divides firms (not just banks) on the basis of the risk they pose to the FSA's objectives. Only around 1 per cent of firms are assessed as 'high impact'.
[114] See Financial Services Authority, above n 112 para 6.7.
[115] One solution to this is to provide similar protection to smaller banks, something that the FDIC has championed. See Goodhart, above n 19.
[116] An approach supported by Taylor, above n 89, 17 at 28.

between its regulatory measures for consumer protection and its work on public awareness.[117]

There can be little doubt that the protection of the consumer is one of the principal objectives of financial regulation, and the need to protect the consumer is one of the principal justifications for financial regulation. Mayer has argued that '[t]he primary issue that regulation is supposed to address, and many people might feel is the only relevant issue, is investor protection'.[118] In an open letter to the FSA, Consumers' Association said that '[t]he FSA must recognise that the needs and wants of consumers must come first when regulating the retail financial services industry'.[119] Consumer protection is certainly central to the regulatory regime.

It is important to say something about the specific elements to which the FSA must have regard when fulfilling the consumer protection objective. The FSA is charged with securing the 'appropriate' degree of protection for consumers. This involves a value judgement, based upon an ideological assessment of the role of the regulator. It is clear from the FSA's publications that it regards market failure as providing the reason for regulation, perhaps calling into question the role for matters such as distributive justice.[120] First, reference is made to the 'differing degrees of risk involved in different kinds of investment or other transaction'. It is widely recognised that financial products vary greatly in relation to the risks they present, and the FSA must have regard to this. Presumably, where there is significant risk, for example in relation to equities, it is important that this is communicated to consumers. However, where there is a high degree of risk, and this is known about, consumers cannot expect to be bailed out.[121] Risk and reward are closely linked and it is important that, where they can, consumers take responsibility for their actions. This is explicitly stated in the objective.

Secondly, paragraph (b) requires the FSA to have regard to 'the differing degrees of experience and expertise that different consumers may have in relation to different kinds of regulated activity.' There is an overlap here with paragraph (a). Where consumers have significant experience, and are likely to possess some expertise, a lighter regulatory touch is likely to be needed, because consumers can be expected to look after themselves. This may explain why the FSA has little responsibility for conduct of business in banking, but is far more involved where investments are concerned.[122]

---

[117] Financial Services Authority, *Towards a National Strategy for Financial Capability* (FSA 2003) at 4.

[118] C Mayer, 'Regulatory Principles and the Financial Services and Markets Act 2000' in Ferran and Goodhart, above n 97, 25 at 26.

[119] The Consumers' Association, 'An Open Letter to the FSA' (29 November 2001).

[120] Financial Services Authority, above n 112 para 1.9.

[121] Except to the extent provided for by the Financial Services Compensation Scheme. See ch 7.

[122] For the role of the *Banking Code* in conduct of business see ch 5.

Unfamiliar areas may, therefore, require more regulation. Research has been undertaken for the FSA about how consumers view different types of financial product, and this will help in identifying the types of products with which consumers are unfamiliar and lack confidence.[123] Another issue to note here is that there is an increasing expectation that consumers should make greater provision for their financial futures. An ageing population, changes in employment patterns and changes in the state pension all play a role here.[124] As consumers are increasingly required to provide for themselves, such as in retirement, they are more likely to be exposed to forms of financial product with which they are relatively unfamiliar.[125] It is important that the FSA has regard to this under this part of the consumer protection objective.

Thirdly, paragraph (c) refers to the FSA having regard to 'the needs that consumers have for advice and accurate information'. The importance of information and advice for consumers has already been alluded to, and is examined in more detail in chapter three. The FSA will seek to improve the quality of information and advice available to consumers. In part the FSA will provide information itself, for example through comparative information, consumer publications and alerts. It also has a role in ensuring that information is provided through other channels, for example, by requiring disclosure by firms.[126] This aspect of the consumer protection objective overlaps considerably with the public awareness objective, and it is worth saying something about the latter now. The public awareness objective is described in s 4(1) as promoting public understanding of the financial system. This includes, in particular, promoting awareness of the benefits and risks associated with different kinds of investment or other financial dealing; and the provision of appropriate information and advice.[127] The FSA has argued that risks to this objective may come from inadequate general financial literacy on the part of the public, and inadequate understanding by consumers of specific products and services. It is clear that the FSA will need to address this in a number of ways, and that improved public awareness should contribute significantly to the other objectives. Better informed consumers should be better able to protect themselves, and avoid financial crime, and should also help to create market confidence. Indeed, market

---

[123] Financial Services Authority, *Better Informed Consumers* (FSA Consumer Research 1, April 2000). For example, 89 per cent of consumers surveyed felt that savings accounts were straightforward, while only 16 per cent felt the same about gilts para 3.7.

[124] See Financial Services Authority, above n 117 at 7.

[125] Fewer than half of those surveyed found personal pensions straightforward. See Financial Services Authority, above n 123 para 3.7.

[126] Financial Services Authority, *Comparative Information for Financial Services* (FSA Consultation Paper 28, October 1999).

[127] Section 4(2).

confidence depends largely on consumer confidence. As Davies has argued

> without regulation to give consumers some independent assurance about the terms on which contracts are offered, the safety of assets which underpin them, and the quality of advice received, saving and investment may be discouraged, again with damaging economic consequences.[128]

There is a close relationship between the consumer protection objective and the FSA's other statutory objectives. Financial crime is identified as one of the risks to the FSA's being able to meet its consumer protection objective, and the financial failure of institutions, which may result from, or lead to, a collapse in market confidence is another risk. But it is the public awareness and consumer protection objectives that are most closely linked. Inadequate understanding of the financial system at large, and of specific products and services is clearly central both to the consumer protection objective and the public understanding objective. It should also be remembered that it is important for consumers to be aware of the role of regulation and, in particular, of what can and cannot be expected of the regulator. The FSA has begun talking about 'financial capability' and has a strategy in place to improve this through financial education, information provision and generic advice.[129]

Finally, paragraph (d) says that the FSA must have regard to 'the general principle that consumers should take responsibility for their decisions.' This element of the consumer protection objective was the cause of some concern, especially from consumer groups. It is a version of the *caveat emptor* or 'let the buyer beware' principle which is well known in consumer law, and doubt could be raised about its appropriateness in the area of financial services law. The National Consumer Council and the FSA Consumer Panel both questioned the utility of this part of the objective. It was as a result of these objections that paragraph (c), which refers to 'the needs that consumers have for advice and accurate information', was added. The government has argued that if s 5 is taken as a whole, it now strikes an appropriate balance between consumers' needs, and their responsibility for their own decisions. The issue is not so much the wording of the provision, but how it is interpreted in practice. Few can deny that where consumers can be expected to take responsibility for their decisions they should be encouraged to do so. The fear is that too much will be expected of consumers who cannot be expected to make informed choices.[130] It should also be noted that if consumers are to be required to

---

[128] Davies, above n 7.
[129] Financial Services Authority, above n 117 at 12.
[130] See ch 3.

take responsibility for their decisions, it is vital that they know what their responsibilities are, compared with those of the bank and the regulator. As well as requirements imposed on banks by the FSA, there are good faith duties in the law of contract, and there may be an increasing movement towards emphasising issues of fairness, which may impose greater obligations on banks than ever before.[131] Furthermore, it is vital that consumers are aware of the limited role the regulator has in protecting them if a product or supplier is badly chosen. In relation to products, the FSA has emphasised that while regulation can limit cases of mis-selling 'consumers need to take responsibility for cases of mis-buying'.[132] In relation to banks, consumers need to know that the regulator will not necessarily step in to save their bank if it finds itself in trouble, and that their protection under the financial services compensation scheme will be limited. It is far from clear that consumers have this knowledge at present.[133] Because of these issues, the FSA's commitment to improving financial capability, mentioned above, is particularly important.

Consumer Protection and Risk-based Regulation

It has already been mentioned that one characteristic of the FSA's approach to banking regulation is that it is risk-based. This means that the FSA makes decisions about how to act based upon an assessment of the risks posed to its statutory objectives.[134] There are several risks to the FSA's ability to meet the consumer protection objective. The FSA has identified these as: financial failure of institutions; financial crime or market abuse; misconduct by, or mismanagement by, institutions; market malfunction, and inadequate understanding by consumers of specific products or services. This demonstrates the close connection between the four objectives that have already been identified. Another way of examining the consumer protection objective is to differentiate between different types of risk that may affect consumers. In *A New Regulator for the New Millennium*, the FSA identified four principal risks that consumers may face in their financial affairs. These are now considered.

First the FSA refers to prudential risk, which is the risk that a firm collapses, for example through weak or incompetent management or lack of capital. As explained above, the FSA has a role in minimising the failure

---

[131] See ch 6.
[132] Financial Services Authority, above n 20 para 2.8.
[133] Research for the FSA found that 19 per cent of those asked believed that regulated firms are not allowed to go bankrupt. See above n 20 para 2.12.
[134] See Financial Services Authority, *Building the New Regulator: Progress Report 2* (February 2002); Financial Services Authority, above n 20.

of institutions where that failure might affect market confidence, but it is clear that this does not mean that firms will be saved at all costs. When examining its market confidence objective, the FSA has stated that it will

> aim to maintain a regime which ensures as low an incidence of failure of regulated firms and markets (especially failures which would have a material impact on public confidence and market soundness) as is consistent with the maintenance of competition and innovation in the markets.[135]

It has already been argued that the public cannot expect the regulator to avoid all financial failures through *ex ante* regulation, nor can they expect the regulator to step in and save all ailing firms *ex post*. As mentioned above, under the public awareness objective, the FSA will need to explain what the public should, and should not, expect the regulator to do. To some extent this has been done, but it is important for the regulator to continue to emphasise that effective financial regulation is not tantamount to a guarantee that an institution is safe.

Second there is bad faith risk, which the FSA describes as 'the risk from fraud, misrepresentation, deliberate mis-selling or failure to disclose relevant information on the part of firms selling or advising on financial products'.[136] There is a close connection between this and the objective of avoiding financial crime. In many cases where there is fraud or deliberate mis-selling a criminal offence will have been committed.[137] However, a crime is not a prerequisite of bad faith. In these circumstances the FSA will still have a role under the consumer protection objective. Perhaps the clearest example of bad faith has been the personal pensions mis-selling.[138] From 1988 to 1994 over eight million people invested in personal pensions, and it has been estimated that between one and two million of those received bad advice. However, this does not mean that there was dishonesty in all these cases.[139] Various measures can be taken to tackle this, such as reducing the chance that rogues become involved in the control of firms via the approved persons regime, challenging unfair terms under the Unfair Terms in Consumer Contracts Regulations, and bringing prosecutions under FSMA.

Third is complexity or unsuitability risk. The FSA describes this as 'the risk that consumers contract for a financial product or service they do not understand or which is unsuitable for their needs and circumstances'.[140]

---

[135] Financial Services Authority, above n 97 para 4.
[136] *Ibid* para 11.
[137] FSMA creates a large number of offences, many of which involve bad faith risk.
[138] See J Black and R Nobles, 'Personal Pensions Mis-selling: The Causes and Lessons of Regulatory Failure' (1998) 61 MLR 789.
[139] G McMeel and J Virgo, *Financial Advice and Financial Products* (Oxford, Oxford University Press, 2001) at 6.
[140] Above n 135 para 11.

This has implications for both the consumer protection and public awareness objectives considered above. It has already been noted that the FSA has identified two main elements of the public awareness objective: improving general financial literacy and improving the information and advice available to consumers. It is perhaps principally through these mechanisms that the FSA will most effectively be able to minimise complexity-unsuitability risk. Steps need to be taken to consider the roles of firms, regulator and consumers here. Improving financial capability is the foundation upon which other initiatives can be built, and better prepared consumers are better able to play the role of the informed, knowledgeable consumer that is central to market discipline. Improving the supply of information will also be fundamental to reducing complexity–unsuitability risk by helping to ensure that consumers understand the products available. The FSA recently emphasised that information to consumers 'must address the questions which they have, be provided in a style with which they feel comfortable and be made available at a time and place which is convenient to them.'[141] In some cases, simplifying the products themselves may also be a solution. In his report *Vulnerable Consumers and Financial Services*, the Director General of Fair Trading made a number of recommendations about how the plight of vulnerable consumers can be tackled where financial services are concerned. Several of these involved changing the types of product that financial services providers make available for consumers.[142] The Government, too, has shown an interest in some of these ideas, particularly that of basic bank accounts. The introduction of CAT (changes, access and terms) standardisation also contributes to this by providing an assurance that products meet minimum criteria through certification. However, as considered in chapter three, the future for CAT standards is uncertain.

Finally, the FSA identifies performance risk, which is the risk that financial products do not deliver the returns hoped for by the consumer. The FSA sees itself as having little, if any, role here:

> [i]t is not the FSA's role to protect consumers from performance risk, which is inherent in investment markets—providing the firm recommending the product has explained to the consumer the risks involved and has not made excessive and unrealistic claims.[143]

It is in relation to investment products that performance risk is of most significance. Many investment products can generally be classified as credence goods because their essential characteristics cannot be determined

---

141 Above n 117 at 12.
142 Office of Fair Trading, *Vulnerable Consumers and Financial Services: The Report of the Director General's Inquiry* (OFT 255, January 1999).
143 Above n 135 para 12.

until long after the contract has been concluded.[144] The regulatory regime will still play an important role after the product has been sold, for example by ensuring that information is disclosed at the appropriate time and that providers are continually supervised, but it will not provide any guarantee of the product's performance.[145]

The FSA's approach to consumer protection can be summed up by the following statement of its former Director of Consumer Relations:[146]

> we clearly need to develop an appropriate level of protection for consumers, and by appropriate, I mean a framework that provides adequate safety for consumers, taking account of their skill, expertise, level of understanding and the risks they face, without placing such an onerous burden on providers that innovation and competition are stifled.

Reducing Financial Crime

Section 6(1) of FSMA states that the reduction of crime objective involves reducing the extent to which it is possible for business carried on, either by a regulated person, or in contravention of the general prohibition, to be used for a purpose connected with financial crime. In considering the objective, the FSA has to have regard to the desirability of regulated persons being aware of the risk that their businesses will be used in connection with financial crime, their taking appropriate measures to prevent financial crime, facilitate its detection and monitor its incidence, and their devoting adequate resources to such matters. Financial crime is broadly interpreted to include fraud or dishonesty, misconduct in, or misuse of information relating to, a financial market, or handling the proceeds of crime. The FSA has identified several risks to this objective. These may arise from fraud or dishonesty, misconduct in or misuse of information relating to, a financial market, and handling the proceeds of crime, for example money laundering. All these activities could have adverse effects on market confidence and consumer protection, and the close relationship between this and the other statutory objectives has already been emphasised.

Dealing with financial crime is one of the most difficult aspects of a financial regulator's work because, by its very nature, it tends to be clandestine. But it remains an objective of considerable importance, not

[144] See ch 3.
[145] Other than the guarantee provided by the financial services compensation scheme should the firm fail. See ch 5.
[146] C Farnish, 'Getting a Fair Deal for Consumers' (11 December 2000) (available at <http://www.fsa.gov.uk/speeches>).

least because of the potential costs involved.[147] Markets cannot function efficiently unless, in the words of Cranston, 'persons can deal with each other in the knowledge that fraud is an exceptional, rather than a regular, feature of the environment'.[148] Financial crime such as fraud also sends confusing signals to the market, leading to resources moving to destinations which appear to be profitable, rather than those which are profitable. Attention needs to be paid both to offences committed by those inside and outside a bank, and the full range of regulatory tools need to be utilised to address these.

THE PRINCIPLES OF REGULATION

As well as having specific statutory objectives, the FSA is also obliged to comply with additional considerations, which are generally referred to as the principles of good regulation.[149] These principles, which are contained in s 2(3) of FSMA seek to ensure that the regulation used by the FSA is efficient, proportionate and takes proper account of competition. The FSA has recently stated:[150]

> the overall effect of these principles is to direct us to operate a regime that is both market-based (i.e. looks to market solutions) and risk-based. Above all, they reinforce the point that in seeking to reduce or remove risk, we cannot pursue our objectives in isolation from the wider economic context.

The first principle states that in discharging its general functions, the FSA must have regard to: '(a) the need to use its resources in the most efficient and economic way'. This is designed to ensure that the FSA is cost-effective in meeting its objectives. It has already been noted that the costs of regulation are not always as transparent as they might be.[151] Costs include direct costs such as people and buildings, charges to fund compensation arrangements, the cost of losing business to other jurisdictions because of expensive regulation, and the cost of reduced competition and the stifling

---

[147] In the USA, it has been argued that fraud in savings and loan institutions could constitute 'the most costly set of white collar crimes in history': HN Pontell and K Calavita, 'Bilking Bankers and Bad Debts: White Collar Crime and the Savings and Loan Crisis' in K Schlegal and D Weisburd (eds), *White Collar Crime Reconsidered* (Boston, Northeastern University Press, 1992) 195 at 195.

[148] R Cranston, above n 36 at 73.

[149] They bear some similarity to the principles of good regulation developed by the Better Regulation Task Force, namely accountability, transparency, proportionality, targeting and consistency. See The Better Regulation Task Force, *Principles of Good Regulation* (January 1998).

[150] Financial Services Authority, above n 112 para 3.4.

[151] These are examined in Goodhart, above n 19.

of innovation.[152] As will be apparent, some of these issues are dealt with under the other principles of regulation. We have already seen that the FSA has developed a risk-based approach, and that this endeavours to ensure that it can assess and prioritise the risks to its objectives on the basis of a common analytical framework.[153] The FSA argues that this enables it to understand better the tools that it can use, and the costs of various options.[154] At 31 March 2003, the FSA was regulating over 11,000 firms (a figure that is set to increase hugely when it takes on responsibility for mortgage advice and general insurance). The FSA's resources are finite, and it needs to be able to focus on those firms that pose the greatest risk to their objectives. This principle is also related to the issue of proportionality, which is considered below.

The second principle states that the FSA must have regard to 'the responsibilities of those who manage the affairs of authorised persons'. This reflects the desire that bank management takes prime responsibility for a bank's activities. Taylor emphasises the importance that supervisors and regulators 'do not become a kind of superior management board', and argues that 'sound corporate governance remains the depositors' and consumers' first and most important protection.'[155] Criticism has been made that FSA regulation sometimes amounts to micro-management of banks, something that the FSA has been eager to refute.[156] There may be a risk that by having a stringent system of regulation, particularly supervision, in place, firms are able to regard themselves as no longer responsible for their decisions. There have been reports of banks' non-executive directors supporting close supervision for the confidence it gave them that their institutions were being well run.[157] The tendency towards more regulation may be further explained by the desire on the part of regulators to avoid financial failures that generate negative publicity. In the words of Goodhart:

> The incentive for regulators, especially when they do not bear the burden of the costs themselves, is to impose such comprehensive regulations that they will not personally be likely to be held responsible for failures and failings during their own term of office. [158]

---

[152] *Ibid.*

[153] Before the creation of the FSA in 1997, the Bank of England was already developing a risk-based approach following Arthur Anderson's review of the appropriateness and effectiveness of its supervision and surveillance operations. See the Bank of England, *Banking Act Report 1996–97*.

[154] Financial Services Authority, above n 34 at 5.

[155] M Taylor 'Accountability and Objectives of the FSA' in M Blair *et al*, above n 89 at 35.

[156] Financial Servicse Authority, *Response of the FSA to the Cruickshank Report on Competition in UK Banking* (July 2000) para 3.15.

[157] See Wood, above n 2 at 357, citing an example from New Zealand.

[158] Goodhart, above n 19 at 451.

Even in the absence of the first principle, it is clear that the FSA is eager to explain that its task is not to ensure the absence of firms failing, and that it is not primarily responsible for firms' mistakes. Ensuring that it is management that takes responsibility for firms' decision-making is closely connected with good principles of corporate governance, transparency and market discipline. This has been recognised at an international level. The *Basel Core Principles for Effective Banking Supervision* emphasise the importance of banks' senior officers taking prime responsibility for their institutions' decisions, stating that supervisors should 'encourage and pursue market discipline by encouraging good corporate governance and enhancing market transparency and surveillance'.[159] The *Basel Core Principles* further state that effective market discipline

> depends on an adequate flow of information to market participants, appropriate financial incentives to reward well-managed institutions, and arrangements that ensure that investors are not insulated from the consequences of their decisions.

It is certainly important that the managers of banks are under appropriate incentives to act prudently, for example by managing risk appropriately. Market discipline will play an important role here, of course, but the regulator can also play a part in ensuring that there are incentives to engage in desirable behaviour.[160]

The third principle states that the FSA must have regard to

> the principle that a burden or restriction which is imposed on a person, or the carrying on of an activity, should be proportionate to the benefits, considered in general terms, which are expected to result from the imposition of that burden or restriction.

This issue, which can be summarised as the principle of proportionality, is a very important one in financial regulation. As mentioned above, there is concern that because consumers cannot signal the extent to which they are willing to pay for regulation, and because there may be a tendency for consumers to underestimate, or even ignore, the cost of regulation, this may lead to over-regulation, with the costs of regulation outweighing

---

[159] Basel Committee, *Core Principles for Effective Banking Supervision* (September 1997).
[160] See H Evans, *Plumbers and Architects* (FSA Occasional Paper 4, January 2000) at 22–23. Writing in 1997 when it still had responsibility for bank supervision, The Bank of England argued that while it was not responsible for banks' remuneration policies, it was legitimate for it to ask questions about whether those policies were likely to provide employees with incentives to act in a way which was inconsistent with the Bank's objectives. See Bank of England, *Banking Act Report 1996–97*, above n 153, at 12. These issues are considered more fully in D Davies, 'Remuneration and Risk' 1997(2) Financial Stability Review 18.

the benefits.[161] The proportionality principle seeks to ensure that the FSA has proper regard to the costs and benefits of any regulation that it might impose. The FSA is required to undertake cost benefit analysis when introducing rules and general guidance, and to consult on this.[162] However, cost–benefit analyses are particularly difficult to make with any precision in the financial sector, largely because of the difficulties in quantifying the benefits of regulation with any degree of accuracy.[163] Despite these difficulties, it is important that all parties recognise that the costs of regulation are ultimately borne by the consumer.

The attention given to the potential costs of regulation and the difficulty in determining the amount that consumers are willing to pay may mask some important issues. First, it is important to remember that it is rational for consumers to demand regulation. Regulation brings clear benefits in terms of improving the soundness of the financial system and ensuring that consumers are not misled. It may be difficult to determine the precise amount that consumers are willing to pay for this, but this should not lead us to conclude that consumers are generally unwilling to pay for such benefits. The benefits to consumers of regulation have been identified as: reinforcement of high standards of integrity, fair dealing and competence; establishment and monitoring of training and competency standards; facilitation of consumers' protecting their own interests through information disclosure; and provision of effective mechanisms for handling investor complaints and for securing redress.[164] Consumers can be expected to demand regulation from which they benefit. Secondly, any tendency to over-regulate may be tempered by the competitive advantages that arise from minimal regulation. Firms may be attracted to states with low levels of regulation and this may counterbalance any move towards over-regulation. This is considered below.

The Principles of Regulation and Competition Policy

There has been considerable debate about the extent to which it is appropriate to charge financial regulators with the objective of encouraging competition.[165] The encouraging or maintenance of competition is

---

[161] See Goodhart *et al*, above n 102, ch 4.

[162] FSMA s 65(2). See I Alfon and P Andrews, *Cost Benefit Analysis in Financial Regulation* (FSA Occasional Paper 3, September 1999).

[163] See Goodhart *et al*, above n 102 at 65–68; Blair, above n 89, at 35. A study of the potential benefits of the disclosure regime being considered for the life assurance industry estimated those benefits at £1 billion per annum. See National Economic Research Associates, *Costs and Benefits of Securities and Investment Board's Proposals to Improve and Commission Disclosure in Life Assurance* (1994).

[164] Goodhart *et al*, above n 102, at 66.

[165] See below.

frequently cited as one of the principal objectives of financial regulation. The House of Commons Treasury Select Committee argued that the FSA should be given competition as one of its statutory objectives, and this received support from groups as diverse as the National Consumer Council and the British Bankers' Association, as well as from the Conservative Opposition.[166] The interim report of the Cruickshank Committee also recommended that the FSA be given a primary competition objective in addition to its regulatory objectives.[167] Although the interim report did not suggest that the FSA be given the duty actively to promote competition, it argued that the FSA needed a specific competition objective. It stated:

> the FSA should be responsible for making the trade-off between regulatory and competition outcomes in financial services: to ensure this happens the FSA should have a primary competition objective, in addition to its regulatory objectives.[168]

Despite these representations, the FSA was highly reluctant to take on such a role. Sir Howard Davies, when FSA Chairman and Chief Executive, argued that such an objective would cut across the remits of other bodies, involve the FSA in commercial activities in an inappropriate way, and could impede the FSA's co-operation with regulators overseas. The FSA's General Counsel, Michael Whittaker, argued that the four regulatory objectives worked well together, whereas a competition objective would do so only partially, and could act as an antithesis to them. This, he argued, would give the FSA 'an unclear and confusing mandate'.[169] Several commentators have emphasised the potential conflicts that may arise between ensuring safety and soundness and encouraging fair competition, and although there is little doubt that competition can aid safety and soundness in some circumstances, it can also threaten them.[170] The FSA has made it clear that it is well aware of the difficult trade-off to be made between competition and the objectives of regulation, including consumer protection and market confidence.

Although competition was not included as one of the statutory objectives, significant emphasis has been given to matters of competition in FSMA's principles of regulation, and the institutional arrangements that

---

[166] See *Joint Committee Report* paras 46–51.
[167] Cruickshank Committee, *Competition and Regulation: An Interim Report* (22 July, 1999) para 49.
[168] *Ibid*, para 76a.
[169] A Whittaker 'The Role of Competition in Financial Services Regulation' (27 April, 2001) para 16.
[170] R Lastra, *Central Banking and Banking Regulation* (London, Financial Markets Group, 1996) at 173; Cranston, above n 36 at 68.

FSMA makes for competition scrutiny. The principles state that the FSA must have regard to:

> (d) the desirability of facilitating innovation in connection with regulated activities; (e) the international character of financial services and markets and the desirability of maintaining the competitive position of the United Kingdom; (f) the need to minimise the adverse effects on competition that may arise from anything done in the discharge of those functions; [and] (g) the desirability of facilitating competition between those who are subject to any form of regulation by the Authority.[171]

These principles help to address the concern that the absence of a specific competition objective will lead the FSA to take too little account of competition matters. However, concern has nevertheless been expressed that the FSA pays too little attention to matters of competition. The Cruickshank Report argued that the FSA sometimes imposed unnecessary regulatory barriers to entry. For example, the Report argued that there was a de facto requirement that new entrants had to be linked to an established bank, a suspicion of applicants whose parent company was not a bank, and a tendency to impose unduly stringent capital requirements on new entrants.[172] The FSA responded robustly to some of these criticisms. It argued that several recent authorisations have not been linked to existing banks, and a significant number of recent authorisations have been of banks owned by non-banks. In relation to capital adequacy, the FSA explained that minimum capital ratios are set on a bank by bank basis, and that '[e]xperience has demonstrated that the absence of a track record is a relevant factor to take into account as part of the risk assessment process'.[173]

It is difficult to judge whether the FSA takes sufficient account of the competition implications of its decisions, and this is something upon which more research is needed. What is clear is that the statutory framework within which it operates demonstrates Parliament's intention that matters relating to competition will be taken seriously. Many of the provisions of FSMA, and initiatives by the FSA will have a positive effect on encouraging competition. For example, the new arrangements for tackling market abuse have been said to be aimed at improving market efficiency rather than enforcing morality, and the work on comparative information should make it easier for consumers to compare retail products.[174]

---

[171] Section 2(3).

[172] Cruickshank, above n 16 para 2.16.

[173] Financial Services Authority, above n 91 para 3.11.

[174] See A Whittaker, 'The Role of Competition in Financial Services Regulation'. Presentation to the Regulatory Policy Institute, 27 April 2001. Available at <http://www.fsa.gov.uk/speeches>.

Indeed, it is important to remember that regulation and competition need not be at opposite ends of a spectrum. In the words of Llewellyn: '[t]he purpose of regulation is not to replace competition but to enhance it and make it effective in the marketplace by offsetting market imperfections which potentially compromise consumer welfare'.[175] It is clear that competition and regulation need not conflict.

CONCLUSIONS

Market failure provides the principal economic rationale for banking regulation. It is widely recognised that financial markets suffer from information asymmetry and the risk of externalities, particularly in the form of systemic risk. Although market failure does not always provide a justification for intervention, the potential failures associated with banking business appear to provide a justification for regulation. There are also sound non-economic, or social rationales for regulation. Societies are entitled to demand that governments ensure a degree of social justice even where this may not be so easily justified solely on economic grounds.

The success of any attempts to regulate banking services can only be assessed against specific objectives. FSMA is ambitious in setting out the statutory objectives that the FSA is charged with achieving, and this forms part of a regime designed to ensure the Authority's transparency and accountability. The consumer protection and public awareness objectives are, of course, central to the FSA's role in protecting the consumer of banking services. But consumer protection issues stretch into other objectives too. The maintaining of market confidence and the prevention of financial crime will play their own parts in a regime designed, above all to 'maintain efficient, orderly and clean markets and help retail consumers achieve a fair deal'.[176]

---

[175] D Llewellyn, above n 3 at 23.
[176] Financial Services Authority, Building the New Regulator, above n 134, para 2.

3

Disclosure, Information and Education

INTRODUCTION

ENSURING THE PROVISION of useful information is essential to an effective consumer protection policy.[1] Chapter two has already set out the rationales for financial regulation. It was argued there that from an economic perspective, consumers can only play the role of rational maximisers of their own utility if they have the information upon which to make an informed decision. In practice, it was argued that financial markets suffer from a high degree of information asymmetry, rendering such decision-making difficult. From a social perspective it is also important that consumers receive appropriate information, whether that be about the financial system at large, the characteristics of different types of product, the terms of individual products, or their legal rights. Consumers also need some appreciation of how their individual position fits into this broader canvass. As the Cruickshank Report stated:

> [k]nowledgeable consumers provide the best incentive to effective competition. With the right information, consumers can take responsibility for their own financial well-being, shop around and exert the pressures on suppliers which drive a competitive and innovative market.[2]

There are several ways in which consumers may lack the information they need to make informed choices. First, they may lack information about the financial system at large, such as the roles of different types of financial products and institutions, and how these relate to their

---

[1] There is copious literature on the role of information in consumer protection. See, for example, H Beales, R Craswell and S Salop, 'The Efficient Regulation of Consumer Information' (1981) 24 *Journal of Law and Economics* 491; WC Whitford, 'The Functions of Disclosure Regulation in Consumer Transactions' (1973) *Wisconsin Law Review* 400; G Hadfield, R Howse and M Trebilcock, 'Information-Based Principles for Rethinking Consumer Protection Policy' (1998) 21 *Journal of Consumer Policy* 131; Office of Fair Trading, *Consumer Detriment Under Conditions of Imperfect Information* (OFT Research Paper 11, prepared by London Economics, August 1997).

[2] *Competition in UK Banking: A Report to the Chancellor of the Exchequer* (the Cruickshank Report) (20 March 2000) executive summary para 50.

individual needs.[3] Secondly, they may lack information about the relative strengths of products within a particular class (how current accounts compare with each other, for example). Thirdly, they may lack information about the standing of individual institutions (how likely it is that their bank will become insolvent, for instance). Finally, they may lack information about the legal framework within which they contract (such as what their rights are and how they can enforce them). Where there is information asymmetry relating to these issues, consumers are likely to suffer detriment.[4] For example, they may not buy appropriate products at reasonable prices, they may not understand the terms on which the products are offered or they may not realise the advantages and disadvantages of different products.[5] Where consumers realise the difficulties they face in making informed choices, they may choose not to purchase, rather than make a mistake. This too gives cause for concern. Given the extent to which the Government is keen to ensure that private provision is made for the future, and the difficulty in playing the part of active citizen without access to certain financial products, the decision not to participate may lead to significant difficulties for the consumer. Llewellyn argues that 'consumer welfare is as much compromised by reluctance (because of lack of confidence in the industry) to purchase appropriate products as it is through being mis-sold inappropriate products'.[6]

The purpose of this chapter is to examine the role of information in protecting the consumer of banking services. The chapter begins by examining why information asymmetry may emerge. It then identifies the different types of asymmetry that are likely to exist in banking markets, and how these might be tackled, with particular reference to the role of the Financial Services Authority (FSA). Next the chapter examines how the supply of false and misleading information can be controlled. Finally, conclusions are drawn.

CONSUMER PROTECTION AND INFORMATION ASYMMETRY

Chapter two examined the economic rationales for financial regulation. It was stated that economic theory makes assumptions about the role of the consumer in the marketplace. It is assumed that consumers are rational

[3] See Financial Services Authority, *Informing Consumers: A Review of Product Information at Point of Sale* (FSA, November 2000) para 35.
[4] Indeed, consumer detriment can be viewed as the difference between the outcome that consumers experience with available information and the outcome they would experience with the further information they could usefully obtain. See Office of Fair Trading, *Consumer Detriment* (OFT Paper 296, February 2000) at 1; Office of Fair Trading above n 1.
[5] Above n 3.
[6] D Llewellyn, *The Economic Rationale for Financial Regulation* ((FSA Occasional Paper 1, April 1999) at 25.

maximisers of their own utility and that they are sovereign in the market. The first point means that consumers (rather than the state, the regulator, or firms operating in the market) are best placed to decide where to deploy their scarce resources. The second point means that when they make such decisions, consumers send signals to suppliers. If suppliers do not take heed of these signals then they will be forced to exit the market. There is, therefore, a clear incentive upon suppliers to respond to consumer demand. However, it was argued that consumers are in part unable to play the role attributed to them in economic theory because of information asymmetry. In the perfect market, all players have perfect information about the nature and values of commodities traded.[7] In reality, financial markets, along with many others, fall far short of this ideal. Consumers, in particular, are likely to know less than would be necessary for them to make fully informed choices. They are at a particular disadvantage when compared with banks and other providers of financial services, and the term 'information asymmetry' refers specifically to this disparity.[8] Although it has been forcefully argued that the market system provides incentives for suppliers to disclose information that is demanded by consumers, there are good reasons to believe that this does not occur in practice.[9] It is worth considering the reasons for this in some detail.

First, some financial products can be classified as credence goods. This means that their essential characteristics cannot be identified until long after the contract is entered, if at all.[10] As a result it is difficult for important information about such products to be transmitted through the market process.[11] Davies comments that the complexity of financial products is particularly problematic for long-term contracts, such as personal pension plans or savings products linked to life assurance. He compares a personal pension with a washing machine stating, 'it is not easy to understand what a personal pension delivers, there is no information on reliability, the price is opaque and the product cannot be tested'.[12] A related problem is that the financial services provider may be able to

---

[7] See I Ramsay, *Rationales for Intervention in the Consumer Marketplace* (OFT, 1984) para 3.3.

[8] This asymmery provides one of the principal justifications for financial regulation, the other being systemic risk. See H Davies, 'Why Regulate?' Henry Thornton Lecture (City University Business School, 4 November 1998); Ramsay, *ibid*.

[9] See G Benston, *Regulating Financial Markets* (London, Institute of Economic Affairs, 1998) at 58–63 for the arguments against mandatory disclosure, and in favour of leaving financial markets to self-regulate. For an excellent and exhaustive examination of the role of information in consumer protection see Office of Fair Trading, above n 4.

[10] MR Darby and E Karni, 'Free Competition and the Optimal Amount of Fraud' (1973) 16 *Journal of Law and Economics* 67.

[11] For example, if a consumer takes out a pension, the pensions key characteristics will not be apparent for many years.

[12] Davies, 'Why Regulate?' above n 8.

change terms during the course of the contract. An obvious example relates to interest rates. Mortgages which operate on a standard variable rate will involve interest rates which change following movements in the money market rates. However, such mortgages do not require the lender to vary the rates payable according to pre-set criteria.[13]

Secondly, suppliers are only likely to provide information to consumers that they believe will place their product in a favourable light, and so lead to an increase in profits. *Consumer Detriment* concludes that suppliers will predominantly provide information that is: easy to understand; easy to verify; effective in attracting customers; and can be provided cost effectively.[14] This means that some information which would benefit consumers will sometimes not be provided. To take a simple example, a supplier will not reveal that one of its products is out-performed by a rival product. As has been noted: 'it is not in the commercial interest of the higher cost creditor that an individual borrower should be sufficiently well informed to be able to identify alternative arrangements that would represent better value'.[15] This does not mean, however, that the information will not be supplied by the market. In the example given, we might expect the rival producer to disclose the superiority of its product. Benston observes that 'vendors have strong incentives to inform consumers effectively about the qualities of their products and of alternatives supplied by other vendors.'[16] But there are reasons to believe that this may not always happen. For example, the rival supplier may fear entering a bidding war, where the other party reveals negative information about its product and so business is picked up by a third rival.[17] Alternatively, the rival supplier may fear that revealing negative information about the first-mentioned supplier may reduce the overall demand for the product in question. For instance, if bank A claims that bank B is in danger of becoming insolvent this may lead to a run on both (and perhaps other banks) owing to a reduction in confidence in the banking system, and the inability of consumers to distinguish accurately between sound and unsound banks. It is important not to overstate this. In some markets consumers do receive a fair picture of the essential characteristics of the products on offer, but the discussion reveals why in some cases, it will not be in the interests of the supplier to provide all the useful information he or she might.

---

[13] See Cruickshank, above n 2 para 4.37. Matters relating to variable rates form a large proportion of complaints to the Financial Ombudsman Service. See further ch 6.
[14] Office of Fair Trading, above n 1 para 3.2.2.
[15] National Association of Citizens Advice Bureaux (NACAB), *Summing Up: Bridging the Financial Literacy Divide* (NACAB, 2001) para 3.7.
[16] Benston, above n 9 at 61.
[17] Office of Fair Trading, above n 4 at 38.

Information need not only be provided by product suppliers and their rivals. It may also come from third parties whose task it is to provide information and advice to the consumer.[18] In some cases, however, the advisor will receive commission from the product provider, and so will be under an incentive to recommend one type of product, or one provider's product, rather than to give the consumer an objective and disinterested assessment. Although regulations attempt to deal with this by using standards of best advice and suitability, in the words of Johnson 'the fundamental incentive structure remains—the regulation is essentially against the natural grain of advisors' incentives'.[19]

In other cases third parties may emerge who provide a genuinely objective account of the merits of different products, but there are reasons to believe that there may be an under-provision of such firms in the market.[20] This is because information has the characteristic of public goods, meaning that it is possible to benefit from it without paying the full cost of its provision.[21] This 'free riding' acts as a form of externality, and provides a disincentive to engage in such business.

A further difficulty with relying on the market to provide information is that it is easier for consumers to see the benefits of some types of information than others. For example, it has been argued that price is more likely to be disclosed than quality: first, because it is easier to communicate convincingly; and secondly, because it is more likely to be effective in winning custom.[22] This may have a negative impact from the point of view of the consumer. Rather than get a balanced picture of all the characteristics of a product, the consumer is told about only one. The consumer then has to make a judgement about quality, which may be difficult. Akerlof argues that in this situation, consumers are liable to conclude that all products are of similar quality, and make a purchasing decision on the basis of price. This provides an incentive for suppliers to deal in cheap, low quality products.[23] The result is focal point competition where suppliers, knowing that consumers are unable to process large amounts of information, focus on one attribute, for example price.

The central reason why suppliers of high quality products may be reluctant to disclose information about quality is that it is difficult to

---

[18] Benston comments that 'if there is a demand [for such information] private information publications ... can and do provide these services' above n 9 at 63.
[19] P Johnson, *CAT Standards and Stakeholders* (FSA, September 2000) at 22. The position of financial advisors is considered briefly below.
[20] Examples might be credit ratings firms such as Standard and Poor and Moody's, and interest groups such as the Consumer Association, which produces the magazine *Which?*.
[21] A Ogus, *Regulation: Legal Form and Economic Theory* (Oxford, Clarendon Press, 1994) at 33–36.
[22] See in particular G Akerlof, 'The Market for "Lemons": Qualitative Uncertainty and the Market Mechanism' (1970) 84 *Quarterly Journal of Economics* 488 at 497.
[23] *Ibid.*

verify and therefore lacks credibility. If there is a move towards low quality products, there may be a tendency on the part of consumers to exit the market, fearing that they might purchase a poor quality product unwittingly. This may lead to individual detriment, with consumers feeling that they are unable to choose the products that they would ideally like. Where consumers are not confident than they can obtain reliable information, then there is the risk that they will decide not to purchase at all.[24] There can be little doubt that consumers treat information from both financial services providers, and financial advisors, with a high degree of scepticism. Research for the FSA showed that governments were also liable not to be trusted by consumers when it comes to providing financial information.[25] The reduction in consumer confidence that this would entail could also, of course, be damaging to the industry. However, it is important to remember that there are different ways that a supplier can communicate information about quality. Although disclosure is the most obvious form of information communication, suppliers also communicate through reputation. This may be more effective than specific disclosure, with consumers trusting suppliers to provide quality products because of their reputation.[26] In a market such as banking, which depends upon consumer confidence for its very existence, reputation is likely to be seen by suppliers as of considerable importance.[27] Research by MORI (Market and Opinion Research Institute) for the Department of Trade and Industry (DTI) found that 77 per cent of consumers felt that in financial services, it is best to go for a well-known brand that can be trusted.[28] Research for the DTI's White Paper on consumer credit reform found that when asked about the important factors in deciding whether to take out credit, 85 per cent said that the reputation of the lender was the most important.[29]

It was stated above that suppliers will provide information if they judge that it will increase their profits. If consumers demand information, there will be some commercial pressure on a supplier to provide it. However, some commentators appear too ready to assume that consumers know which questions they should be asking to find the information they would

---

[24] Llewellyn, above n 6 at 25
[25] BMRB (British Market Research Bureau) survey conducted for the FSA, July 1999. Advice agencies and the FSA performed best here.
[26] As Stigler comments in one of the classic works on the topic: 'when economists deplore the reliance of the consumer on reputation,.they implicitly assume that the consumer has a large laboratory, ready to deliver current information quickly and gratuitously'. G Stigler, 'The Economics of Information' (1961) 3 *Journal of Political Economy* 213 at 214. Benston also emphasises the utility of relying upon reputation above n 9 at 61).
[27] Fractional reserve banking could not exist without a high degree of confidence. See ch 2.
[28] DTI, *Consumer Knowledge Survey*, Consumer Affairs Report Series no.1 (DTI, 2001).
[29] This was even more important than the advertised APR (Annual Percentage Rate). (*Ibid* at 14).

ideally want. Even if search costs are low, which they will frequently not be, consumers may be confused about how to obtain the information they would like. A consumer taking out a mortgage may be so concerned with the monthly repayments that he or she does not ask about redemption penalties. The assumption that consumers will ask if they need to know is unrealistic where complex products are concerned.[30]

An additional difficulty with relying upon the market to supply information is that consumers suffer from bounded rationality. This means that their ability to receive, process and act upon information is limited.[31] Not only do consumers not know which questions to ask to get the result they want, but in some cases they will be unable to deal with any information that is supplied, even if the information appears to be useful. The problems that consumers experience in processing information mean that there is a limit to the utility of providing information, particularly where it is relatively complex or detailed. One of the principal difficulties here is that consumers differ significantly in relation to the extent to which they can process a given type and amount of information. From a bank's point of view, it will be under an incentive to provide the information that it deems most profitable. This may mean that information that would be important to some consumers, for example the most vulnerable, will not be provided. As will be seen below, it is important that the distributional effect of information provision is addressed.

The discussion above reveals some of the reasons why the market may not provide consumers with the information they need to make informed choices. It is important now to consider what types of information consumers need to be able to make those choices, and so play the role of informed consumer. The existence of information asymmetry informs a good deal of the thinking behind the Financial Services and Markets Act (FSMA).[32] As the FSA has argued: 'retail consumers frequently lack the necessary information, knowledge or understanding to shop around effectively and exert their buying power in the marketplace'.[33] When examining this topic it is important to look at the consumer protection and public awareness objectives together. As explained in chapter two, both objectives are premised upon the idea that if consumers are better

---

[30] This issue is partly addressed by the argument that provided some consumers ('marginal consumers') are prepared to take action, this will have the effect of raising standards. However, although individual action can have benefits, its effect is frequently limited. See ch 6.

[31] Ogus, above n 21 at 41. See also H Simon, *Models of Bounded Rationality* (Cambridge, MA, MIT Press, 1982).

[32] See ch 2.

[33] Financial Services Authority, *Comparative Information for Financial Services* (FSA, October 1999) para 1.2.

informed then they are more likely to be able to play a role in disciplining the market and protecting themselves. It is suggested that the information that consumers need can roughly be divided into four main categories: financial education, product information, institutional information, and legal rights.[34] These are examined below. First, however, it is helpful briefly to say something about the necessity and sufficiency of correcting information asymmetry.

Necessity and Sufficiency of Correcting Information Asymmetry

It is important to emphasise that although information deficits are an example of market failure, this does not necessarily mean that the regulator should always take steps to correct them. On an economic basis, intervention will only be justified where its benefits outweigh its costs and in some cases, correcting information asymmetry would simply be uneconomic. In producing its *Regulatory Checklist*, which provides guidelines for improving regulation, the Organisation For Economic Cooperation and Development (OECD) argued that:

> government intervention should be based on clear evidence that government action is justified, given the values at stake and current government policies; the likely benefits and costs of action … and alternative mechanisms for addressing the problem.[35]

The *Checklist* adds that 'a clear assessment of total costs and benefits … is crucial information for decision makers.'[36] Weighing the costs and benefits of regulation is an important part of the regulatory scene in the UK. For example, the FSA is obliged to comply with the principles of regulation, and these principles make it clear that the FSA must have regard to the cost-effectiveness of its actions. The FSA must also publish a cost–benefit

---

[34] It is not suggested that this is a perfect list. However, it is hoped that it provides a helpful framework for analysis. Alternative approaches are taken by McMeel and Virgo, who distinguish between advice regulation, information regulation and product regulation, and Johnson, who distinguishes between regulating the advice process, disclosure, consumer education and product regulation. See G McMeel and J Virgo, *Financial Advice and Financial Products*, (Oxford, Oxford University Press, 2001) paras 1.60–1.68, and P Johnson above n 19 at 31.

[35] Organisation for Economic Cooperation and Development, *Recommendation of the Council of the OECD on Improving the Quality of Government Regulation* (including the *OECD Reference Checklist for Regulatory Decision-Making and Background Note*) (Paris: OECD, 1995) at 9. For discussion see MTrebilcock, 'Rethinking Consumer Protection Policy' in C Rickett and T Telfer (eds), *International Perspectives on Consumers' Access to Justice* (Cambridge, Cambridge University Press, 2003) 68.

[36] Organisation for Economic Cooperation and Development, *ibid* para 29.

analysis (CBA) as part of the process of consultation. However, undertaking a cost–benefit analysis of regulatory action is enormously difficult, and is particularly so where financial services are concerned.[37] As discussed in chapter two, the FSA adopts a risk-based approach to regulation. In so doing, it makes a judgment about the risks posed to its objectives, and decides what action to take accordingly. In some cases there may be clear evidence of information failure, but it may nevertheless not pose a sufficient risk to the FSA's statutory objectives to warrant action. This will be particularly so if the consequences of the market failure in question are not particularly severe. It should also be remembered that there may be sound reasons for intervention based upon distributive justice. Even if the financial costs of a particular provision outweigh the financial gains, those gains may be clustered among those who are most in need. This has been increasingly recognised.[38] Indeed, the CBA used by the FSA allows benefits to be assessed in qualitative terms.[39]

Types of Information Asymmetry

Financial Illiteracy and Financial Education

An important part of a consumer protection information strategy is consumer education. The United Nations Guidelines for Consumer Protection state that '[g]overnments should develop or encourage the development of general consumer education and information programmes' and argue that '[c]onsumer education should, where appropriate, become an integral part of the basic curriculum of the educational system'.[40] However, it is clear that general awareness of financial products and the financial ssystem may be lacking. The FSA suggests that 'many [consumers] are confused by the range of products on offer and do not understand which sorts of product might be most suitable to meet

---

[37] A Alfon and P Andrews, *Cost–Benefit Analysis in Financial Regulation* (FSA Occasional Paper 3, September 1999). See also C Briault, 'The Costs of Financial Regulation' ZEW/AEI Conference on Regulation and Supervision of Financial Markets and Institutions in the EU, Mannheim, 10 July 2003; and J Hamilton and M Wisniewski, 'Economic Appraisals of Rulemaking in the New Society: Why, How and What Does It Mean? The Challenge for the Consumer' in Rickett and Telfer (eds), above n 35 at 196.
[38] D Simpson, G Meeks, P Klumpes and P Andrews (eds), *Some Cost–Benefit Issues in Financial Regulation* (FSA Occasional Paper 12, October 2000).
[39] Alfon and Andrews, above n 37 at 8. It is also possible to apply distributional weights to take into account the value of a fixed cost to different groups. See generally RN Vaughan, *Distributional Issues in Welfare Assessment and Consumer Affairs Policy* (OFT, January 1999).
[40] UN Guidelines for Consumer Protection (UNGA Res 39/248 (9 April 1985)) paras 31 and 32. This has been met with the introduction of citizenship (which includes consumer education) into the English national curriculum.

their particular needs.'[41] Consumers will be unable to make informed decisions if they are unaware of the different types of financial product available, and lack a general understanding of the financial system.

Under FSMA's public awareness objective, the FSA has responsibility for promoting awareness of the benefits and risks associated with different kinds of investment and financial dealing as well as providing appropriate information and advice.[42] The FSA has stated that it intends to fulfil this objective by promoting a higher level of financial literacy as well as by improving the advice and information available to consumers.[43] Financial literacy can be seen as underpinning the entire system, and a wide range of initiatives are currently examining issues relating to promote this.[44] As the Cruickshank Report commented: '[t]he strongest curb against the mis-selling of financial products is to equip customers with the knowledge and confidence to ask the right questions and to seek out the best products or the ones which suit them best.'[45] With these skills in place, the FSA is able to make assumptions when deciding how best to intervene. In the words of the National Association of Citizens Advice Bureaux (NACAB) '[f]inancial literacy is no longer a desirable trait that consumers should be encouraged in, it is an essential requirement to play an informed consumer role today'.[46] The National Consumer Council (NCC) also emphasises how fundamental financial literacy is: '[b]uilding on basic skills such as literacy and numeracy as a foundation, consumer education empowers people so they can interpret information, negotiate, make judgements and choices, enquiries and complaints'.[47] The NCC further argued that: 'in a fast changing and complex marketplace, consumers need more than just information—they need the skills to be able to analyse and use that information'.[48]

There can be little doubt that financial illiteracy is widespread.[49] If consumers are to be able to make informed choices, they need to have an

---

[41] Above n 33 para 1.3.

[42] FSMA s 4(2).

[43] Financial literacy can be defined as 'the ability to make informed judgements and to take effective decisions regarding the use and management of money'. M Noctor, S Stoney and R Stradling, *Financial Literacy* (Slough, National Foundation for Educational Research, 1992). This definition has been approved by the FSA (*Promoting Public Understanding of Financial Services: A Strategy for Consumer Education*, (FSA, November 1998)) para 1.4.

[44] See for example the work of the Personal Finance Education Group, the FSA, and the Basic Skills Agency. For a useful although now slightly outdated account see J Vass, *A Guide to the Provision of Financial Services Education for Consumers* (FSA, 1998).

[45] Cruickshank, above n 2 para 4.127.

[46] National Association of Citizens Advice Bureaux, above n 15 at 1.

[47] National Consumer Council (NCC), *Consumer Education: Beyond Consumer Information* (NCC, 2001).

[48] *Ibid.*

[49] See in particular The Adult Financial Literacy Advisory Group, *Report to the Secretary of State for Education and Employment* (DFEE, December 2000).

appropriate perspective on the financial system. They need to be aware of the different types of products on offer, and how these relate to their needs and expectations. Where such information is not readily available, they need to know how to find the information, for example by research or by going to a financial advisor. In addition, consumers sometimes need to be told that a financial product may not be suitable for them because of the likelihood of the consumer's situation changing. In the case of financial advice for, say, a personal pension, neither the consumer nor the advisor is likely to know whether the consumer will stop payments, thus making the product inappropriate. However, the advisor should be able to tell the consumer about the effects of allowing a policy to lapse in the early years, and that a significant proportion of consumers who allow such policies to lapse.[50] There is ample evidence that people save too little because they underestimate their vulnerability to economic risks.[51] A further issue is that consumers need to be aware of the importance of shopping around. Research suggests that consumers generally do not shop around where financial services are concerned. One survey found that more than one third of consumers believed that the financial market is so competitive that 'there is little difference between the charges and costs of different companies'.[52] The facts tell a different story. FSA research found that by taking out an average priced product rather than the cheapest on offer, a typical consumer would lose out £230 a year on variable rate mortgages and more than £100 a year on a savings account.[53]

Identifying that there is a problem of financial illiteracy, and that consumers need to have better skills if they are to be able to make informed choices is one thing; deciding how to address this is another. The first point to note is that different organisations will be able to tackle different elements of financial illiteracy. The information deficits that lead to consumer detriment should perhaps be seen as existing on a spectrum. At one end of the spectrum consumers lack the basic skills of literacy and

---

[50] There are several reasons why consumers allow policies to lapse, some of which might have been anticipated at the point of sale. See Financial Services Authority, *Persisting—Why Consumers Stop Paying into Policies* (FSA Consumer Research Report 6, 2000). See also the discussion in S Smith, *Stopping Short: Why Do so many Consumers Stop Contributing to Long-Term Savings Policies?* (FSA Occasional Paper 21, January 2004).
[51] BD Bernheim, 'Personal Saving, Information and Economic Literacy: New Directions for Public Policy' in Tax Policy for Economic Growth in the 1990s (Washington DC, American Council for Capital Formation 1994). Cited in Johnson, above n 19 at 24. The DTI Task Force on Overindebtedness argued that too few consumers give thought to the possibility of their circumstances changing when they take out a loan. *Report by the Task Force on Tackling Overindebtedness* (DTI July 2001) para 4.6.
[52] Financial Services Consumer Panel, *Consumers in the Financial Market* (FSCP, 2001).
[53] M Cook et al, *Losing Interest: How Much Can Consumers Save by Shopping Around for Financial Products?* (FSA Occasional Paper 19, October 2002) at 5.

numeracy that provide the foundations upon which further initiatives are built. This absence of basic skills on the part of many consumers is perhaps the fundamental problem. An *International Numeracy Survey* for the Basic Skills Agency found that only 20 per cent of those tested were able to complete all tasks accurately. This placed the UK bottom of a league of seven developed nations. The Basic Skills Agency is the national development organisation for literacy and numeracy in England and Wales.[54] The Agency works in partnership with other bodies such as the FSA, with whom it developed the Adult Financial Capability Framework. This supports the creation of learning programmes and resources, and covers a wide range of issues in money management and consumer finance. Another important group involved in addressing financial illiteracy through education is the Personal Finance Education Group (PFEG). Launched in 1996, the PFEG's goal is 'to promote and facilitate the education of all UK school pupils about financial matters so that they can make independent and informed decisions about their personal finances and long-term security'. To achieve this it brings together a variety of parties including teachers, consumer bodies, government, the FSA and representatives from the financial services industry. A remarkable variety of other bodies have a role in addressing financial illiteracy, and it is not possible to consider them here. It is important to note that the FSA will not have much of a role, if any in the provisions of basic skills of literacy and numeracy. The FSA recently stated that its financial capability strategy (considered below) 'is not about teaching consumers basic numeracy skills, which is better led by government'.[55]

If we move further along the spectrum from lack of basic skills to a lack of a satisfactory understanding of the financial system, the principal issue for consideration in this part of the chapter, other players take on a more prominent role. The FSA has perhaps the principal responsibility for this under FSMA's public awareness objective. As has been noted, FSMA describes the public awareness objective as promoting public understanding of the financial system, which includes promoting awareness of the benefits and risks associated with different kinds of investment or other financial dealings and the promotion of appropriate information and advice. Although the FSA works closely with others to address the lack of fundamental basic skills, it has a major responsibility for improving public understanding of the financial system. It is clear that the FSA sees itself as having the central role in addressing these issues and it looks as

---

[54] Basic skills are defined as 'the ability to read, write and speak English/Welsh and use mathematics at a level necessary to function and progress at work and in society in general.' See <http://www.basic-skills.co.uk>.
[55] Financial Services Authority, *Towards a National Strategy for Financial Capability* (FSA, 2003) at 12.

though major changes may be afoot. In particular, the FSA has announced that it is setting up a Financial Capability Steering Group. The Group will work to develop a national strategy for financial capability with the objective of providing consumers with the education, information and generic advice that they need to be able to make their financial decisions with confidence.[56] The FSA has taken the view that there is a pressing need to engage more fully with a wider variety of stakeholders and potential partners concerned with these issues, and that there is currently something of a leadership vacuum in relation to such matters. The FSA's role in this will be to lead and facilitate the development of the strategy, and to implement it, taking particular responsibility for elements of its delivery.[57] The strategy is due to be published in March 2004 and is awaited with interest. It should be noted that financial education forms only part of the strategy for financial capability. To the extent that financial illiteracy is characterised by a lack of generic financial information, it may be that the solution lies in providing generic financial advice.[58] Furthermore, the provision of information will also play a role. These issues are considered below.

Although improving the provision of financial education will undoubtedly be an important element in addressing problems of financial illiteracy, it will not be a panacea. The Financial Services Consumer Panel argued that they 'doubt that it will be possible to raise the understanding and skills of the general population to a level at which they will fully understand the complex products on offer'.[59] There can be little doubt that this is correct. However, this does not mean that consumer education does not have a valid role to play for all consumers. The more that consumers are able to make informed choices, the more that incentives are placed upon providers to improve information and raise product standards. An Executive Director at the OFT has recently commented that 'consumer education is as much about culture and attitude as it is about information'.[60]

Product Information

Improving basic skills and an understanding of the financial system are necessary but not sufficient for creating capable, informed consumers. The FSA has argued that consumers also lack:

---

[56] *Ibid* at 12.
[57] *Ibid* at 15.
[58] *Ibid* at 12.
[59] Financial Services Consumer Panel, *Response to FSA Consultation Paper 15* (10 February 1999) para 5.
[60] P Boys, quoted in 'Empowering Consumers, Adding Value' in (2003) 36 *Fair Trading* 6 at 6.

clear, meaningful information on the key characteristics of products of a particular type so that once they have decided what sort of product they need, they can take better-informed decisions about which particular one might offer them the best deal.[61]

Ideally, consumers will want to know the price, quality and terms of trade of all products of a particular category that they are considering purchasing.[62] However, as explained above, there may be reasons to assume that the market will not necessarily provide this information. The provision of appropriate information will be important for a wide range of consumers, many of whom will have different needs. As will be seen, this is a major policy problem. However, the important point is that the regulatory regime addresses the question of what kind(s) of information are needed. As the FSA has noted in the context of its financial capability strategy:

> in order to be fit for purpose, the information provided to consumers must address the questions which they have, be provided in a style with which they feel comfortable and be made available at a time and place which is convenient to them.[63]

The discussion below should be viewed in this context.

Mandatory Disclosure   Where the consumer wants information about individual products, but that information may not be supplied by the market, one solution is to use mandatory disclosure.[64] Although disclosure is not always championed by adherents to free market ideology, it is a relatively 'pro-market' regulatory response because it facilitates the consumer's making of an informed choice.[65] Disclosure may therefore be attractive from the perspectives both of efficiency and ideology. In terms of efficiency, disclosure enhances and encourages competition. In the words of Page and Ferguson '[t]he modern rationale for compelling disclosure stresses its role in fostering the efficient functioning of markets through providing investors with the information which they

---

[61] *Ibid*.

[62] Office of Fair Trading, above n 1 at 5.

[63] Above n 55 at 12.

[64] See generally W Whitford, 'The Functions of Disclosure Regulation in Consumer Transactions' above n 1.

[65] See H Beales, R Craswell and S Salop, 'The Efficient Regulation of Consumer Information' (1981) above n 1 at 514, C Scott and J Black, *Cranston's Consumers and the Law* (London, Butterworths, 2000) at 339. It can be described as 'freedom with disclosure' (M Taylor, 'Accountability and Objectives of the FSA' in M Blair *et al*, *Blackstone's Guide to the Financial Services and Markets Act 2000* (London, Blackstone Press, 2001)) 17 at 29.

require in order to arrive at informed decisions'.[66] As Breyer similarly argues:

> since freely functioning markets require adequate information—which disclosure helps provide—disclosure ... can be viewed as augmenting the preconditions of a competitive marketplace rather than substituting regulation for competition.[67]

From the point of view of ideology, disclosure may be attractive as once the consumer's decision is made, that consumer's choice is respected. It is therefore possible to commend disclosure for the respect it gives to personal autonomy. However, this carries with it inevitable risks. In the words of Loss it does not take away the consumer's 'inalienable right to make a fool of himself'.[68]

In theory at least, a well-organised disclosure regime can ensure that helpful information is supplied in a way that enables consumers to make informed decisions.[69] Disclosure regimes exist for a wide range of financial products, and this work will not attempt to provide an exhaustive examination of these regimes. However, it is worth briefly saying something about some of the principal examples. First, under the Consumer Credit Act 1974 disclosure of credit prices in terms of APR (Annual Percentage Rate) and of terms is a significant part of the regulatory regime.[70] Several reasons were set out by the Crowther Committee for the introduction APR disclosure. First, it was argued that such disclosure would help consumers to make comparisons between suppliers and so shop around for the best deal.[71] Secondly, disclosure would enable consumers to compare the interest payable on a loan with interest received on savings, and so to decide how best to order their financial affairs.[72] Thirdly, it was argued that disclosure would make credit suppliers more conscious of how their rates of interest compare with their competitors, and so stimulate competition.[73] Finally, the Committee argued that disclosure would help consumers to ensure that they do not

---

[66] A Page and R Ferguson, *Investor Protection* (London, Weidenfeld and Nicolson, 1992) at 45.
[67] S Beyer, *Regulation and its Reform* (Cambridge MA, Harvard University Press, 1982) at 151.
[68] L Loss, *Fundamentals of Securities Regulation* (1983) at 86, cited in Page and Ferguson, above n 66 at 46.
[69] See D Llewellyn, above n 6 at 33; *Report of the Committee on Consumer Credit* (the Crowther Committee) (Cmnd 4596, 1971) para 3.8.3.
[70] For example, disclosure is required in advertising (s 44), in quotations (s 52), before execution of the contract (s 55), in the document itself (ss 60 and 61) and during performance or on default (s 87). For discussion of the role of disclosure in this context see I Ramsay, *Consumer Protection: Text and Materials* (London, Weidenfeld and Nicolson, 1989) at 327.
[71] Crowther Committee, above n 69 para 3.8.3.
[72] *Ibid.*
[73] *Ibid.*

over-extend their financial resources by 'ill-informed and rash use of credit facilities'.[74] One aspect of disclosure under the Act relates to providing certain information in advertisements. The Consumer Credit (Advertisements) Regulations 1989 divides advertisements into three types: simple, intermediate and full.[75] There are different rules about what has to be disclosed, depending upon how the advertisement is classified. The rationale behind the Regulations is that advertisements should provide a fair and reasonably comprehensive indication of the nature and true cost of the credit terms being offered. This is done by regulating both the content and the form of the advertisement. It seems that the provisions are generally viewed as unnecessarily complex, and there have been calls for them to be significantly reformed.[76] The 2003 Consumer Credit White Paper argues that 'the current rules have resulted in a highly technical and complex regime, creating confusion for lenders, enforcers and consumers'.[77] The Government has stated its desire to introduce new measures that will 'ensure greater consistency and transparency in credit advertising, so that consumers can compare financial products with confidence and make informed purchasing decisions'.[78] The changes have only been outlined at the time of writing, but it is clear that the Government intends to bring the regime more into line with that proposed for the regulation of mortgages.[79] The Government has stated that the new advertising regulations will have a number of effects. First, they will ensure that all advertisements for credit are clear, fair and not misleading. Secondly, the distinction between simple, intermediate and full credit advertisements will be replaced with a new hierarchy, aimed at ensuring consistency in how key information is used and presented. Thirdly, the new regime will require a single set of assumptions to be used by credit card issuers in determining the APR, helping consumers to compare costs more easily. Where there is personal pricing, lenders will be able to quote a typical APR, but this will have to be 'the highest rate reasonably expected to be given to at least 66 per cent of the eventual number of consumers who accept a credit agreement in response to the advertisement'. In addition, in order to prevent additional charges and costs being hidden in small print, where certain

---

[74] *Ibid* para 3.8.13.

[75] SI 1989/1125 as amended by SI 1999/3177 and SI 2000/1797.

[76] See for example Better Regulation Task Force, *Consumer Affairs* (May, 1998). Details of the Regulations are contained in the OFT booklet *Credit Advertising* (OFT, 2003).

[77] Department of Trade and Industy, *Fair, Clear and Competitive: the Consumer Credit Market in the 21st Century* (Cm 6040, December 2003). Hereafter 'The White Paper', para 2.5, basing its conclusions on 'Research Findings: Consumer Credit Advertising' (Report for the DTI prepared by Research Business International Ltd, July 2002).

[78] White Paper para 2.7.

[79] Considered below.

items of information linked to the cost of a loan are displayed, they must be 'shown together and with equal prominence'.[80] In such circumstances the APR will have to be given in the same place as the other information, but will be double the size and more prominent.

The White Paper also contains some details of the Government's intention to improve the pre- and post-contractual information provided for consumers, and to ensure that agreements are presented in a clear and transparent format. A few brief points should be noted. First, in relation to pre-contractual information, the Government intends to ensure that certain information be provided before any agreement is concluded, so that the consumer is able to reflect on that information before making a final decision. In practice, the result will be that the provisions of the Distance Marketing Directive will be extended to all contracts.[81] One advantage of this for lenders will be that they will no longer feel obliged to produce separate pre-contractual information for those contracting at a distance, and those contracting face to face.[82] In relation to making the format of agreements clearer and more transparent, the Government believes that the way that information is presented discourages consumers from reading credit agreements. It has therefore proposed that there should be a requirement to state key information on rights and responsibilities. For example, such information would include, where applicable, information on early settlement, cancellation and statutory wealth warnings.[83] The Government will consult with industry about how information about the ways in which card issuers calculate interest on the use of credit cards can be standardised and made more transparent. With regard to clear post-contractual information, the White Paper suggests that consumers need regular information during the course of their contracts, such as the outstanding amount they owe, and should also be informed if they fall into arrears or have incurred additional charges upon which interest will be charged. The Government has also stated that consumer should receive warnings about the implications of only making minimum payments on credit card debt and the consequences of defaulting on payments.[84]

---

[80] The types of information include deposits, total amount payable and frequency, amount and number of payments. White Paper para 2.11.

[81] Directive 2002/65/EC. The Directive aims to protect retail consumers when entering into a financial services contract sold at a distance. See Financial Services Authority, *Implementation of the Distance Marketing Directive* (FSA Discussion Paper 21, March 2003). The Directive must be implemented by 9 October 2004.

[82] White Paper para 2.23. Examples of the required pre-contractual information are the APR, the amount, frequency and number of repayments the total charge for credit and also a 'wealth warning' for any loan secured on a consumer's home.

[83] 81% of borrowers surveyed stated that they would welcome more information on their rights according to the DTI's *Consumer Credit Awareness Survey*.

[84] White Paper para 2.32.

Disclosure will also become important under the FSA's proposed rules on mortgage regulation. The FSA will have responsibility for regulating mortgage sales from 31 October 2004 and an important element of the regulatory regime will be the requirement for disclosure. As mentioned above, the consumer credit regime will to some extent borrow from that relating to mortgages. Under the proposed regime, when consumers and firms make initial contact, consumers will be given an initial disclosure document (IDD) which describes the services that the firm will offer the consumer in a set format. Before the consumer applies for a mortgage, firms must give him or her a key facts illustration (KFI). This will set out product information in a set format so that consumers are able to compare different mortgages. At the offer stage, the lender will give the consumer an offer document which includes an updated KFI. The FSA states that this will allow consumers to see the impact of any changes in the product or details such as interest rates, since they received the KFI.[85] Before the consumer applies for a product switch, a further advance, or the addition or removal of a party to the mortgage contract, firms will be obliged to give out a KFI. In addition, if the consumer applies for any other variation to the mortgage, firms will have to give out key information specified in FSA rules.

As the examples considered above in part demonstrate, there are strengths of, but also limitations to, the use of mandatory disclosure as a method of protecting the consumer. One point to emphasise is that it seems likely that disclosure will be of least benefit to the most vulnerable consumers. Wilhelmsson argues that the emphasis that policy makers have placed on consumer information acts to reproduce injustice, because those consumers most in need of protection derive the least benefit from the protection offered. He states:

> information measures are neutral as to their recipients, which in practice means an advantage for the consumers who are well-equipped to use the information. In this sense, therefore, measures based on the information paradigm may reproduce and even strengthen existing social injustice.[86]

Certainly, the empirical evidence on disclosure of the price of consumer credit raises doubts about the effectiveness of disclosure as a regulatory tool. APR disclosure should in theory be beneficial. Consumers are presented with a simple percentage figure that enables them to make meaningful price comparisons. However, the extent to which it works in practice is unclear. Crow, Howells and Moroney found that although

---

[85] Financial Services Authority, *Mortgage Regulation*, para 4.1.
[86] T Wilhelmsson, 'Consumer Law and Social Justice' in I Ramsay (ed), *Consumer Law in the Global Economy* (Aldershot, Dartmouth, 1997) 217 at 224.

over three-quarters of debtors had heard of the term APR, only one in
seven had a reasonable understanding of its meaning.[87] Whitford reviews
the plethora of studies on truth in lending in the USA and concludes that
the main beneficiaries of truth in lending legislation in the USA have been
those in higher income groups.[88] Studies of other sectors have come to
similar conclusions.[89] Similar concerns have been expressed in relation to
key features documents. In the words of Johnson 'in the face of a population, a large proportion of whom have difficulty with such simple concepts as percentages, understanding the implications of Reduction in
Yield figures is likely to be limited'.[90]

Although some traders doubt the need for mandatory disclosure, it
does not appear that there are significant difficulties in persuading
traders to comply with the law. Scott and Black comment that

> the major problem with disclosure regulation is not in securing business
> compliance, but rather that consumers are unaware of the information dis-
> closed, do not appreciate its significance, or simply do not employ the infor-
> mation provided in the marketplace.[91]

As mentioned above, the view that consumers rarely act upon the information supplied appears to be backed up by some empirical studies,
particularly in the USA.[92] One response to the doubts raised about the
effectiveness of mandatory disclosure regimes is to focus more attention
on the design of the disclosure in question. For example, information disclosed should generally be objective and verifiable and presented in a
clear and accessible manner.[93] In some cases this will be extremely difficult. Although APR disclosure in theory enables comparisons to be made
relatively easily, it is not always accurate as an indicator of cost. A study
by the Consumers' Association found that for the same transactions and

---

[87] I Crow, G Howells and M Moroney 'Credit and Debt: Choices for Poorer Consumers' in
I Crow, G Howells and M Moroney, *Aspects of Credit and Debt* (London, Sweet and Maxwell,
1993) 11 at 35–37.
[88] W Whitford, above n 1 at 414; See also L Mandell, 'Consumer Perception of Incurred
Interest Rates' (1971) 26 *Journal of Finance* 1143. In response to this, it can be argued that all
consumers benefit from actions taken by those few marginal consumers who take the time
to shop around.
[89] See K Monroe and P La Placa 'What Are the Benefits of Unit Pricing?' (1972) 36 *Journal of
Marketing* 16.
[90] Johnson, above n 19 at 22. As noted above, the FSA will be changing aspects of the KFDs
regime with these sorts of issues in mind.
[91] Scott and Black, above n 65 at 372.
[92] See for example W Brandt and G Day, 'Information Disclosure and Consumer Behaviour:
An Empirical Evaluation of Truth in Lending' (1973) *University of Michigan Journal of Law
Reform* 297. S Breyer, *Regulation and its Reform* above n 67 at 164.
[93] Note the principles for comparative information provided by the FSA. Above n 33
para 1.17.

APR, interest charges could vary by up to 36 per cent. This depended upon the specific interest rate calculation used.[94] The major banks have accepted that the APR is not sufficient alone to work out the cost of credit, and efforts have been made to address this. Even firm supporters of market-based regulation have recognised the limitations of disclosure. Cayne and Trebilcock argue that 'disclosure laws can be an effective means of protecting the poor ... because they enhance the operation of free market forces', but also recognise disclosure's boundaries. In particular 'they can only be of value if the consumer is intellectually and psychologically equipped to apply the information which disclosure regulation entitles him to have.'[95] This points to the importance of efforts to tackle financial literacy, as discussed above.

Another argument that is sometimes advanced is that mandatory disclosure is unnecessary. An interesting debate has emerged between Llewellyn and Benston about the utility of this form of regulation in the area of financial services. Benston argues that governmental regulation of financial services is likely to work against the interests of consumers.[96] First, he accepts that information asymmetry exists in financial services markets, but argues that 'the potential market failures ... apply with equal or greater force to many products and services that are not regulated'.[97] Indeed, he suggests that financial products are easier for consumers to evaluate than non-financial products. It is doubtful whether Benston's conclusions are correct. Although it is true that information asymmetry exists in other markets, it is likely to be particularly great in relation to some financial products. As many are credence goods, it is not possible for information to be communicated through the normal market process (as might be the case for search or experience goods). Llewellyn sets out the key differences between financial and many other products. For example, they are purchased infrequently, faults cannot be rectified, the value of the contract is frequently lost if the firm becomes insolvent during the maturity of the contract, and that the contract may create a fiduciary relationship with the company. In total, Llewellyn identifies 19 significant differences between (some) financial and non-financial services.[98] Many of these, it is submitted, provide at least some justification for regulatory intervention. Secondly, Benston suggests that correcting information

---

[94] *Treasury Select Committee First Report* (10 December 2003) para 49.

[95] D Cayne and M Trebilcock, 'Market Considerations in the Formulation of Consumer Protection Policy' (1973) 23 *University of Toronto Law Journal* 396 at 424. In relation to comparative tables, it is recognised that they be of limited use to less financially literate consumers. See below.

[96] Benston, above n 9 at 58.

[97] *Ibid* at 60.

[98] Llewellyn, above n 6 at 37–38.

asymmetry may not be an appropriate task for the regulator. He continues '[n]either Llewellyn nor anyone else [to my knowledge] has explained why a government agency is more likely than suppliers to determine what information consumers would find useful for making 'informed' decisions'.[99] The reasons why there might be incentives for suppliers not to provide consumers with an optimal amount of information are considered above, and will not be repeated here. Suffice it to say that there are reasons to believe that if there are incentives for suppliers to withhold or mask potentially useful information, this may provide a justification for the information to be provided by, or at the insistence of, the regulator. As already mentioned, and as is generally recognised, regulation is not cost-free, and the existence of market failure does not automatically justify regulation.[100] But where information can be provided in a cost-effective way outside normal market mechanisms, there are arguments for requiring its provision.[101]

Certification and CAT Standards   Another limitation with disclosure is that it is likely to be more effective in relation to some types of information than others. Akerlof suggests that it is far easier for consumers to compare price than quality, and that there is an incentive for suppliers to compete on price, leading to poorer quality goods driving out higher quality goods.[102] It is possible for the law to insist on firms disclosing information about quality, but quality–disclosure regimes are notoriously difficult to design effectively.[103] However, alternative information schemes can be designed to deal with terms other than price. One way of doing this is to use some form of certification. With certification, products or suppliers which meet certain minimum standards are given some form of mark of approval which shows the consumer that they meet those standards. It differs from prior approval, in that prior approval requires all products or suppliers to meet minimum standards.[104] By contrast, there is no obligation to be certified. In the words of Ogus: '[c]ertification thus constitutes an indicator of quality to those consumers who wish to make use of it; but freedom of choice between certified and uncertified activities is preserved'.[105]

---

[99] Benston, above n 9 at 60. The author also questions Llewellyn's argument that economies of scale and the need to maintain confidence justify regulation.

[100] Llewellyn too accepts this. Above n 6 at 50.

[101] On a related point, see the FSA's cost–benefit analysis of comparative tables (Comparative Tables, Bulletin One, Annex A).

[102] G Akerlof, above n 22.

[103] Scott and Black, above n 65 at 346–47.

[104] See ch 4.

[105] Ogus, above n 21 at 215. The standards in question will frequently be developed voluntarily by business, eg through the British Standards Institution.

In the area of financial services perhaps the best example of certification is that of CAT standards.[106] Financial products which meet certain minimum standards in relation to charges, access and terms can advertise themselves as meeting the Government's CAT standards. Products are not obliged to meet these standards, and suppliers are free to offer better, worse, or simply different terms. The Government has thereby avoided some of the criticisms of anti-competitiveness that might emerge from the introduction of a system of mandatory minimum standards. Those who are willing to shop around can use CAT standards as a benchmark for comparing rival products.[107]

An idea behind CAT standards is to enable customers to 'identify safe harbour products offering decent value and reliable standards'.[108] In the words of the Treasury's consultation paper of 1998, CAT standard products 'should always offer savers a reasonable deal. The deal may not be the very best on the market, but savers using products which meet—or better—the standard should not get ripped off'.[109] This will lead to a second benefit—CAT products should give consumers confidence in the products they have chosen, thus encouraging them to take on particular types of product. This is important where the Government is keen for consumers to take on particular types of product, but where consumer confidence may be lacking. A third factor which influenced the Government in setting up the CAT regime was the evidence that many people who did take out products chose inappropriately. This is particularly so of some investment products.[110]

The principles behind CAT standards were given a broadly warm welcome by the Sandler Report.[111] The Sandler Committe was set up to 'identify the competitive forces and incentives that drive the industries concerned, in particular in relation to their approaches to investment, and, where necessary, to suggest policy responses to ensure that consumers are well served'. Although the Report was concerned with the retail savings industry, some of its observations about CAT standards are pertinent to our discussion. The Report enthusiastically supported the vision of: 'a market characterised by a small number of simple products available at a modest cost, enabling consumers to be more confident and effective in exerting pressure on price and quality'.[112] Some commentators

---

[106] See P Johnson, above n 19.
[107] HM Treasury, *CAT Standard Benchmarks for Mortgages* (2000).
[108] HM Treasury, *Standards for Retail Financial Products* (London, February 2001) at 45.
[109] HM Treasury, *Making Savings Easy* (May 1998). Cited in Johnson, above n 19 at 10. In March 2000 the Government extended the CAT standard to domestic residential mortgages.
[110] Johnson, above n 19 at 20.
[111] *Review of Medium and Long Terms Savings in the UK* (the Sandler Review) (July 2002).
[112] *Ibid*, summary para 51.

have argued that the regime should be significantly extended. For example, the National Association of Citizens Advice Bureaux has argued that CAT standards should be extended to all products within the personal finance sector, and that advertising for all personal finance products should have to show whether or not the product meets the CAT standard.[113] The HM Treasury document *Standards for Retail Financial Products* considers the role that CAT standards might play for a basic bank account and for credit cards, although, as will be seen below, their future is uncertain. However, there has been criticism of the regime. The Cruickshank Report noted that while the government does not set the price of CAT standards, it does establish a ceiling that prices must not exceed.[114] The Report argued that '[t]his has the dangerous effect of providing a focal point for suppliers offering these products'. It continued '[t]he Government is not well-positioned to prescribe the prices of these products, and there is a real risk that introducing government determined prices into the market will suppress price competition'.[115]

It now looks as though the Government will put its efforts into product regulation rather than certification, and the expansion of 'stakeholder products' may signal the end of the CAT brand. In examining the competitive forces at work in the financial service industry, the Sandler Report argued that such forces lead towards the complexity of products which make it difficult for low and middle income consumers to access financial products.[116] The Report concluded that the solution lay with product regulation. It recommended 'a suite of simple and comprehensible products, the features of which would be sufficiently tightly regulated to ensure that, with certain additional safeguards, these could be purchased safely without regulated advice'.[117] The Report envisages that the products (which it refers to as 'stakeholder products') would be promoted as a specific and separate set of products with an overall brand identity. The Government supports the idea of moving towards greater product regulation under the 'stakeholder' brand. While this would focus mainly on investment products, it remains to be seen to what extent the stakeholder brand could apply to retail banking products.[118] The Government has stated that it does not propose to remove the CAT standard for mortgages at this stage, but its future must be in doubt. In addition, it is unclear whether standards are

---

[113] National Association of Citizens Advice Bureaux, above n 46 para 6.7.
[114] Cruickshank, above n 2 para 4.119.
[115] *Ibid.*
[116] Sandler, above n 111 para 126.
[117] *Ibid* para 1.28.
[118] *The Government Response to the Consultation on Sandler 'Stakeholder' Product Specifications* (HM Treasury/DWP July 2003) found little support for products other than a pension and a medium term savings vehicle. (para 9).

likely to be developed in the future for retail banking products such as basic bank accounts and credit cards.

Comparative Tables   Much of the debate on the utility of information remedies has centred upon the effectiveness and desirability of mandatory disclosure. One of the weaknesses of mandatory disclosure is that it tends to require the consumer to shop around in order to make comparisons. Although disclosure helps to reduce the costs of search, in many cases they will still be significant. Certification reduces search costs, but may not provide much information to the consumer who wants to be able to make a detailed comparison between rival products. An important tool in the FSA's armoury which involves product information, but which addresses some of these concerns is the comparative table.[119] The FSA has commented that

> consumers lack clear, meaningful information on the key characteristics of products of a particular type so that once they have decided what sort of product they need, they can take better informed decisions about which particular one might offer them the best deal.[120]

It further suggests that '[e]asy access to clear simple and comparative information from an authoritative source would help consumers to shop around and make better-informed financial decisions'.[121] In addition to correcting information asymmetry, comparative tables should also improve competition among firms by providing incentives for them to meet consumer demand and by 'illuminating in a public document the extent to which products of the same type offer better or worse value for money for the consumer'.[122] The Cruickshank Report agreed with the view that comparative tables will benefit competition, arguing that comparative information 'provides a further incentive to keep prices down and to justify the value to consumers of apparently small differences in product features'.[123]

As mentioned above, comparative tables will only be useful if consumers are not only aware of them, but also aware of the benefits of using them. This brings us back to the importance of encouraging public understanding of the environment in which financial services operate, in

---

[119] Baldwin and Cave see the use of the phrase disclosure as appropriate, arguing that 'disclosure regulation may also involve the supply of information to the public directly by a scrutinising regulator or governmental official'. R Baldwin and M Cave, *Understanding Regulation* (Oxford, Oxford University Press, 1999) at 49.
[120] Financial Services Authority, above n 33 para 1.3.
[121] *Ibid* para 2.2.
[122] Financial Services Authority, *Response to CP 28* (FSA, June 2000) para 2.3.
[123] Cruickshank, above n 2 para 4.123.

particular the benefits that arise from making comparisons between rival products.

One limitation of comparative tables is that the consumers who need them most may be least likely to have access to them. To some extent this is inevitable. The most flexible and effective tool for providing information is probably the internet, and the FSA decided to concentrate its efforts on that medium. There can be little doubt that this is the most useful format for consumers who are computer-literate. For example, it enables consumers to select tables for the appropriate product type, rank products on the basis of the indicators they want, and filter out unwanted products. The risk with using the internet, of course, is that it will exclude many people for whom the tables would be useful. The FSA has recognised this, and has discussed linking the tables to a telephone helpline. The FSA is realistic about the consumers who are likely to be able to benefit from comparative tables. Although arguing that it wishes the tables to be as accessible to as many people as possible, the FSA admits that 'it would be very difficult to design a service that is easily usable by those consumers whose level of financial understanding is below "able average" '.[124] The NACAB also suggests that comparative tables with principally benefit 'relatively skilled consumers'.[125]

A further potential difficulty is that consumers might use tables at too early a point in the decision-making process. The tables are not designed to suggest whether products are suitable, and do not constitute advice.[126] The FSA faces some difficulty here. On the one hand, if they give information about suitability of a particular type of product they could be accused of giving advice. On the other, if there is no background information accompanying the tables there is a risk that consumers will not see the information in context. The FSA has addressed this by providing 'background information about the nature of the products, about the sorts of circumstances for which they might be appropriate, and about the need for professional advice if the consumer is at all confused'.[127]

The FSA has not, at the time of writing, produced comparative tables for mainstream banking products. As already mentioned, the Cruickshank Report favoured the use of comparative tables for banking products, and it is hoped that they will be introduced in the future.[128] The FSA has stated: 'in principle, we would extend the Comparative Tables to

---

[124] This is the terminology used in the report *Consumer Reactions to Comparative Information on Six Financial Products* by Reflexions Communication Research (October 1999).
[125] National Association of Citizens Advice Bureaux, *Summing Up*, above n 46 para 6.8.
[126] Although in the protocol sent to firms who have been invited to participate, the FSA does state that it runs the scheme 'in order to provide information and generic advice to consumers'. *The Protocol* para 4.
[127] Above n 122 para 3.2.
[128] This was strongly supported by NACAB (above n 46 para 6.8).

cover all those products for which there is an identified need. In the future we may well look at banking products, but we intend to build the scope of the Tables in the light of experience'.[129]

Warnings   Another form of product information that may have some relevance in relation to banking products is the use of warnings. As Trebilcock argues '[s]imple warnings, unlike bans, actually retain consumer choice, but do not have the information cost problems associated with more sophisticated disclosure devices'.[130] Warnings play a part in a number of relevant areas. For example, advertisements and quotations for secured loans are obliged to carry the warning that 'your home is at risk if you do not keep up repayments on a mortgage or other loan secured on it'.[131] Such warnings provide a simple way of raising public awareness by bringing to the consumer's attention one of the inherent risks of a particular product.

Advice   A link between product information and financial education is provided by financial advice. It is presented here as a sub-heading of product information, but, as mentioned above, it could be seen as appropriately placed elsewhere. Some commentators draw a distinction between the provision of information and the provision of advice. Unfortunately, there appears to be no definitive statement of the distinction between the two concepts. This is surprising, as the FSA, in one of its main consumer documents advises: 'Don't confuse information with advice'. McMeel and Virgo argue that 'information and advice exist on a spectrum and the two concepts merge imperceptibly into one another'.[132] It is clear that consumers can receive information through different channels. On the one hand, the consumer may receive information and advice from a firm offering only its own products. At the other extreme, the consumer may go to an independent financial advisor and want advice about products throughout the market. Where certain investment products are concerned, the concept of 'polarisation' applies. The polarisation regime was introduced in 1988 by the Securities and Investment Board (then the appropriate regulator). Under this regime, those advising on what are known as 'packaged products' had to be either independent (and so advise on products from across the market) or tied, and sell only the products of one company.[133] The effect on banks was that nearly all opted for

---

[129] Above n 122 para 6.8.
[130] M Trebilcock, above n 35 at 75.
[131] See the Consumer Credit (Advertisement) Regulations SI 1989/1125 and the Consumer Credit (Quotations) Regulations SI 1989/1126.
[132] Above n 34 para 1.59.
[133] The products covered are life assurance, personal pensions policies, collective investment schemes and investment trust savings schemes.

tied status. In 1999 the Director General of Fair Trading reported to the Treasury that the polarisation rules have the effect of restricting or distorting competition to a significant extent by preventing innovation in retail markets. In November 2002 the FSA announced that it would remove the polarisation restrictions (de-polarise). Firms will therefore be able to sell not only their own products, but also those of any other product provider. Firms will have a product 'range' from which they make choices. Under the new regime, firms will have to explain to consumers clearly the scope of their advice or service. There will be a new initial disclosure document which is 'designed to give consumers relevant core information in an easily digestible form'.[134] In some cases, this will simply make it clear that there is a single range. It is up to the firms themselves to decide which providers they represent. The standard of advice for provider firms (those that market only their own products) or advisors who are tied to a particular group is that they must recommend the most suitable product from the disclosed range.[135]

Following de-polarisation, those who wish to continue as independent financial advisors and advise across the whole market, will be able to do so. However, the FSA has decided that for a firm to hold itself out as an independent financial advisor, it must both offer whole of market advice and offer its customers the choice of paying a fee for advice.

The polarisation and de-polarisation issues apply only to packaged investment products, and discussion of these is beyond the scope of the book. However, it is important to say something about the nature of advice, and its relationship with this chapter. Advice is an obvious way of addressing information asymmetry, and of overcoming some of the problems caused by financial illiteracy. The introduction of the requirement to give customers the opportunity to pay for advice (rather than through commission) addresses in part one of the inherent problems of addressing information asymmetry—that the advisor may not be under the right incentives to recommend the most appropriate product where commission is involved. However, a remaining problem is that of affordable financial advice. Many of those who responded to the FSA's consultation paper on polarisation felt that while there were strengths of a fee charging environment 'consumers would be unable, or unwilling, to pay the level of fees required to allow the market to work'.[136] There is undoubtedly a mismatch between the needs of less affluent consumers for basic financial advice, and the interests of advisors who will, understandably,

---

[134] Financial Services Authority, *Reforming Polarisation: Removing the Barriers to Choice* (FSA, January 2003) para 1.6.
[135] *Ibid*, para 4.14. See also *FSA Handbook*, 'Conduct of Business' (COB) 5.3.6 R.
[136] Financial Services Authority, *Policy Statement in Response to the CP121 Consultation* (FSA January 2003) at D23.

be drawn to more affluent consumers. The need to encourage consumers, and particularly the less affluent, to seek independent advice has been emphasised by a large number of commentators, but it is clear that there are significant barriers to persuading them that it is in their best interests to seek, and pay for, advice. The solution may be to provide some form of funded independent and affordable financial advice. The Chairman of the Financial Services Consumer Panel has called for the Government to establish a nationwide chain of money advice centres. She describes such an approach as 'prevention rather than cure for people who don't think of going to independent financial advisors'.[137] The National Consumer Council (NCC) recommended the establishment of a taskforce on financial advice.[138] The NCC also considered possible methods of delivering advice, including expanding the existing network of citizens advice bureaux and money advice trusts, and establishing a publicly funded consumer advice service.[139] A similar view has been put forward by the Consumers' Association as part of its 'Campaign for Fair and Accessible Financial Advice'.[140]

As mentioned above, comparative tables will play some part in delivering 'advice' in a loose sense. Although the FSA has argued that they are not designed to tell consumers whether products are suitable, and cannot be said to constitute advice, the FSA has also argued in the protocol sent to firms that it runs the scheme 'in order to provide information and generic advice to consumers.'[141] The FSA has argued that by providing background information about 'the nature of the products, about the sorts of circumstances for which they might be appropriate, and about the need for professional advice if the consumer is at all confused' it can ensure that consumers get information in context, although it clearly is keen not be seen as giving specific advice.[142]

Institutional Information

There may be additional categories of information that consumers need to be able to make informed choices about banking products. First, a consumer may be more concerned with the financial stability of the firm offering a product, than the different types of financial product available. Davies observes that where long-term contracts are concerned, the

---

[137] 'Watchdog's Watchdog Wants Chain of Advice Centres for All', *The Independent*, (1 November 2003).
[138] National Consumer Council, *Independent and Affordable?* (NCC, May 2002) at 20.
[139] *Ibid* at 21.
[140] See <http://www.which.net/campaigns>.
[141] *The Protocol* para 4.
[142] Above n 122 para 3.2.

consumer relies heavily upon both the behaviour and the solvency of the firm long after the original contract is entered.[143] In fact, as he acknowledges, where firms offer long-term savings products, the value of the solvency increases over time as the consumer's stake in the firm increases. Even where simpler banking products, such as current accounts, are concerned, the continued solvency of the bank will be of great importance to the consumer. The difficulty that consumers face in getting reliable and helpful information about the solvency of a firm is an important, if sometimes overlooked, element of information asymmetry.[144]

In an ideal world, the consumer would be able to judge the solvency of the firm, and make a decision accordingly. Indeed, it has been argued that '[t]he public availability of meaningful information sufficient for people to make informed decisions about the likely standing of banks both individually and relatively is the keystone of market discipline'.[145] However, it is unrealistic in practice to expect consumers to make an informed judgment about a firm's solvency. Although it is possible in theory that firms will emerge to provide monitoring and information services to consumers, it seems unlikely that this will provide a practical solution.[146] So how might the matter be addressed? Although it may appear fanciful to rely upon disclosure as a method of enabling consumers to make an informed choice about the likelihood of a bank becoming insolvent, such an approach can be found in New Zealand. The New Zealand regime attempts to give consumers the information they need to make such decisions. A Key Information Summary (KIS) has to be supplied prominently in every branch and are aimed at the consumer, rather than the professional analyst.[147] This contains information about the bank's credit rating, its capital ratios, and information about peak exposure concentration, asset quality, shareholder guarantees and profitability.[148] Although targeted at the consumer, it is questionable how effective the KIS is in practice. One of the leading supporters of market-oriented financial regulation has admitted that few consumers consult the documents

---

[143] Above n 8.

[144] The FSA has made it clear that information disclosed would not include confidential information obtained by the FSA for the purpose of its supervision of firms. (Above n 33 para 3.5). Although this does not preclude the presentation of information about financial soundness of banks which is public, it does not look as though the FSA is inclined to expect consumers to make judgements about financial soundness.

[145] D Mayes, *A More Market Based Approach to Maintaining Market Stability* (FSA Occasional Paper 10, August 2000).

[146] Rating agencies provide such services for businesses, but it seems unlikely that there would be much consumer demand for these services. See Davies above n 8.

[147] By contrast, the General Disclosure Statement of a bank is aimed at analysts. As might be expected, it is far more detailed than the KIS. See D Mayes, L Halme and A Liuksila, *Improving Banking Supervision* (Basingstoke Palgrave, 2001) at 153–56.

[148] Mayes, above n 145 at 35.

and that it has not achieved its aim of meeting the needs of private consumers.[149] It is interesting to note that the Reserve Bank of New Zealand has fallen back on trying to improve financial and economic literacy, particularly in schools, in order to try to encourage consumers to exercise market discipline.[150]

If consumers cannot be expected to make informed choices about a bank's solvency, this might provide a justification for intervention. One of the risks that consumers face in their financial affairs is classified by the FSA as 'prudential risk', ie the risk that a firm collapses with damaging consequences for the consumer. The regulatory system is designed to allow the FSA to identify possible causes of prudential risk, such as incompetent management or lack of capital, and to take action to address them.[151] However, as discussed in chapter two, the FSA's statutory objectives do not extend to bailing out failing institutions to protect consumers. The FSA has made it clear that it will not intervene to save firms where there is no threat to the soundness of the financial system. The FSA has commented that

> [c]onsiderable dangers would arise if consumers or market participants believed that no firm would be allowed to collapse; this would reduce the incentive for individuals or firms to take due care in assessing the risk attaching to their financial decisions.[152]

There is an expectation that consumers should take responsibility for their decisions, even though the reality is that this may not always be possible.[153] It is accepted that there are good reasons for not stepping in to save ailing firms. As the FSA has recognised, it would raise the spectre of moral hazard, where decision-makers would no longer bear the consequences of their decisions, and might be under an incentive to pursue the highest returns, safe in the knowledge that the survival of a firm is 'guaranteed'. However, whether there is significant moral hazard relating to the decisions of consumers to choose particular banks is questionable. This is addressed in more detail in chapter seven. In the context of deposit protection schemes. Such schemes acknowledge the difficulties that consumers face in making informed decisions about the solvency of a bank. Although this does not fully reimburse consumers, it provides for the return of a proportion of their deposits in the event of a firm failing.

---

[149] Mayes, above n 145 at 36.
[150] *Ibid.*
[151] See further, ch 4.
[152] Financial Services Authority, A New Regulator for the New Millenium (FSA, January 2000) para 6.
[153] See further ch 7.

Rights and Redress

The final category can be loosely identified as 'legal rights'. As noted above, great faith is sometimes placed in the role of the consumer in disciplining the market. In theory, where consumers are dissatisfied with a product or a provider, they can play a role in providing market discipline by switching to an alternative. In practice, at least where some financial products are concerned, this will be difficult.[154] For example, front-loading means that switching at an early stage of a long-term investment product may be costly. Furthermore, the existence of tie-ins and lock-ins may make switching uneconomic or impossible. The existence of barriers to switching has been identified by the FSA as an element in unfairness.[155] In addition, as recent research has demonstrated, it is frequently difficult for the consumer to judge whether switching would be advantageous. This is particularly so where complex financial products are concerned.[156] There is clearly overlap here with category one. One part of financial literacy and education can be seen as greater awareness of the possible means of seeking redress.

Where the consumer is not just dissatisfied, but believes that a legal wrong has been committed, then the appropriate response may not be switching, but suing. However, cost also presents a difficulty here. The transaction costs of taking action to enforce legal rights frequently make it unrealistic for consumers to do so. Rational consumers are only likely to enforce their legal rights when the expected benefits exceed the expected costs, and Leff has commented that consumers sometimes need 'superspite' to implement their rights.[157] As a result of the transaction costs involved in switching or suing, such action will frequently be inappropriate. So long as suppliers are aware of that, they are under inadequate incentives to correct the matters in question.

The principal solution to the barriers that consumers face to obtaining redress is to facilitate redress, in particular through mechanisms for alternative dispute resolution. The main example of this relating to banking regulation is the Financial Ombudsman Service (FOS). Another solution is to require firms to have in place effective internal mechanisms for the handling of consumer complaints. These issues are looked at in chapter six.

---

[154] Financial Services Authority, *Treating Consumers Fairly After the Point of Sale* (FSA Discussion Paper, June 2001) para 4.36.
[155] *Ibid*.
[156] I Alfon, *To Switch or Not to Switch, That's the Question* (FSA Occasional Paper 18, September 2002).
[157] This means 'infliction by the consumer of greater harm on himself than he could inflict on his enemy'. A Leff, 'Injury Ignorance and Spite' (1970) *Yale Law Journal* 1 at 21.

Important as these issues are, they provide only a partial solution. The discussion of the inadequacy of private law remedies mentioned above assume at least that the consumer is aware of the true position and decides, rationally, not to take action. In many cases, action is not taken through inertia, or because consumers are not aware of the true position. If the well-informed consumer is under inadequate incentive to take action, the poorly informed consumer faces more significant hurdles. Lack of knowledge of legal redress leads not only to inefficient outcomes, with banks not being disciplined appropriately, but also to socially unjust outcomes.[158] The solution here is to raise awareness of the possible forms of redress.[159] It has been argued that one possible response to some of these concerns is for the state to provide some form of public legal education. This could be done both to enable individuals to avoid disputes by ordering their affairs accordingly, or to help them to prosecute complaints effectively on a self-help basis.[160] It may be that this should be viewed as part of the public understanding objective of the FSA.

TACKLING FALSE AND MISLEADING INFORMATION

As well as ensuring that consumers have accurate information, regulators may also have a role in ensuring that consumers do not receive inaccurate information. Although the literature on information tends to focus on the correcting of information gaps through disclosure and certification, it is also important to consider the role of the law in controlling false and misleading information. Tackling false information can be justified on both economic and social grounds. From an economic point of view, it is clear that markets cannot function effectively unless 'persons can deal with each other in the knowledge that fraud is an exceptional, rather than a regular, feature of the environment'.[161] From a social perspective, fraud, and other forms of dishonesty, are hugely damaging. In the words of Cayne and Trebilcock 'the community will not and should not tolerate dishonesty, whatever the economic consequences of preventing it'.[162] Although the provision of false or misleading information will generally give rise to a civil action in contract or tort, we have seen that there are

---

[158] See ch 2 and Wilhelmsson, above n 86.

[159] There is evidence that knowledge of some forms of redress mechanisms has been low in the past. See for example C Graham, M Seneviratne and R James, 'Publicising the Bank and Building Societies Ombudsman Schemes' (1993) 3(2) *Consumer Policy Review* 85.

[160] M Trebilcock, above n 35 at 85. See also G Kane and E Myers, 'The Role of Self-Help in the Provision of Legal Services' in R Evans and M Trebilcock (eds), *Lawyers and the Consumer Interest: Regulating the Market for Legal Services* (Toronto, Butterworths, 1982).

[161] R Cranston, *Principles of Banking Law*, 2nd edn (Oxford, Oxford University Press, 2002) at 68.

[162] Above n 95 at 422.

good reasons to assume that those affected will not always pursue their rights. As Breyer comments:

> [t]he rationale for governmental action to prevent false or misleading information rests upon the assumption that court remedies and competitive pressures are not adequate to provide the consumer with the true information he would willingly pay for.[163]

The FSA has identified one of the risks to its being able to meet its consumer protection objective as 'bad faith risk'. This is 'the risk from fraud, misrepresentation, deliberate mis-selling or failure to disclose relevant information on the part of firms selling or advising on financial products'.[164] Another of the FSA's objectives is reducing financial crime, and in many instances where false information is provided a criminal offence will be committed. Furthermore, where false or misleading information is provided financial crime may be furthered, for example by persuading consumers to invest in illegal schemes and scams.[165] However, it should be remembered that the supply of false information will not always be an offence, and offences will not always require proof of dishonesty.

It is common for legislation to address the risk of consumers' receiving inaccurate information by criminalising the making of false and misleading statements in the course of business. Where false information is provided, for example where a clearly false statement has been made, there is no social utility in its supply and there are strong arguments that such behaviour should be criminalised. This is particularly so where *mens rea* can be proved, although most offences of this type impose strict liability.[166] One example is s 46(1) of the Consumer Credit Act 1974 which states '[i]f an advertisement to which this part applies conveys information which in a material respect is false or misleading the advertiser commits an offence'.[167] Others are contained in s 397 of FSMA which deals with a number of misleading statements and practices.

The offences mentioned above refer to information which is false or misleading. Difficulties are raised by including 'misleading' information

---

[163] S Breyer, *Regulation and its Reform* above n 67. For the argument that providing misleading information to consumers does not ultimately pay, see B Klein and K Leffler, 'The Role of Market Forces in Assuring Contractual Performance' (1981) 89 *Journal of Political Economy* 615.
[164] Above n 152 para 11.
[165] Financial Services Authority, *The FSA's Regulatory Approach to Financial Promotions* (FSA, April 2002) para 2.3.
[166] An exception concerns the offences contained in s 397 of FSMA which require proof of *mens rea*. This is an amended version of s 47 of the Financial Services Act 1986.
[167] An interesting recent example of s 46 was the OFT's taking action against Barclaycard for advertising a '0 per cent forever credit card'. See 'Barclaycard Withdraws Misleading Adverts' OFT Press Release (PN 149/03, 18 November 2003).

alongside 'false' information. In particular, legislation is generally silent about how the misleading character of information is to be judged. For example, it is generally unclear how far the courts should consider how different consumers might interpret the information in question. Such guidance as can be gleaned from the case law in UK consumer protection statutes indicates that the question to ask is how the average consumer would have interpreted the information in question. In *Burleigh v Van den Berghs and Jurgens Ltd* it was stated that a description must be likely to mislead 'the average member of the shopping public' and that 'it is not enough that we should be sure that an unusually careless person might be misled ... [or] a person who is dyslexic, short-sighted, or of less than average intelligence'.[168] This is consistent with the Molony Committee Report's aspiration that consumers should be encouraged 'to go shopping with their eyes open and their wits reasonably alert'.[169] It is also consistent with the requirement in FSMA that when considering the protection of consumers, the FSA must have regard to 'the general principle that consumers should take responsibility for their decisions'.[170] There are clear reasons for this objective approach, particularly from the point of view of the need for certainty. This need for certainty requires us to make a decision about the extent to which we take account of the differences among the consumer collective. Sunstein suggests that 'almost all substantive advertisements will deceive at least some of the people in the light of the exceptional heterogeneity of listeners and viewers'.[171] If this is so, it may point towards our having to set an objective test and to accept that some consumers will inevitably be misled. The European Court of Justice, for example, uses the concept of the average consumer, who is 'reasonably well-informed and reasonably observant and circumspect'.[172]

An alternative view is that we should pay greater attention to the different ways in which information can be interpreted. Wilhelmsson suggests six possible images of the consumer: the fully informed consumer, the information seeker, the passive glancer, the snatcher, the irrational consumer and the consumer without choice.[173] The objective

---

[168] [1987] Butterworths Trading Law Cases 337. See R Bragg, *Trade Descriptions* (Oxford, Clarendon Press, 1991) at 43 and P Cartwright, *Consumer Protection and the Criminal Law* (Cambridge, Cambridge University Press, 2001) at 180–84.

[169] *Report of the Committee on Consumer Protection* (the Molony Committee) (1962 Cmnd 1781) para 813. The Trade Descriptions Act 1968 was largely based upon the Report's recommendations.

[170] FSMA s 5(2)(d).

[171] C Sunstein, *Free Markets and Social Justice* (New York, Oxford University Press, 1997) at 284.

[172] Case C–210/96, *Gut Springheide GmbH v Oberkreisdirektor des Kreises Steinfurt* [1998] ECR I–4657 para 37.

[173] See T Wilhelmsson, 'Consumer Images in East and West' in H Micklitz (ed), *Rechtseinheit oder Rechtsvielfalt in Europa?* (Baden Baden, Nomos, 1996) 53.

test apparently favoured by the courts in England and Wales is consistent with the first two images, but less so with the others. Another possible distinction would be between the credulous and the sceptical consumer. Of course, there is no clear dividing line here, but some consumers are likely to be more credulous than others. This credulity may result from a number of factors, such as lack of education, lack of experience and lack of intellect. The need to protect the most vulnerable would suggest that providers of financial services should at least consider how more credulous consumers might interpret information and guard against ambiguity and exaggeration where this might lead to consumers' being misled. It is particularly important that the law requires those financial services providers who target groups of consumers, such as those on low income, have regard to how their advertisements and promotional literature might be construed. Low income consumers are more likely than most to be poorly educated, less experienced in financial matters and not to have English as their first language. It is submitted that such consumers are particularly susceptible to ambiguous and exaggerated claims. Some states have adopted concepts which are designed to ensure that consumers less worldly or intelligent than the average receive protection.[174] For example, standards such as the 'least attentive consumer' and the 'casual observer' have been used in Belgium and Germany respectively.[175]

A further issue in relation to information is that firms work hard to create an impression of trust and competence in the minds of consumers. They do this in a variety of ways, from guarantees/warranties to subtle messages generated through advertising. Consumers' credulity may result from efforts of the financial services industry to create this trustworthy image. Ramsay argues that:

> many financial institutions stress the importance of the relationship of trust and confidence which they wish to develop with consumers and this is part of their advertising image ... It does not seem far fetched to argue that these images and stories may raise consumer expectations that they will be treated fairly.[176]

This may point towards the need to think carefully about what it is reasonable for consumers to expect from suppliers, and how they may view information that the supplier provides. Indeed, Ramsay goes so far as to suggest that rather than view advertising through the lens of

---

[174] See R Bradgate, R Brownsword, and C Twigg-Flesner, *The Impact of Adopting a Duty to Trade Fairly* (Sheffield, Institute for Commercial Law Studies, July 2003) para 3.26.
[175] *Ibid.*
[176] I Ramsay, *Advertising, Culture and the Law* (London, Sweet and Maxwell, 1996) at 18.

truth and falsity, we might focus instead on questions of exploitation and unfairness.[177] A market-failure based approach to regulation would require us to rely on the rational consumer to rid the market of unfair and exploitative information through purchasing decisions, and to rid the market of false information through the private law. Recognition of the transaction costs facing the consumer might lead us to support agencies to deal with false information through enforcement action. But how far we go beyond that, and provide remedies or enforcement action based upon unfair or exploitative information (or indeed, conduct) is more difficult.

CONCLUSIONS

If consumers are to receive an appropriate degree of protection, and in particular if they are to be able to protect themselves, then they need access to information. From an economic perspective, consumers will only be rational maximisers of their own utility if they are able to make informed decisions. Although there are some incentives upon suppliers to provide information to consumers, there are good reasons to believe that these are inadequate to ensure that consumers get the information they need. In addition to the economic justifications for intervention, there are also social, in particular distributive, reasons for wanting to intervene in the market to ensure that certain types of information are provided.

It is important to remember that more information is not necessarily the answer. Gabriel and Lang's observation that 'in theory the consumer can be helped with information. In practice choice is doomed to be a stab in the twilight' is perhaps a little too defeatist.[178] Although more information will make it easier for consumers to access information, it will not necessarily improve their ability to use it. As Tanner argues '[m]ore effective policies are likely to include education programmes to raise financial literacy and ensuring that information is clearly written, jargon-free and relatively easy to understand'.[179]

---

[177] *Ibid* at 19.
[178] Y Gabriel and T Lang, *The Unmanageable Consumer* (London, Sage, 1995) at 42.
[179] S Tanner, *The Role of Information in Saving Decisions* (Institute of Fiscal Studies, Briefing Note no 7, 2000).

4

Authorisation and Continued Supervision

INTRODUCTION

A VARIETY OF TECHNIQUES are available to regulate banks and protect consumers. The previous chapter focused on the role of the law in addressing the information gaps that exist between banks and their customers. Just as information deficits provided 'the key analytical basis for early consumer protection law', so, it might be argued, did information remedies provide its solution.[1] Broadly interpreted, information remedies encompass not only disclosure, but also measures such as educational initiatives and sanctions against the provision of false and misleading information. The purpose of this chapter is to consider another principal regulatory technique, that of prior approval. Where banks are concerned, this most interventionist form of regulation is central. Authorisation is required before banking business can be undertaken. As will be seen, banking is viewed as an industry which demands close scrutiny, both in terms of licensing and continued supervision.

The chapter begins with an overview of the regime for the authorisation and supervision of banks under the Financial Services and Markets Act 2000 (FSMA), and that under the Consumer Credit Act 1974. It then moves on to consider the strengths and weaknesses of this form of regulation with particular reference to these statutes. It will be argued that there is the potential for such regulatory schemes to lead to inefficient and unintended outcomes, and that the weaknesses of this form of regulation should be taken seriously. However, the chapter concludes that a well-organised and well-resourced system of prior approval and continued supervision is essential to meeting the principal objectives of banking regulation.

---

[1] G Hadfield, R Howse and M Trebilcock, 'Information-Based Principles for Rethinking Consumer Protection Policy' (1998) 21 *Journal of Consumer Policy* 131 at 134.

THE NATURE OF PRIOR APPROVAL

Prior approval by licensing is central to the regulation of banks in the UK. Sometimes known as screening or authorisation, prior approval involves giving a body the power to screen out institutions which fail to meet minimum standards.[2] It is an example, of 'command and control' regulation, backed up with stringent powers. Ogus identifies several characteristics of prior approval. First, the licences in question are issued before the regulated activity has taken place, the ostensible purpose of this being to prevent a socially undesirable occurrence. Secondly, the potential quality of all engaged in the activity is assessed to see if they achieve the minimum standards. Thirdly, the conditions of the licence involve only minimum and uniform standards. Fourthly, the ultimate sanction, which is revocation of the licence, and so removal from the sphere of activity, is particularly severe. Fifthly, the administrative costs of operating the scheme are high, and opportunity costs resulting from the delay before the licence is granted should be considered. Finally, welfare losses arise if the system is used anti-competitively to create barriers to entry.[3] These issues will be returned to below, when the strengths and weaknesses of prior approval are considered.

THE DEVELOPMENT OF PRIOR APPROVAL FOR BANKS

Banks have been subject to a prior approval regime since the passing of the Banking Act 1979. The 1979 Act was introduced in part as a response to the secondary banking crisis of the 1970s, although the principal reason for its introduction was the need for the UK to have an authorisation regime in place to meet the requirements of the First Banking Co-ordination Directive.[4] The 1979 Act was perceived by some as having fundamental weaknesses, chief among which was the two-tier system of supervision, which divided institutions into recognised banks and licensed deposit takers.[5] Following the rescue of Johnson Matthey Bankers Ltd (JMB) in 1984, the Banking Act 1987 was introduced. The JMB affair had illustrated some of the weaknesses of the 1979 Act as well as revealing the Bank of

[2] See A Ogus, *Regulation: Legal Form and Economic Theory* (Oxford, Clarendon Press, 1994); S Breyer, *Regulation and its Reform* (Cambridge MA, Harvard University Press, 1982) ch 7. Banks are licensed in order to control their activities in the public interest. Licensing for other purposes, such as to develop natural resources or to allocate scarce resources are beyond the scope of the chapter.
[3] Ogus, *Ibid* at 214.
[4] Directive 77/780/EEC. See C Hadjiemmanuil, *Banking Regulation and the Bank of England* (London, Lloyds of London Press, 1996) ch 1.
[5] For background see the White Paper 'The Licensing and Supervision of Deposit Taking Institutions' (Cmnd 6584, August 1976).

England's supervisory practices to be problematic.[6] With the 1987 Act came the requirement that deposits could only be accepted by those authorised by the Bank of England. The two-tier system was abolished and a far stronger and more detailed regime of authorisation introduced. Despite the improvements that the 1987 Act brought, problems with its implementation were revealed following the collapse of the Bank of Credit and Commerce International (BCCI). Although it would be wrong (as this chapter will emphasise) to see failure of a firm as conclusive evidence of regulatory failure, the inquiry into the supervision of BCCI ('the Bingham Report') showed evidence of shortcomings in law and practice.[7] Ten years after the 1987 Act, the incoming Labour administration re-drew the financial regulatory map of the UK with its decision to introduce a single financial regulator. The Financial Services Authority (FSA) was set up soon after the 1997 election, effectively gaining the Bank of England's principal regulatory powers through the Bank of England Act 1998.[8] The FSA only assumed its powers under FSMA on 1 December 2001.

PRIOR APPROVAL UNDER FSMA

The authorisation regime under FSMA is detailed and complex. Although this chapter provides merely an overview of the regime's principal elements, it is submitted that this is helpful in order to illustrate the role of prior approval as a regulatory technique. According to the *FSA Handbook of rules and guidance* (hereafter *FSA Handbook*) (which contains the details of the regime) the purpose of authorisation of firms (in our case banks) under FSMA is 'to allow only those persons which satisfy the necessary conditions … to engage in a regulated activity', while the purpose of approval of persons is 'to seek to ensure that only fit and proper persons perform controlled functions in the financial services industry'.[9] The term 'regulated activities' covers a variety of matters, the chief one for the purposes of this book being the accepting of deposits.[10]

---

[6] Hadjiemmanuil describes the Bank's supervisory practices at the time as 'naïve and complacent' above n 4, at 43.

[7] 'Inquiry into the Supervision of the Bank of Credit and Commerce International' HC 198 (1991–92).

[8] Initially, powers were transferred from the Bank of England to the Securities and Investments Board (SIB). Legally, the FSA was merely a re-named SIB. The Bank of England retains responsibility for the overall stability of the financial system and has powers to intervene in money market operations. As a result it could be said to retain some regulatory powers.

[9] *FSA Handbook*, 'Authorisation Manual' (hereafter, AUTH) 1.1.2 G.

[10] Others include managing investments and effecting contracts of insurance. They are set out in the Financial Services and Markets Act 2000 (Regulated Activities) Order 2001(SI 2001 no 544). This is made by the Treasury under FSMA s 22.

Under FSMA there is a single authorisation regime for the majority of financial services business, although in practice firms apply for permission to conduct specific activities. Anyone wishing to accept deposits by way of business in the UK has to be authorised or exempt.[11] There are two categories of authorised person under FSMA: first, a person who has Part IV permission (that is, permission granted under Part IV of FSMA), and secondly a person who qualifies for authorisation. Under Single Market Directives, banks (or, more precisely, credit institutions) which are established and authorised under the law of an EEA (European Economic Area) State (known as the home state) may accept deposits and conduct certain other business in other EEA states (known as host states) without the need to be authorised by the host state.[12] The home state regulator has responsibility for authorisation and prudential supervision of the firm, with the host state able only to impose minimum rules. Once authorised, the 'passporting' firm (as it is known) can provide services cross-border to the host state, or can establish branches there, provided it notifies its home regulator (who will then notify the host regulator). In some cases, the passporting firm's authorisation from its home state may be wider than the activities which are regulated by the host state. In other cases, passporting firms will require 'top up authorisation' from the host state regulator. Where the home state permission covers consumer credit, the firm will be exempt from the need to seek a licence under the Consumer Credit Act 1974 to offer loans to UK consumers.[13]

It was noted above that prior approval regimes generally involve the application of mandatory minimum standards by the regulator. In the case of banks, some of these are relatively objective—what Cranston refers to as 'measurable factors', such as solvency, liquidity, provisioning and initial capital.[14] Others are far more subjective—what might be called 'open textured criteria'.[15] This reflects the tradition in the UK, considered below, for relying on broad and flexible criteria in the authorisation

---

[11] Exempt persons include the Bank of England, other EEC central banks, various international institutions, as well as various other bodies affiliated to local or central government. See the Financial Services and Markets Act 2000 (Exemption Order) 2001 (SI 2001 no 1201) and the discussion in E Ellinger, E Lomnicka and R Hooley, *Modern Banking Law*, 3rd edn (Oxford, Oxford University Press, 2002) at 41.
[12] This European passport has existed for credit institutions since the establishment of the Second Banking Co-ordination Directive of 1989 (known as the 2BCD (1989/646/EEC)). This was supplemented by a host of other Directives, including the Own Funds Directive (1989/299/EEC), the Solvency Directive (1989/647/EEC) and later the Consolidated Supervision Directive (1992/30/EEC), the Large Exposures Directive (1992/121/EEC), the Deposit Guarantees Directive (1994/19/EEC), and the Post-BCCI Directive (95/26/EC). Passporting is now covered by the Banking Consolidation Directive (2000/12/EC).
[13] See further below.
[14] R Cranston, *Principles of Banking Law*, 2nd edn (Oxford, Oxford University Press, 2002) at 85.
[15] *Ibid* at 86.

of banks. Under FSMA, the FSA has the power to refuse, vary or cancel permission, and can also restrict a bank's permission by imposing the limitations or requirements that it considers appropriate. The key to permission is meeting the minimum standards, or 'threshold conditions', as they are known. These are now considered.

Threshold Conditions

Schedule 6 of FSMA contains details of the five 'threshold conditions', which represent the minimum conditions that firms must satisfy and continue to satisfy, to be given and retain Part IV permission.[16]

The first threshold condition concerns the legal status of the applicant. Schedule 6(1)(1) provides that a person who wishes to carry on a regulated activity which constitutes accepting deposits or issuing electronic money must be a body corporate or a partnership.[17] This ensures that the provisions of Article 1 of the Banking Consolidation Directive are met. Threshold condition two, which deals with the location of offices, reflects the requirement under Article 6 of the post-BCCI Directive.[18] It states that if the person concerned is a body corporate, constituted under the law of any part of the UK, its head office and, if it has a registered office, that office, must be in the UK.[19] Neither FSMA, nor the Directive, defines the term 'head office'. The *FSA Handbook* provides that the head office will not necessarily be the place of incorporation, nor even the place where the business is wholly or mainly carried on. The FSA will instead focus on identifying the location of the firm's senior management and control. They will look at those who make decisions relating to the bank's central direction, its material management decisions and also at the bank's central administrative functions. Examples of the latter might be internal audit and central compliance.[20] The purpose of the provision is to ensure that business is organised in a way that can be supervised effectively.

The third threshold condition is concerned with 'close links', and implements the requirements of the post-BCCI Directive.[21] Paragraph 3 of Schedule 6 of FSMA states that if the person concerned ('A'), has close links with another person ('CL') the FSA must be satisfied: first, that those links are not likely to prevent the effective supervision of A by the FSA, and secondly, that if it appears to the FSA that CL is subject to the laws,

---

[16] *FSA Handbook*, 'Threshold Conditions' (hereafter COND) 1.2.1.
[17] Different obligations apply to other sectors, eg insurance and investment business.
[18] Directive 95/26/EC of 29 June 1995.
[19] COND 2.2.1.
[20] COND 2.2.3.
[21] COND 2.3 and Directive 95/26/EC.

regulations or administrative provisions of a territory which is not an EEA state (known as 'the foreign provisions'), that neither those foreign provisions, nor any deficiency in their enforcement, would prevent the effective supervision of A by the FSA.[22] The *FSA Handbook* indicates some of the factors that the FSA will consider when deciding if this threshold condition is met. For example, first, it will look at whether it is likely to receive adequate information both from the bank and those with whom it has close links, to establish whether the bank meets minimum standards, and to identify and assess the impact on the regulatory objectives in s 2 of FSMA. Secondly, the FSA will consider whether the structure and geographical spread of the bank, its group, and other persons with whom it has close links, might hinder the provision of information to the FSA. Thirdly, the FSA will look at whether the bank and its group are, or will be, subject to consolidated supervision. Finally, it will consider whether it can assess the group's overall financial position with confidence at any one time. The provision aims to ensure that the FSA can supervise the person in question effectively, taking the factors mentioned into account.

The fourth threshold condition concerns the adequacy of resources. Under schedule 6 paragraph 4 resources of the person concerned must, in the FSA's opinion, be adequate in relation to the regulated activities that he seeks to carry on, or carries on. In deciding this, the FSA may take into account the membership of any group, and the provision made for liabilities, and the means for managing the incidence of risk in connection with its business. The FSA has to ensure that the bank has adequate resources in relation to the specific regulated activity, or activities, which it carries on, or seeks to carry on. Under the *FSA Handbook*, 'adequate' means sufficient in terms of quantity, quality and availability. 'Resources' includes all financial and non-financial resources and means of managing its resources, including capital, provisioning, liquidity, personnel and risk-management.[23] The FSA will consider whether the firm is ready, willing and organised to comply with these requirements. A variety of factors will need to be taken into account when determining whether a firm will satisfy, and continue to satisfy, this threshold condition. Relevant matters identified in the *FSA Handbook* include: whether the bank is likely to be able to meet its debts as they fall due, whether there are any implications for the adequacy of its resources arising from its

---

[22] The Schedule explains that A is deemed to have close links with CL if: CL is a parent undertaking of A; CL is a subsidiary undertaking of A; CL is a parent undertaking of a subsidiary of A; CL is a subsidiary undertaking of a parent undertaking of A; CL owns or controls 20% or more of the voting rights or capital of A; or A owns or controls 20% or more of the voting right or capital of CL. See also COND 2.3.1.
[23] COND 2.4.2 G(2).

history, and whether it has taken reasonable steps to identify and measure any risks of regulatory concern that it may encounter in conducting its business and has installed appropriate systems and controls and appointed appropriate human resources to measure them prudently at all times.[24]

Suitability is the final threshold condition. Schedule 6 paragraph 5 states that the person concerned must satisfy the FSA that he is a fit and proper person having regard to all the circumstances, including: his connection with any person; the nature of any regulated activity that he carries on or seeks to carry on; and the need to ensure that his affairs are conducted soundly and prudently. This focuses upon the bank's suitability, rather than that of individuals connected with it.[25] The FSA will consider all relevant matters, including whether the firm: conducts or will conduct its business with integrity and in compliance with proper standards; has or will have a competent and prudent management; and can demonstrate that it conducts, or will conduct, its affairs with the exercise of due skill, care and diligence.[26]

Conducting Business with Integrity and in Compliance with Proper Standards

This is primarily concerned with probity, and a few matters can be noted by way of illustration.[27] For example, the first factor is whether the firm has been open and co-operative in all its dealings with the FSA and any other regulatory body, and is ready, willing and organised to comply with appropriate requirements and standards. This is fairly self-explanatory, and is concerned with requirements and standards under the regulatory system and other legal, regulatory and professional obligations. Another factor is whether the firm or any person connected with it has been convicted of any unspent offence involving specified matters, including fraud, money laundering, and offences under legislation relating to insurance, banking or other financial services, companies, insolvency, consumer credit or consumer protection. A further factor is whether the firm has taken reasonable care to establish and maintain effective systems and controls for compliance with applicable requirements and standards under the regulatory system that applies to the firm and the regulated activities for which it has, or will have permission.

---

[24] COND 2.4.4.
[25] Under the approved persons regime, the FSA also has to assess the suitability of each person who performs something classified as a controlled function. This is considered below.
[26] COND 2.5.4 G(2).
[27] COND 2.5.6 G. For more detail see A Campbell and P Cartwright, *Banks in Crisis* (Aldershot, Ashgate, 2002) ch 2.

Competent and Prudent Management and Exercise of Due Skill, Care and Diligence

The focus here is less on probity and more on competence and experience. Again, some factors are noted by way of illustration. First, the FSA will consider if the governing body of the firm is made up of individuals with an appropriate range of skills and experience to understand, operate and manage the firm's regulated activities. Another factor the FSA will consider is whether the governing body of the firm is organised in such a way as to enable it to address and control the regulated activities of the firm, including those carried on by managers to whom particular functions have been delegated. In addition, the FSA will consider whether the firm has approached the control of financial and other risk in a prudent manner and has taken reasonable care to ensure that robust information and reporting systems have been developed, tested and properly installed. A final factor is whether the firm has conducted enquiries that are sufficient to give it reasonable assurance that it will not be posing unacceptable risks to consumers or the financial system.[28]

The FSA endeavours to set out in detail the factors that it will consider in deciding whether the threshold conditions are met. In some cases, there is a very close relationship between whether the firm meets minimum standards, and whether people connected with the firm (in particular approved persons performing controlled functions) meet those standards. Although there is a separate regime for determining whether approved persons are fit and proper, the fitness and propriety of those persons will also be relevant to the fitness and propriety of the firm. The ways in which the regulatory system deals with directors of banks is considered briefly below.

The Interim Sourcebook and Prudential Rules

The *Interim Prudential Sourcebook for Banks* (IPRU) forms part of the *FSA Handbook*. The purpose of the standards contained in IPRU is to ensure that banks maintain the capital resources that are commensurate with their risks, and appropriate systems and controls so that they can manage those risks. Although the FSA refuses, quite correctly, to guarantee that banks will not fail, it has been noted already that it has an important role in minimising the risk that banks will fail.[29] The rules are now considered briefly.

---

[28] COND 2.5.7 G.
[29] See ch 2.

First, the 'four eyes requirement' demands that at least two individuals effectively direct the business of a bank.[30] The requirement means that at least two independent minds must be applied to the formulation and implementation of the bank's policies. Where there are only two people involved in running the bank, each must play a part in the decision-making process on all significant decisions.[31] The individuals do not have to be involved in the day to day execution of policy, but need to concern themselves with strategy and general direction, and have input into the way this is carried out. Each individual requires 'sufficient experience and knowledge of the business and the necessary personal qualities and skills to detect and resist any imprudence, dishonesty or other irregularities by the other individual'.[32] Where a single individual is particularly dominant in a bank, this will raise doubts about whether the requirement is met.

The next factors can be looked at together, with capital adequacy coming first. Adequate capital is a vital part of prudential regulation. Capital acts as a cushion against loss, ensuring that any loss is borne internally by the bank's shareholders, as well as increasing the confidence of counterparties and helping finance the infrastructure of the business.[33] Under IPRU a bank must, at the time it obtains a permission which qualifies it as such, have initial capital of at least €5 million, and maintain own funds of at least €5 million.[34] Banks are also required to maintain adequate capital resources which are commensurate with the nature and scale of its business and the risks inherent in that business.[35] Where a bank is a member of a group, those capital resources must also be commensurate with the risks inherent in the activities of other members of the group insofar as those risks are capable of affecting the bank. Next comes liquidity. Liquidity is necessary to ensure that banks meet their obligations as they fall due.[36] Where a bank is unable to meet its liabilities it is liable to lose its business rapidly, and illiquidity can quickly turn to insolvency. Banks must maintain adequate liquidity taking into account the nature and scale of its business so that it is able to meet its obligations as they fall due.[37]

---

[30] IPRU 3.3.2 G.
[31] IPRU 3.3.6 G.
[32] IPRU 3.3.7 G.
[33] D Ware, *Basic Principles of Banking Supervision* (London, Bank of England, 1996) at 9–10. The Basel Committee aims to complete a new Accord on capital adequacy (known as Basel II) by mid 2004. For the latest developments towards this see Basel Committee 'Continued progress toward Basel II' (Basel Committee 15 January 2004). The weaknesses of the original Capital Accord are well trodden. For a helpful overview see Cranston, above n 14 at 89–92.
[34] IPRU 3.3.9 R and 3.3.11 R.
[35] IPRU 3.3.13 R.
[36] The main function of banks is maturity transformation, and liquidity is essential to their ability to fulfil this function.
[37] IPRU 3.3.15 R.

The next factor is that of adequate provisions. Banks must maintain adequate provisions for the depreciation or diminution in the value of its assets, for liabilities which will or may fall to be discharged by it and for losses which will or may occur.[38] Details of how a bank should comply with this are set in the chapter of IPRU on provisioning policy statements. The FSA will pay close regard to the provisioning policy of the bank. Large exposures are next. A bank must have adequate systems and controls to enable it (a) to monitor and control its large exposures in conformity with its large exposures policy statement, and (b) to calculate its large exposures accurately and promptly.[39] Details of how a bank should comply with this are set out in the chapters of IPRU on large exposures and incremental capital for large exposures. If it proposes to enter into a transaction, or transactions which would result in it having an exposure which exceeds 25 per cent of its capital, a bank must notify the FSA.[40] The final factor is auditing. A bank should have an internal audit function, which may be in-house, or outsourced.[41] It should also have an audit committee, which should be chaired by a non-executive director of the bank, or be an audit committee of non-executive directors of the bank's holding company where that committee fulfils the role of audit committee in respect of the bank itself.[42]

Controlled Functions

It is perhaps trite to say that the success of a bank depends in large part on the competence and integrity of those who perform key functions on its behalf. The Basel Committee's *Core Principles for Effective Banking Supervision* refer to the need for the licensing authority to assess 'the banking organisation's ownership structure, directors and senior management'.[43] The competence, integrity and qualifications of proposed management, is central to the authorisation process. Under s 59 of FSMA, when a bank enters into an arrangement in relation to carrying on a regulated activity, any person performing a 'controlled function' under that arrangement must be approved by the FSA to perform that function. A function can be controlled if it is likely to enable the person responsible for its performance to exercise a significant influence on the conduct of the authorised person's affairs, so far as relating to the regulated activity,

---

[38] IPRU 3.3.17 R.
[39] IPRU 3.3.19 R.
[40] IPRU 3.3.21 R.
[41] IPRU 3.3.23 E.
[42] IPRU 3.3.25 E.
[43] Basel Committee, *Core Principles for Effective Banking Supervision*, Principle 3.

if it will involve the person performing it in dealing with customers of the authorised person in a manner substantially connected with the carrying on of the regulated activity, or if it will involve the person performing it in dealing with the property of customers of the authorised person in a manner substantially connected with the carrying on of the regulated activity.[44] Where an authorised person applies for approval, the FSA will only grant the application if satisfied that the person making the application ('the candidate') is fit and proper to perform the function in question.[45] The FSA may withdraw approval if it considers that the person to whom the approval was given is not a fit and proper person. If it proposes to withdraw approval the FSA must give each interested party a warning notice. If it decides to withdraw its approval it must give each of the interested parties a decision notice, and each interested party will be allowed to refer the matter to the tribunal.

Continued Supervision and Enforcement

A criticism sometimes levelled at prior approval regimes is that they can pay insufficient attention to whether minimum standards continue to be met *post* authorisation. Commenting on the licensing of professional occupations, Ogus observes that 'conditions typically involve a test only of a minimum standard at the outset of an individual's professional career; they provide no guarantee of continuing competence'.[46] In relation to banking, however, this criticism is unlikely to apply. Most banking regulatory regimes, including that in the UK, use continued supervision to ensure that banks and their key personnel continue to meet minimum criteria as long as they remain in the market. It is this continued supervision that distinguishes banking from some other forms of prior approval.

In theory, it might be possible for bank customers to monitor continuously the conduct of banks in order to assess the risks they pose. In practice, however, this would be impractical. Transaction costs, which include search, monitoring and enforcement costs cannot be carried out effectively by consumers.[47] They have neither the time nor the expertise to obtain, process and act upon the information that would be necessary. Economies of scale, the need for expertise, and the absence of effective

---

[44] Section 59(5)(6) and (7). It is clear that some controlled functions will not, however, be undertaken by senior management. See AUTH 6. Procedural matters are found in FSMA ss 60–63.

[45] Section 61(1).

[46] Ogus, *Regulation*, above n 2 at 223. As will be seen below, there are proposals that the OFT should take on a more supervisory role under changes to the Consumer Credit Act 1974.

[47] See I Ramsay, *Rationales for Intervention in the Consumer Marketplace* (London, OFT, 1984) para 3.6.

enforcement powers on the part of private individuals require this to be performed by a specialist regulatory agency. Llewellyn argues as follows:[48]

> [i]n effect, consumers delegate the task of monitoring to a regulatory agency ... There are strong efficiency reasons for consumers to delegate monitoring and supervision to a specialist agency to act on their behalf as the transaction costs for the consumer are lowered by such delegation.

Once a bank has received authorisation the FSA engages in what is known as 'baseline monitoring', to ensure that the bank continues to comply with the minimum regulatory requirements.[49] The FSA has identified four principal supervisory tools that it has at its disposal.[50] First, 'diagnostic tools' are designed to identify, assess and measure risks. An example might be a visit from a team of inspectors, although on site inspections have not been as common a part of the process of banking supervision as they have in other jurisdictions, such as the USA. Secondly, 'monitoring tools' are concerned with tracking the development of identified risks wherever they arise. An example given by the FSA is of a desk-based review of financial information provided by an institution.[51] Thirdly, 'preventative tools' aim to limit or reduce identified risks and so prevent them crystallising or increasing. An example might be the provision of comparative information to consumers. Finally, 'remedial tools' are used to respond to risks once they have materialised. The FSA gives the example of the delivery of restitution or compensation to consumers who have suffered loss.[52] A variety of tools, is therefore available to the regulator in carrying out supervision.

Fundamental to effective supervision is appropriate information, and the role of the FSA is in large part one of obtaining accurate information from firms, upon which it can make informed judgments. As discussed in chapters two and three, one of the key economic rationales for regulation is information asymmetry. The better the supply of information to participants in banking markets the lower the likelihood of inappropriate decision-making. This applies to regulators as well as consumers. There are therefore obligations on banks to report a variety of information. For example, FSMA requires a potential controller, or an existing

---

[48] D Llewellyn, *The Economic Rationale for Financial Regulation* (FSA, Occasional Paper 1, April 1999) at 24.

[49] Llewellyn suggests that there may be a distinction between supervision and monitoring. See ch 1 and Llewellyn, *ibid* at 6.

[50] *FSA Handbook*, 'Supervision' (SUP) 1.4.2 G. See also Financial Services Authority, *Building the New Regulator* (FSA, December 2000).

[51] *Building the New Regulator, ibid* para 49.

[52] *Ibid*.

controller who is proposing to increase control through specified thresholds to notify the FSA of this proposal.[53] The FSA may require a bank to provide specified information or information of a specified description, and to produce specified documents or documents of a specified description.[54] The FSA may also require banks to provide it with a report on any matter about which the FSA has required, or could require the provision of information or the production of documents under s 165.[55] In addition, there are powers to appoint competent persons to conduct investigations.[56] Once the FSA has received the information it needs it then has a number of other regulatory techniques available including, ultimately, formal disciplinary action.

Regulation through prior approval and continued supervision is only likely to meet its objectives if there are effective powers of enforcement in the hands of the regulator. There is a huge body of literature on the subject of enforcement in regulation, much of it involving empirical studies of specific industries.[57] What follows is a brief outline of some of the FSA's enforcement powers under FSMA, and a brief examination of some of the key issues relating to enforcement in general.[58]

Section 45 of FSMA deals with what is termed the FSA's own initiative power. The FSA may vary or cancel an authorised person's permission if it appears that: he is failing, or is likely to fail, to satisfy the threshold conditions; that he has failed, during a period of at least 12 months, to carry on a regulated activity for which he has a Part IV permission; or that it is desirable to exercise that power in order to protect the interests of consumers or potential consumers. Permission may be varied by: adding a regulated activity to those for which it gives permission; removing a regulated activity from those for which it gives permission; varying the description of a regulated activity for which it gives permission; cancelling a requirement imposed under s 43; or varying such a requirement. Under s 46 if the FSA considers that a person has acquired control over a UK authorised person who has Part IV permission, and it appears to the FSA that the likely effect of this acquisition is uncertain, the FSA can impose or vary a requirement under s 43 as if the person were applying for permission.

The own initiative powers are subject to a review procedure. It is important that banks which are subject to this action be given the opportunity to make representations on an informed basis. Section 54 deals

---

[53] Section 178(1).
[54] Section 165(1).
[55] Section 166(1).
[56] Section 167(1).
[57] There has not, to my knowledge, been such a study in relation to banking.
[58] There is also some discussion of enforcement in ch 6 and the comments here should be read in conjunction with that chapter.

with cancellation of Part IV permission and s 53 with variation of such permission. Section 54(1) states that if the FSA proposes to cancel an authorised person's Part IV permission otherwise than at his request, it must give him a warning notice. Section 54(2) states that if the FSA decides to cancel an authorised person's Part IV permission, otherwise than at his request, it must give him a decision notice. Details of what constitutes warning and decision notices are contained in ss 387(1) and 388(1) of FSMA. Under s 53, where the FSA exercises its own initiative power to vary an authorised person's Part IV permission, it must give the authorised person written notice, including such matters as the details of and reasons for the variation, the right to make representations, and the right to refer the matter to the tribunal. This written notice is referred to as a supervisory notice.[59] If, having considered any representations the FSA decides to vary the permission in the way proposed or (if the permission has already been varied) not to rescind the variation, it must give written notice, again, informing the person of the right to refer the matter to the tribunal. If having considered any representations the FSA decides not to vary the permission in the way proposed, to vary the permission in a different way, or to rescind a variation which has effect, it must give him written notice. Detailed requirements relating to notices are set out in Part XXVI of FSMA. The FSA obviously has considerable powers under FSMA to cancel and vary permission. Section 45(1), which sets out when the FSA can use its own initiative power, is couched in broad language. The FSA can take action if it appears to it that an authorised person is likely to fail to meet the threshold conditions, and if it appears to it that it is desirable to exercise that power in order to protect the interests of consumers or potential consumers. The combination of a subjective test ('if it appears to [the FSA]') and very general threshold conditions, means that the FSA has considerable power to take action at the first sign of trouble.

Enforcement, Discipline and the FSA

Chapter 11 of the *FSA Handbook* (ENF 11) is helpful in giving an indication of the FSA's overall approach to disciplinary measures. The main disciplinary measures available to the FSA under parts V and XIV of FSMA are: public statements and public censures; and financial penalties. One point to emphasise is that the FSA is aware of the need to use informal measures to secure compliance with its regulatory objectives. For example, where the FSA has concerns about a bank's behaviour, but decides not to take formal action it 'considers that it will be helpful for a firm or approved person to be made aware that they came close to being

---

[59] See FSMA s 395.

subject to formal disciplinary action, and may to that end, give a private warning.'[60] Examples of where private warnings might be used are where the matter in question is minor in nature or degree, or where the firm or approved person has 'taken full and immediate remedial action.'[61] Private warnings form part of a compliance history, and may influence the FSA in deciding whether to take disciplinary action in the future.

In deciding whether to take disciplinary action, the FSA will take account of all the circumstances of the case. The principal factors will be: the nature and seriousness of the breach (which includes whether the breach was deliberate or reckless, the amount of any benefit gained or loss avoided, and the loss or risk of loss caused to consumers or other market users); the conduct of the firm or the approved person after the breach (including matters such as whether remedial steps have been taken to identify whether consumers have suffered loss and compensating them); and the previous regulatory record of the firm or approved person.[62] This bears some similarity to regulatory compliance strategies. A compliance strategy has as its aim 'to secure conformity with law by means of ensuring compliance or by taking action to prevent potential law violation without the necessity to detect, process and penalise violations.'[63] It 'seeks to prevent a harm rather than punish an evil'.[64] The empirical evidence on enforcement in regulation in a number of sectors suggests that compliance strategies are frequently used, with prosecution seen very much as a last resort.[65] Although there are critics of compliance strategies, bargaining and negotiation may be the most effective options for the regulator. If compliance with legislation can be ensured by informal measures then the prime purpose of the legislation is fulfilled cost-effectively with a minimum of ill will. The cost of regular enforcement might be prohibitive, and also damaging to relations between regulator

---

[60] *FSA Handbook*, 'Enforcement' (hereafter ENF) 11.3.1 G.

[61] ENF 11.3.2 G.

[62] ENF 11.4.1 G.

[63] AJ Reiss, 'Selecting Strategies of Social Control Over Organisational Life' in K Hawkins and J Thomas (eds), *Enforcing Regulation* (Dordrecht, Kluwer Nijhoff, 1984) at 23–24. Reiss contrasts these with deterrence strategies, the aims of which are 'to secure conformity with the law by detecting violation, determining who is responsible for the violation, and penalising violations to deter violations in the future, either by those who are punished or by those who might do so were violations not penalised.'

[64] C Veljanowski, 'The Economics of Regulatory Enforcement' in K Hawkins and J Thomas (eds), *Enforcing Regulation, ibid* at 172. This contrasts with deterrence strategies and retributive strategies. The aim of a deterrence strategy is 'to secure conformity with the law by detecting violation, determining who is responsible for the violation, and penalising violations to deter violations in the future, either by those who are punished or by those who might do so were violations not penalised' (Reiss, *ibid*).

[65] Although it is possible for an enforcement agency to adopt a compliance strategy in relation to most types of wrong but a deterrence strategy in particular types of case. See J Rowan-Robinson, PQ Watchman and CR Barker, 'Crime and Regulation' (1988) Crim LR 211 at 216–17.

and regulated. As Ayres and Braithwaite argue, "adopting punishment as a first choice strategy may be seen as 'unaffordable, unworkable, and counter productive in undermining the good will of those with a commitment to compliance.'[66]

Where a private warning is not sufficient, the FSA may decide to issue a public censure or a public statement, or may impose a financial penalty. In deciding on the appropriate course of action, all the circumstances will be taken into account. As to whether public censure, public statement or financial penalty is appropriate, regard will be had to *inter alia* any profit that was made or loss avoided, the severity of the misconduct, the steps taken to ensure consumers are compensated, the record of the firm or approved person in question, the FSA's approach in similar cases, and the means of the firm or approved person. In short, financial penalties are likely to be imposed in the more serious cases.[67] If the FSA 'proposes' to publish a statement under s 205 or impose a penalty under s 206 it must give a warning notice that sets out the terms of the statement and the amount of the penalty. If the FSA 'decides' to publish such a statement or impose such a penalty, it must give a decision notice.

It is appropriate at this point to say something more about the role of public censures and public statements. The FSA states that it regards a public censure or public statement as a serious sanction.[68] As well as helping to promote market confidence, the FSA argues that

> public censures and public statements promote public awareness of the standards of behaviour expected of firms and approved persons. Increased public awareness also contributes towards greater consumer protection.[69]

It seems likely that the use of such powers can play an important role in consumer protection. By raising public awareness about how the FSA regards certain contraventions, this helps consumers to be aware of what they can expect from banks. As explained in chapter three, one of the difficulties consumers face is having inadequate information, and this includes information about what they can expect from those with whom they do business. By raising public awareness of contraventions by individual institutions, consumers will be able to make a decision about whether to do business with that institution in the future. As Gobert and Punch observe 'adverse publicity orders in effect give members of the public, through their purchasing power, a voice in determining

---

[66] I Ayres and J Braithwaite, *Responsive Regulation: Transcending the Deregulation Debate* (Oxford, Oxford University Press, 1992) at 26.
[67] ENF 12.3.3 G.
[68] ENF 12.2.2 G.
[69] *Ibid.*

the ultimate sanction incurred by a corporate offender.'[70] Fisse and Braithwaite argue that 'corporations fear the sting of adverse publicity attacks on their reputations more than they fear the law itself.'[71] The issue of adverse publicity is considered further in chapter five.

The final enforcement powers to consider here are those relating to the prosecution of criminal offences. Under s 401 of FSMA, the FSA has the power to prosecute a wide variety of offences, such as making false claims to be authorised or exempt, and misleading the FSA.[72] When deciding whether to prosecute, the FSA will apply the principles contained in the *Code* for Crown prosecutors.[73] There are two main issues here. First, under the evidential test, the FSA will consider whether there is sufficient evidence to provide a realistic prospect of conviction against the defendant (ie that it is more likely than not to secure a conviction).[74] Secondly, under the public interest test, the FSA will consider whether, having regard to the seriousness of the offence and all the circumstances, criminal prosecution is in the public interest. This will involve consideration of all the circumstances of the case.[75]

PRIOR APPROVAL AND CONSUMER CREDIT

Prior approval is central to the regulation of consumer credit as well as banking.[76] Indeed, the scheme under the Consumer Credit Act 1974 (CCA) was the first major prior approval system in the financial area in the UK.[77] Although the credit licensing regime is not considered in great depth here, it is important to say something about it as it provides an example of an alternative prior approval regime under which banking activity is controlled. It should be remembered that banks require a licence to conduct consumer credit business in addition to the authorisation they receive under FSMA.

The justification for prior approval of all credit providers is somewhat different from that of banks. First, the failure of a credit provider,

---

[70] J Gobert and M Punch, *Rethinking Corporate Crime* (London, Butterworths, 2003) at 238.
[71] B Fisse and J Braithwaite, *The Impact of Publicity on Corporate Offenders* (Albany, State University of New York Press, 1983) at 249.
[72] Under ss 24 and 398 respectively.
[73] ENF 15.5.1 G.
[74] ENF 15.5.3 G.
[75] ENF 15.5.5 G.
[76] In fact, the licensing regime covers not only consumer credit, but hire, credit brokerage, debt adjusting and debt counselling, debt collection and credit reference agencies. The term 'consumer credit licensing' is being used in this chapter in a loose sense to cover licensing under the Consumer Credit Act 1974. In practice, most applicants ask for and receive a licence which covers all these categories.
[77] As discussed above, banks were not subject to prior approval until 1979.

unlike that of a bank, will not generate systemic risk.[78] Secondly, the regime under FSMA covers investment business, where the trader will have possession of the consumer's money, and where there is a risk of loss through the process of investment. These factors do not apply in the credit market, where it is the consumer who has the trader's money, and the costs are set at the beginning.[79] It was mentioned above that prior approval should only be used in relatively limited circumstances. Whether concerns about consumer protection are sufficient to justify such an interventionist scheme of regulation is a subject for debate.

The focus of the licensing scheme for credit is very much the protection of the consumer, and there are many risks to the consumer in the consumer credit market. In trying to categorise types of consumer detriment that may occur in credit markets, the Department of Trade and Industry (DTI) identified the following: irresponsible lending, high costs of credit, misinformation or lack of adequate or clear information, debt escalation, high pressure sales tactics and harassment and threats of violence.[80] It seems that consumers may be particularly vulnerable when contracting for credit. Lack of knowledge has long been identified as one element of this, and information asymmetry is likely to be great where credit is concerned. However, the Crowther Committee identified other reasons why consumers may be at risk, including inertia, recklessness, improvidence and having inadequate incomes.[81] As well as information asymmetry, the extent of potential harm that might result from inadequate regulation is another justification for prior approval. As has already been noted, these are two of the principal justifications for prior approval regimes. However, where credit is concerned, the risk is that there will be significant harm to individual consumers who deal with a particular creditor. Where banking is concerned, the risk is that consumers of a perfectly well-run bank may lose out through systemic risk.[82] Nevertheless, as seen below, there are strong arguments for using prior approval where credit is concerned.

The key to the CCA test is the fitness test contained in s 25. Section 25(1) provides that an applicant will be awarded a licence if he satisfies the Director General of Fair Trading that: '(a) he is a fit person to engage in activities covered by the licence, and (b) the name or names under which

---

[78] See ch 2.
[79] Department of Trade and Industry, *A Consultation Document on the Licensing Regime under the Consumer Credit Act 1974* (DTI, 2002) para 2.4.1.
[80] *Ibid* para 2.2.
[81] *Report of the Committee on Consumer Credit* (the Crowther Committee), (Cmnd 4596/1971) paras 6.1.4–6.1.10.
[82] See ch 2.

he applies to be licensed are not misleading or otherwise undesirable.' Section 25(2) states than in deciding if an applicant is a fit person, the Director General shall have regard to:

> any circumstances appearing to him to be relevant, and in particular any evidence tending to show that the applicant, or any of the applicant's employees, agents or associates (whether past or present) or, where the applicant is a body corporate, any person appearing to the director to be a controller of the body corporate or an associate of any such person, has—
>
> (a) committed any offence involving fraud or other dishonesty, or violence,
>
> (b) contravened any provision made by or under this Act, or by or under any other enactment regulating the provision of credit to individuals or other transactions with individuals
>
> [bb] contravened any provision in force in an EEA State which corresponds to a provision of the kind mentioned in paragraph (b);]
>
> (c) practised discrimination on grounds of sex, colour, race, or ethnic or national origins in, or in connection with, the carrying on of any business, or
>
> (d) engaged in business practices appearing to the Director to be deceitful or oppressive, or otherwise unfair or improper (whether unlawful or not).

At least one previous Director General of Fair Trading has emphasised that the standard is a high one. Writing in 1982, Sir Gordon [now Lord] Borrie stated: 'I have a statutory duty to be satisfied that an applicant is a fit person to hold a licence and I cannot possibly be fully satisfied in this respect if doubts and reservations are raised and not answered.'[83] The DTI has recently questioned the extent to which the OFT is able to construct a detailed view on the fitness of an applicant to hold a licence. It is interesting to contrast the test under the CCA with the fit and proper test under FSMA, which is examined above. The DTI argues that 'whereas regulators like the Financial Services Authority operate authorisation regimes that place a great deal of emphasis on tests of competence and active checking and monitoring for determining whether an applicant is qualified to hold a licence, the consumer credit licensing system as administered by the Office of Fair Trading (OFT) has traditionally applied a less rigorous test for qualification.'[84] The details of the regime are evaluated as part of the general discussion of prior approval below.

---

[83] G Borrie, 'Licensing Practice Under the Consumer Credit Act' (1982) *Journal of Business Law* 91 at 94–95.
[84] Above n 79 para 2.1.

A CRITIQUE OF PRIOR APPROVAL

There are some very clear strengths to the use of prior approval in banking. Most developed countries now have some form of authorisation requirement in place and the Basel Committee's *Core Principles for Effective Supervision* stress the need for states to have a licensing authority which has the right to set criteria and reject applications that fall short of those criteria.[85] Above all, prior approval has a prophylactic role in screening out those institutions, or individuals, who are most liable to pose risks to the FSA's statutory objectives. The FSA has declared that it has a 'bias towards proactivity', with a focus on identifying and reducing risks at an early stage.[86] The Authority continued:[87]

> Vetting at entry aims to allow only firms and individuals who satisfy the necessary criteria (including honesty, competence, and financial soundness) to engage in the regulated activity. Experience in the UK and elsewhere shows that regulatory objectives are more likely to be achieved by setting and enforcing standards for entry, rather than having to deal with major problems later.

There can be little doubt that there are good reasons to exclude the dishonest, the incompetent and the financially unsound from banking business, and that prior approval plays an important role in fulfilling that. As has been seen, the threshold criteria that apply to institutions, and the powers over those performing controlled functions mean that the FSA has considerable scope to exclude those who fail to meet minimum standards. In relation to consumer credit, the Crowther Committee supported the use of licensing for credit providers, fearing that lesser modes of regulation would not be adequate.[88] The Committee said:

> The more unscrupulous type of credit grantor may well take the view that the occasional check on his malpractices by a determined consumer in an isolated transaction is not a serious deterrent, and is outweighed by the financial advantages he may derive from evading the law. There is thus a need for an agency entrusted with the continuing supervision of consumer credit grantors, with power to investigate trading practices, require

---

[85] Principle 3.
[86] Financial Services Authority, *A New Regulator for the New Millennium* (FSA, January 2000) at 12.
[87] *Ibid* at 29.
[88] Licensing was already in existence for some groups, notably moneylenders and pawnbrokers, but the lack of adequate oversight and enforcement led some commentators to argue that it was ineffective. See I Ramsay, *Consumer Protection: Text and Materials* (London, Weidenfeld and Nicolson, 1989) at 323; C Scott and J Black, *Cranston's Consumers and the Law* (London, Butterworths, 2000) at 465.

production of accounts and records and, in the vase of serious malpractices, suspend or revoke the offender's licence.[89]

Although the extract above compares prior approval with regulation through the private law, and there are many other regulatory techniques, the Crowther Committee's Report makes it clear that the Committee did not see those other types of regulation as adequate by themselves.[90] It could also be argued that the very introduction of a prior approval regime has an effect upon unscrupulous traders. That introduction might remove traders who realise that, because of their past behaviour, they will not gain authorisation. It has been pointed out, for example, that when moneylenders were first subjected to prior approval, around 60 per cent did not apply for a licence, in many cases, presumably, because they believed that one would be refused.[91]

A further argument in favour of prior approval is that it allows the regulator to take action against improper behaviour which does not breach the criminal law. For example, under FSMA, when deciding if a firm is a fit and proper person for the purposes of the suitability test, the FSA can take into account conduct which is not criminal, but casts doubt upon whether the firm conducts, or will conduct, its business with integrity and in compliance with proper standards. This might include, *inter alia*, whether the firm or any person connected with it has contravened statements of principles or codes of practice of other regulatory bodies. Under the CCA, the OFT can also consider a wide variety of factors, including whether the person has 'engaged in business practices appearing to the Director to be deceitful or oppressive, or otherwise unfair or improper (whether unlawful or not).'[92] However the breadth of this discretion might give cause for concern. Ramsay, for example, argues that while licensing can be an effective bargaining lever in such circumstances '[t]here may be a justified concern where licensing is used to persuade traders to refrain from practices not prohibited by law.'[93] While it is important that a regulator should be careful to take account of the legality of conduct, it is nevertheless important to recognise that there may be examples of conduct that, while not infringing specific legal obligations, is deceitful, oppressive or otherwise unjust.

---

[89] Crowther Committee, above n 81 para 6.3.3. This was so, even though the Committee also thought that 'the state should interfere as little as possible with the consumer's freedom to use his knowledge of the consumer credit market to the best of his ability and according to his judgement of what constitutes his best interests.' (para 3.9.1).
[90] The Consumer Credit Act does make use of other techniques, such as disclosure, cooling-off periods and restrictions upon creditors' remedies to mention but three.
[91] C Scott and J Black, above n 88 at 449.
[92] Consumer Credit Act 1974 s 25(2)d.
[93] Ramsay, above n 88 at 326.

There are undoubtedly advantages to prior approval but there are also concerns about its use as a regulatory technique. Some of these concerns are also applicable to other forms of regulation, for example, mandatory minimum standards, but are particularly significant where prior approval is concerned. The discussion below considers both the risks attached to the use of prior approval in general, and the particular concerns raised by the FSMA and CCA regimes.

First, the effect of prior approval is to limit the number of suppliers in a market and, therefore, to limit competition.[94] There may be good reasons to support this where it is done in the public interest with the aim of protecting the consumer, but there is concern that prior approval may be used for anti-competitive purposes.[95] For example, a state that wishes to protect the position of its own banks could use prior approval as a way of limiting competition, but under the guise of the public interest. It has been forcefully argued that prior approval tends to be supported by those who are already in the marketplace because it limits the competition that they are likely to face.[96] Gelhorn, for example, notes that 'licensing has only infrequently been imposed upon an occupation against its wishes'.[97] When new legislation is introduced, existing firms are frequently 'grandfathered' into the new regime, removing from them the costs of meeting the new standards.[98] However, this does not mean that firms will always support changes in a licensing regime which increases regulation. There was opposition from many parts of the financial services industry to much of FSMA, and there are still fears that the FSA represents something of a leviathan.[99] Furthermore, the cost of existing regulation is lower to incumbent firms than to newcomers as their presence in the market gives them contacts, expertise and a cost advantage.[100] There is certainly an incentive upon banks to try to restrict the amount of competition that they

[94] Its aim is not to limit the number of suppliers, but to screen out those who are unfit. It differs from what might be called 'public interest allocation', or 'governmental franchising'. See S Breyer, *Regulation and its Reform*, (Cambridge MA, Harvard University Press, 1982) ch 4; R Baldwin and M Cave, *Franchising as a Tool of Government* (London, Centre for the Study of Regulated Industries, 1996).

[95] Ogus, *Regulation*, above n 2 at 214–15.

[96] See for example M Friedman, *Capitalism and Freedom* (Chicago, University of Chicago Press, 1962) at 144–49; A Maurizi, 'Occupational Licensing and the Public Interest' (1974) *Journal of Political Economy* at 399. G Benston, *Regulating Financial Markets* (London, Institute of Economic Affairs, 1998) at 80–85.

[97] W Gelhorn, 'The Abuse of Occupational Licensing' (1976) 44 *University of Chicago Law Review* 6 at 11. The one exception he notes from the US is stockbrokers who were subjected to such a scheme following the financial scandals of 1929.

[98] Ogus, *Regulation*, above n 2 at 220. Grandfathering is used by the FSA. For a discussion of its role see P Thorpe 'The Final Stages of Preparation by the FSA and the Industry'. Available at <http://www.fsa.gov.uk/speeches>.

[99] See for example A Alcock 'A Regulatory Monster' (1998) *Journal of Business Law* 371, A Tyrie and M McElwee, *Leviathan at Large* (London, Centre for Policy Studies, 2000).

[100] Benston, *Regulating Financial Markets*, above n 96 at 96.

face, but in an increasingly internationalised financial environment, there may be as much concern at losing business to institutions operating overseas as there is to new entrants into a domestic market.

If there is potential for prior approval schemes to be used to protect incumbents, it is vital that regulators see that this is not realised. However, there are theories that suggest why regulators might wish to be complicit in a conspiracy with industry to restrict competition. One possible result of having a relatively small number of firms in a market which form a close relationship with the regulator is that the relationship may become too close, with the regulator becoming 'captured' by the firm.[101] Capture is possible, in theory at least, in all regulatory environments, and not just where there is prior approval. The process of standard setting, the making of rules on disclosure and the exercise of discretion about whether to prosecute may all be influenced by the nature of the relationship between regulator and regulated. Perhaps the best-known version of capture theory is found in the work of Bernstein. Bernstein's theory that regulators have a 'life cycle' was summarised memorably by J K Galbraith as follows:

> Regulatory bodies, like the people who comprise them, have a marked life-cycle. In youth they are vigorous, aggressive, evangelistic, and even intolerant. Later, they mellow, and in old age—after a matter of ten or fifteen years, they become, with some exceptions, either an arm of the industry they are regulating or senile.[102]

One reason why capture may emerge is explained by 'revolving door theory'. This suggests that regulators aspire to well-paid jobs in the firms they are regulating and are therefore eager not to harm their career prospects by alienating the regulated. Regulatory studies are inconclusive on the subject of capture and it seems that the majority of commentators are unconvinced that it is a major problem.[103] It does not seem to be a particularly great threat where banking is concerned in the UK. There are a large number of banks operating in the jurisdiction, and while there is some subjectivity in the process of authorisation, most of the minimum standards are relatively objective and uniform. Indeed, it appears that before the creation of a system of authorisation and continued supervision, there was a closer and far less formal relationship between regulator and regulated. The Bank of England was well known for regulating banks

---

[101] See M H Bernstein, *Regulating Business by Independent Commission* (Princeton, Princeton University Press, 1955).

[102] J K Galbraith, *The Great Crash* (Boston, Houghton Mifflin, 1955) at 171.

[103] Ogus, *Regulation*, above n 2 at 107. See also T Makkai and J Braithwaite 'In and Out of the Revolving Door: Making Sense of Regulatory Capture' (1995) 1 *Journal of Public Policy* 61.

on the basis of 'moral suasion'.[104] It favoured informal meetings, flexibility and co-operation over more formal methods of regulation. It has been argued that this approach was largely successful. Tidball describes the regulation of banks from the Second World War to the early 1970s as 'quiet and consistent, untarnished by controversy, where banks followed the gentlemanly tradition of accepting the Bank's authority.'[105] Quinn stated that he firmly believed 'that there is an important place within the [Banking] Act [1987] for moral suasion' and considered that 'the use of the bank's traditional influence can in many circumstances be a better protection for depositors and for the financial system as a whole than the application of the Bank's formal powers'.[106] However, weaknesses in regulation were a major contributory factor to the secondary banking crisis, which in turn provided a major reason for the creation of the Banking Act 1979.[107] Furthermore, while such informality and co-operation may have been possible in the homogeneous world of banking in the three decades or so after the Second World War, the internationalisation of finance in the 1980s would have made this impossible.[108] It should also be noted that it is far from clear that the close relationship between regulator and bank in the period before 1979 was either the result of, or a factor leading to, capture. The Bank had (admittedly limited) powers to make recommendations and issue directions under the Bank of England Act 1946 and it may be that these powers, coupled with the Bank's importance, were sufficient to give it the necessary authority to control those under its jurisdiction. Indeed, it could be argued that the flexibility that characterised moral suasion was a great concern to the regulated, because of the paucity of safeguards it encompassed.[109]

A further, but related, concern with prior approval is that by limiting the number of suppliers, the regulator may also be limiting the choice of the consumer. In chapter two, it was argued that in the perfect market, consumers are viewed as sovereign maximisers of their own utility. They should be able to make choices about where to place their deposits from the broadest choice possible. As well as the efficiency gains that would be

---

[104] See B Quinn, 'The Influence of the Banking Acts 1979 and 1987 on the Bank of England's Traditional Style of Banking Supervision' in J Norton (ed), *Bank Regulation and Supervision in the 1990s* (London, LLP, 1991) 1.
[105] S Tidball, 'The Development of Banking Regulation' in E J Swan (ed), *The Development of the Law of Financial Services* (London, Cavendish, 1993) 95 at 99.
[106] B Quinn, 'The Influence of the Banking Acts', above n 104 at 6.
[107] The 1979 Act was described as a 'memorial to the secondary banking crisis', but it is clear that the adoption of the First Banking Co-ordination Directive was perhaps a more significant factor. See Tidball, above n 105 at 101.
[108] See M Moran, *The Politics of Banking: The Strange Case of Competition and Credit Control*, cited in K McGuire, 'Emergent Trends in Bank Supervision in the United Kingdom' (1993) 54 MLR 669 at 673.
[109] Quinn, above n 104 at 5.

brought in theory by increased competition, consumers would also be able to take risks that they were prepared to, but that a regulator would avoid. Freedom of choice encompasses, inevitably, the freedom to make mistakes.[110] One of the effects of prior approval is to limit that choice. As we have seen in chapter two, there are both social and economic arguments for limiting that choice. Paternalist doctrine suggests that individual choice must sometimes be surrendered for the individual's own good. Furthermore, it is also necessary to limit individual choice in the interests of efficiency, particularly where it can be assumed that relatively few consumers would be willing to run the risks in question. From an economic perspective there are good reasons why consumers should be prevented from making decisions which have an adverse effect on the soundness of the financial system.[111] Systemic risk, avoidance of which is one of the principal aims of financial regulation, is an externality. Regulation is generally viewed as essential to reducing the likelihood of such a risk and limiting its effect should it materialise. Prior approval is likely to play a key role in such regulation, particularly when coupled with continued supervision.

An additional concern with prior approval is that it is expensive both to establish and to operate. The FSA's budget for 2002–03 was £220.4 million.[112] Regulatory costs come in a variety of forms, however. These have been said to include direct costs, such as people, equipment and buildings, costs financing compensation funds, the costs of failing to attract additional resources because of the regulatory burden and the costs of reduced competition and innovation.[113] It has been argued by both supporters and critics of financial regulation that there is a tendency to regard regulation as a free good: 'the potential benefits of extra regulation/supervision are patent, and the costs are nearly indiscernible.'[114] In practice, regulation is paid for by the taxpayer and the consumer, but the lack of visibility of its costs compared with its benefits can lead to an over-demand.[115] As will be seen below, however, while it is difficult to quantify the costs of regulation with any degree of precision, it is even more difficult to quantify its benefits.[116] Any attempts at informing consumers about the costs and benefits of regulation in anything other than

---

[110] See T Schelling, *Choice and Consequence* (Cambridge MA, Harvard University Press, 1984) at 144–46.
[111] See ch 2.
[112] Financial Services Authority, *Annual Report 2002–03* (FSA, 2003) at 112. For a discussion of the costs of regulation see Benston, above n 96 at 91–97.
[113] C Goodhart, *The Central Bank and the Financial System* (Basingstoke, MacMillan, 1995) ch 19.
[114] Goodhart *et al*, *Financial Regulation: why, how and where now?* (London, Routledge, 1998) at 63.
[115] That is, more demand than there would be were the costs and benefits better understood.
[116] See C Goodhart, above n 113; R Baldwin and M Cave, *Understanding Regulation: Theory, Strategy and Practice* (Oxford, Oxford University Press, 1999) ch 7. Goodhart *et al*, *Financial Regulation*, above n 114, at 62–63.

general terms is therefore likely to be difficult. Furthermore, even if there is a tendency upon the part of consumers to treat regulation as a free good, this should not lead us to conclude that strict regulation is inappropriate. Consumers may be willing to pay for the sense of security that is derived from the feeling that banks are being monitored in the public interest. Provided this is not taken as a guarantee that banks will be saved at all costs, with the moral hazard that this necessarily involves, this should not be unduly damaging. Indeed, despite the difficulties present in quantifying costs and benefits, cost–benefit analysis has become an important part of the financial regulatory landscape.

A possible result of the expense of prior approval regimes is that they are forced to operate with inadequate resources. This criticism has been levelled at the CCA regime. There are approximately 215,000 live consumer credit licences. It seems fanciful to believe that the OFT has the resources at its disposal to adequately monitor and enforce their operation. Indeed, the DTI notes that:

> [t]here is widespread concern among the finance industry, the trading standards community and consumer bodies that the current licensing system is not appropriately resourced or structured to be both efficient and effective in keeping rogues out of the marketplace and consumers protected.[117]

Inadequate resourcing leads to difficulties that have already been mentioned.

A further concern with prior approval is that it may provide regulators with incentives to make sub-optimal decisions. For example, when the FSA is deciding whether to authorise an applicant it can make two principal types of error. First, it can authorise a firm which, in retrospect, it should not have authorised. Secondly, it can refuse to authorise a firm that, in retrospect, it should have authorised. Both types of mistake involve welfare losses, but the former is far more visible, and far more likely to lead to negative publicity, than the latter. There may, therefore, be incentives upon regulators to be ultra cautious, refusing to authorise except in the clearest of circumstances.[118] Goodhart argues that in an attempt to reduce the extent to which they are held responsible for the failure of financial institutions, regulators tend to push for detailed and comprehensive regulations. He continues '[s]ince the success for a regulator, when the costs of regulations are not taken fully into account, can be

---

[117] Above n 79 para 1.1.

[118] K Shrader-Frechette, 'Uncertainty and the Producer Strategy: The Case for Minimising Type II Errors in Rational Risk Evaluation', ch 9 in K Shrader-Frechette, *Risk and Rationality* (Berkeley, University of California Press, 1991); S Breyer, *Regulation and its Reform*, above n 94 at 133.

measured by the absence of newsworthy failures, the incentive will be for over-regulation.'[119] Even under regulatory regimes where significant efforts are made to take costs into account, as under FSMA, it is doubtful that the public, faced with the collapse of a major bank, will appreciate the trade-offs involved.[120] In some cases, the caution shown by regulators may be based upon uncertainty or ignorance on their part. Benston writes of 'the tendency of naturally conservative supervisors to disapprove of or disallow innovations that appear to be risky or that they do not understand.'[121] The techniques used by banks, for example to measure risk, may develop quickly, and if regulators are unable to keep pace with these developments, there is a risk of welfare losses.

Another risk with prior approval is that it may lead to a false sense of security on the part of consumers. Where consumers are aware that there is a developed system of prior approval in place, in particular where it also encompasses continued supervision, there is a risk that they will no longer recognise the risks that remain. Trebilcock argues that instruments such as prior approval 'may actually increase the gap between [consumer] expectations and reality by giving the impression that a licence or permit indicates an actual level of safety or competence.'[122] This impression may be particularly strong where continued supervision is concerned. Here, the consumer may think, not only that the bank has been approved, but that its subsequent conduct is so closely monitored and supervised that all its major decisions are approved by the regulator. If this is the perception given, then it is highly problematic. The role of the FSA is not to act as an alternative to senior management. As Taylor comments:

[a] long-standing matter of concern in Britain and in many other countries has been that a regulatory regime might result in a shifting of responsibility from the firms' management to the supervisory authorities ... It is important that supervisors and regulators do not become a kind of superior management board ...[123]

There are provisions to guard against the FSA's taking on of this role. Chief among these is the principle in s 2(3)(b) of FSMA that the FSA must

---

[119] Goodhart, 'The Costs of Regulation', above n 116 at 451.
[120] Ian MacFarlane of the Reserve Bank of Australia has commented that 'in an optimal system of supervision the occasional failure should occur. But the public [in the UK], despite an enormous amount of effort, have never accepted this'. Cited in Goodhart *et al, Financial Regulation*, above n 114 at 215.
[121] Benston, above n 96 at 111.
[122] M Trebilcock, 'Rethinking Consumer Protection Policy' in C Rickett and T Telfer (eds) *International Perspectives on Consumers' Access to Justice* (Cambridge, Cambridge University Press, 2003) 68 at 75.
[123] M Taylor, 'Accountability and Objectives of the FSA', in M Blair *et al, Blackstone's Guide to the Financial Services and Markets Act 2000* (London, Blackstone Press, 2001) 17 at 35.

have regard to 'the responsibilities of those who manage the affairs of authorised persons'. However, it is under the public awareness objective that the FSA needs to make it clear to consumers what the respective roles of supervisor and supervisee are. An additional problem here is that consumers' over-reliance on the regulator may generate moral hazard. If consumers are lulled into a false sense of security then they will not take sufficient care when making decisions, believing that the approval provided by the regulator acts as something akin to a guarantee. The risk may be particularly great where the regulator is so under-resourced that it cannot adequately monitor the traders in question. Moreover, under the consumer credit regime, the OFT does not have responsibility for continually supervising holders of credit licences the way the FSA does for those under its wing. The risk is that consumers will see the holding of a licence as a guarantee that the trader is reputable.[124] Some changes in this respect are likely to emerge from the review of the Consumer Credit Act. The Consumer Credit White Paper envisages the OFT playing a greater role in the monitoring of licence holders, using a risk-based approach, similar to that adopted by the FSA.[125] Licences will be granted for an indefinite period (rather than for the current period of five years) and the OFT will monitor licence holders throughout the period of the licence. The risk-based approach will mean that the intensity of monitoring will be reflected by the degree of risk to the consumers that the licence holder is deemed to pose. Those who are deemed to pose little threat because of their past record or the nature of their business will experience a light touch. By contrast, those who are thought to pose a greater threat because of the sectors in which they operate or their previous conduct can expect to be monitored more closely. Some of the powers discussed below should assist the OFT in fulfilling its obligations, but whether it will have the resources to monitor effectively must be a matter for concern.

An additional risk with prior approval concerns the powers available to the regulator. Scott and Black sum up the problem by observing that 'enforcement agencies are handicapped if there is a discrepancy between the sanctions they can initiate and the objectionable behaviour they are charged with eliminating.'[126] It is obvious that if the powers of the regulator are weak then they are likely to be inadequate as a deterrent. However, it has been argued that there are also difficulties where the only available sanctions are severe. The ultimate sanction in the regimes

---

[124] Above n 79.

[125] Department of Trade and Industry, *Fair Clear and Competitive: The Consumer Credit Market in the 21st Century* (the White Paper) (Cm 6040, December 2003); Financial Services Authority, A New Regulator for the New Millennium (FSA, January 2000) ch 2.

[126] Scott and Black, above n 88 at 450. See also R Arens and D Lasswell, *In Defence of Public Order* (New York, Columbia University Press, 1961) at 224–25. Cited in Scott and Black, above n 88 at 450; Ayres and Braithwaite, Responsive Regulation, above n 66.

we are examining, namely revocation of a licence, is indeed severe.[127] As a result, it is only likely to come into effect in extreme cases. As Ayres and Braithwaite observe, licence revocation is so drastic a sanction that 'it is politically impossible and morally unacceptable to use it with any but the most extraordinary offences.'[128] Even the use of less draconian powers such as suspending or varying a licence may impact adversely upon the livelihood of the trader and so be justified in only exceptional circumstances. This leads to a paradox where especially stringent laws produce under-regulation.[129] The risk of this is significantly reduced where the regulator has a wider variety of tools at its disposal. By contrast with the OFT, the FSA has a wide variety of disciplinary and remedial tools.[130] It is interesting to note that the Crowther Committee recommended that the regulator should have a variety of powers at its disposal. This would include the ability to apply to the courts for injunctions and to initiate prosecutions, as well as to initiate civil proceedings on behalf of private individuals.[131] Crowther's original vision appears to be of a regulatory regime with some similarities to that under FSMA. This has been addressed by the White Paper, which states that the Government intends to introduce powers for the OFT to impose special conditions on, or take undertakings from, licence holders. Breach of a condition or undertaking could lead to the OFT imposing a financial penalty or, ultimately, the revocation, suspension or variation of the licence.[132] Following consultation with the DTI, the OFT will be required to issue guidance on penalties when the provisions go through Parliament. In addition, the provision that allows an applicant or licence holder to appeal to the Secretary of State for Trade and Industry against certain decisions of the OFT relating to licensing will be reformed. In particular, responsibility for appeals will pass to a new Tribunal service that is being planned by the Department for Constitutional Affairs.[133]

An additional difficulty with prior approval regimes concerns whether the minimum standards upon which they are based are set at the optimum level. Although prior approval in theory involves the disinterested use of [relatively] objective criteria, it is difficult to judge the extent to which this occurs in practice. Some standards, such as capital adequacy,

---

[127] The White Paper describes the sanction as 'draconian', above n 125 para 3.7.
[128] Ayres and Braithwaite, *Responsive Regulation*, above n 66 at 36.
[129] *Ibid*. See also C Sunstein, *After the Rights Revolution: Re-conceiving the Regulatory State* (Cambridge MA, Harvard University Press, 1990) at 90–91.
[130] For example, the FSA can publicly censure, impose penalties, vary or revoke permission, require restitution, and seek court orders. See E Lomnicka, 'The Reform of Consumer Credit in the UK' (1994) *Journal of Business Law* 129.
[131] Crowther Committee, above n 81 para 7.4.3.
[132] The White Paper, above n 125 para 3.21.
[133] *Ibid* para 3.24.

are relatively easy to quantify in advance.[134] Others will be far more subjective. Perhaps the best example of this is the fit and proper test under the approved persons regime. Commenting on the provisions of Schedule 3 of the Banking Act 1987,[135] in particular the test for assessing competence and soundness of judgment, Hadjiemmanuil argued that the test 'increases the risk of discriminatory or arbitrary treatment of specific individuals, raising a potential threat to the freedoms of employment and economic activity in the field of banking'.[136] This is addressed to some extent by the Statements of Principle and Code of Practice, which clarify how the discretion is likely to be used. Nevertheless, concerns remain. There must be a risk that the powers of the regulator are so broad that some individuals may be excluded on dubious grounds.

Despite these concerns, it is clear that the discretion that such open-ended criteria give to the regulator means that a wide variety of factors can be taken into account. Indeed, it has been suggested that in order to exclude undesirable traders from the credit marketplace the fitness test under the CCA will have to be developed further. It appears that in practice, the test for fitness is set at a relatively low level. In 2000–01 the OFT only rejected around 0.2 per cent of new licence applications, about the same proportion as the previous year. This has since risen to 0.6 per cent, or 95 of around 16,000 new applications.[137] Indeed, it has been suggested that the test should be more closely aligned with that under FSMA. To the extent that the aim of the provisions is to screen out rogue traders, it will be important to improve the implementation of the current regime to ensure that the OFT has accurate information about matters relating to probity. However, the FSMA test is concerned not only with probity, but also with competence. The White Paper argues that the OFT needs to be able not only to look back to a trader's past conduct, but also forward 'to assess their preparedness for running their credit business.'[138] The proposals lack detail at the time of writing. The White Paper states that the OFT will be given responsibility for producing initial guidance on what it considers are the standards of fitness required for the conduct of credit business. Guidance would take account of 'current and relevant market practice' and would be the subject of public consultation before being issued.[139] It is not clear how close the new approach is likely to be to the test under FSMA, which emphasises matters of competence and skill. The DTI had suggested that the test under the CCA could include wording

---

[134] Although there will be doubt about what is appropriate to count as capital, and whether the capital adequacy requirements are set at an appropriate level.
[135] A forerunner of the regime discussed.
[136] C Hadjiemmanuil, above n 4 at 235.
[137] Above n 79 at 2.6.1.
[138] The White Paper para 3.8.
[139] *Ibid* para 3.10.

similar to that found in FSMA, imposing an obligation 'to ensure business is conducted with integrity and in compliance with proper standards; whether it has or will have a competent and prudent management; and whether it conducts itself with due care, skill and diligence.'[140] This would be a significant change, and would bring consumer credit much more closely into line with the approach in FSMA.

It was mentioned above that one of the strengths of prior approval concerned the extent to which it enabled the regulator to obtain useful information about the trader and the industry at large. However, some regimes may lack bite in this respect. One of the principal difficulties facing the OFT under the CCA regime appears to be that of accessing data about convictions. The OFT does not have access to the National Police Computer, nor the Criminal Records Bureau databases. Although the OFT obtains details of convictions from the National Identification Service if it suspects that a conviction has not been disclosed, it cannot routinely check against criminal records.[141] Another difficulty, which was emphasised by the Parliamentary Accounts Committee (PAC), is that of falsified applications. In 2002–02 around 30 per cent of refusals or revocations of licences were because of incomplete or misleading information. Although the OFT is able to prosecute a trader for providing misleading information it has never done so, arguing that such action would not present value for money. The PAC argued that '[t]here appears to be little to deter applicants from obtaining licences on the basis of false information and then trading until they are caught.'[142] The PAC recommended that the OFT should monitor prosecutions by local authorities and step in to prosecute 'until such time as local enforcement agencies can be relied upon to act against traders who falsify their applications.'[143] The DTI has also recognised that the information that the OFT can collect 'is insufficient to enable it to carry out risk assessment or to target action in those areas causing the greatest problems as effectively as it might.'[144] The White Paper accepts that the OFT has limited powers when trying to establish whether a trader is unfit to hold a licence. It suggests that the OFT should have powers to seek additional information from licensees and third parties.[145] In addition, the Government proposes extending the

---

[140] *Above* n 79 at 2.4.3.

[141] See the 37th Report from the Committee of Public Accounts, *The Office of Fair Trading: Protecting the Consumer from Unfair Trading Practices* (HC 501, Session 1999–2000), and the Comptroller and Auditor General's Report, *The Office of Fair Trading: Progress in Protecting Consumers' Interests* (HC 430, Session 2002–03).

[142] 34th Report from the Committee of Public Accounts, *The Office of Fair Trading: Progress in Protecting Consumers' Interests* (*Hansard* HC 546, Session 2002–03) at 13.

[143] *Ibid.*

[144] Above n 79 para 2.1.

[145] This might include the requirement to produce books, documents and records and powers to carry out compliance visits (White Paper, above n 125 para 3.16).

duties under s 36 of the Consumer Credit Act so that licensees will have to inform the OFT of material changes in their circumstances relating to their fitness to hold a licence, such as county court judgments, disqualification from acting as a director, bankruptcy or criminal convictions.[146] The White Paper will also be consulting on how to ensure 'a more effective flow of information' from the courts to the OFT about judgments or convictions.[147] It is not clear at this stage how far any changes are likely to go.

The discussion above has highlighted some concerns with the use of prior approval. In some cases the concern is focused on the specific provisions of the legislation discussed. As will be apparent, some of the concerns posed by the regime for regulating consumer credit are addressed by the White Paper, although there is still the risk that any reforms will not go far enough. In others cases concern attaches to the very nature of prior approval as a regulatory technique. While it is important to take these concerns seriously, it is equally important not to over-state them. The key strength of prior approval is that it gives the regulator considerable power to screen out those suppliers who do not meet, or are expected not to meet minimum standards. The success of this depends in large part of the specific wording of the provisions and on the need for regulators of competence and integrity. It should also be remembered that strict regulation of this type can bring benefit to the extent that it raises consumer confidence. Even stern critics of financial regulation recognise that consumer confidence is raised by governmental regulation.[148] One of the FSA's statutory objectives is to maintain confidence in the financial system. The nature of fractional reserve banking is such that confidence is vital for its success. Although systemic risk is unlikely to emerge from the failure of a trader with a credit licence (unless of course, that trader is a bank), consumer confidence is still important. Research for the DTI has suggested that consumers are more concerned with the reputation of a lender than they are with the advertised APR.[149] Consumer confidence is vital for the success of the financial services industry as a whole, and this requires confidence in firms, regulators and the environment in which they operate. Chapter two considered the role of community values in providing a rationale for regulation of the financial marketplace. Many commentators have emphasised the central roles of mutual trust and confidence in the successful operation of the market, and Ramsay points to both the Consumer Credit Act 1974 and the Financial Services Act 1986 as examples of legislation intended to stimulate consumer confidence in these

---

[146] White Paper, above n 125 para 3.18.
[147] *Ibid* para 3.19.
[148] Benston, above n 96 at 79.
[149] Cited in the White Paper para 3.9.

markets at a time of rapid change.[150] By its very nature, prior approval is a regulatory technique likely to promote consumer confidence. As mentioned above, however, it is important that this confidence does not lead to the abdication of consumer responsibility that generates moral hazard.

There are doubts about whether banking, and financial markets generally, are as inherently unstable as some commentators have suggested. Dowd cites with approval the 'great deal of work [that] has been done which suggests that laissez-faire in banking ought to be highly stable and that traditional fears of its "inherent" instability are, at the very least, much exaggerated'.[151] He concludes that there is nothing in the experience of the USA to suggest that free banking does not work, and much to suggest that it does.[152] He sees the solution as a removal of government from the monetary system, on the assumption that it is markets that work, and governments that fail.[153] The arguments about the relative ills of market and government failure, and about the impact of regulation are clearly important. But even if regulation does not provide a guarantee about the safety of a bank, or of the banking system, it cannot be doubted that it has an important role in giving consumers confidence. They will at least have the confidence that banks are being regulated, and so certain types of risk, such as profligate lending, inadequate capital and fraud will be reduced. These risks will not be eliminated of course. Nor should they be. The importance of persuading consumers to take responsibility for their actions where they are able to should remain part of the regulatory system. As the FSA itself has stated, 'given the risks inherent in financial markets, a zero failure regime is neither achievable in practice, nor desirable in principle.'[154]

Prior approval is not appropriate for all sectors of the economy, but there are some areas where such a strict form of regulation can be justified. It is perhaps best suited to those areas where the risks of making incorrect decisions have the gravest consequences, where it is particularly difficult to obtain reliable information, where there is near-uniform demand for high quality services, and where externalities are present.[155] Banking is an area that appears to meet these criteria. First, consumers have a good deal to lose through making incorrect decisions. Secondly, as chapter three has shown, there are significant difficulties for consumers in

---

[150] Ramsay, above n 88 at 54.

[151] K Dowd, *Laissez-faire Banking* (London, Routledge, 1993) at 180–81. I am grateful to Kevin Dowd for our discussions on this subject.

[152] *Ibid* at 201.

[153] *Ibid* at 204.

[154] Financial Services Authority, *Building the New Regulator* (FSA, December 2000) para 4.

[155] See P Cartwright, *Consumer Protection and the Criminal Law* (Cambridge, Cambridge University Press, 2001) at 41–44. J Kay and J Vickers, 'Regulatory Reform: An Appraisal' in G Majone, *Deregulation or Re-regulation?* (London, Pinter, 1990) 223 at 241.

obtaining optimal information about banks and their products, and while addressing these through information remedies such as disclosure is one solution, it is important to bear in mind the limitations of this approach. Thirdly, there are certain criteria that virtually all consumers are likely to want banks to meet. As Kay and Vickers comment: 'if appropriately informed, few would want to buy financial services from crooks'.[156] Finally, the spectre of systemic risk, the chief externality that banks face, remains perhaps the principal reason for the use of prior approval.[157]

In relation to credit too, prior approval can be justified. Although systemic risk is unlikely to arise from credit business, the other justifications for prior approval apply. The regime under the CCA is not perfect, and there are concerns about the extent to which it is effective in delivering its aims, but the White Paper addresses many of these. Moreover, the successes of the regime should be remembered. Sir Gordon (now Lord) Borrie, when Director General of Fair Trading pointed out that:

> [r]esults can often be obtained without going to the extreme of refusing, revoking or suspending a licence, including the drawing up of fairer agreements and the provision of compensation to members of the public who have been overcharged or unfairly treated.[158]

This reflects the idea of the regulator as a benign big gun, with a variety of powers at its disposal, but relying on strategies of persuasion to ensure compliance.[159] Borrie also makes reference to ways in which the very existence of a licence changes the behaviour of a trader. He emphasises

> those businesses which have declined, after consideration, to carry on or launch a particular scheme because they think it might endanger their licences; or those businesses which, in order to safeguard their licence, are now issuing firm instructions to employees on their behaviour; or those businesses which have tightened up their own procedures and redrafted their agreements and publicity material to the same end.[160]

It is always difficult accurately to estimate how firms would have behaved were regulatory provisions not in place. However, it is likely that where there is a significant power, such as that to withdraw a licence, it will have a chilling effect on a proportion of traders, particularly if the regime is accompanied by a range of potential sanctions. It has been

---

[156] J Kay and J Vickers, 'Regulatory Reform: An Appraisal', *ibid* 223 at 241.
[157] See ch 2.
[158] G Borrie, above n 83 at 100–1.
[159] Ayres and Braithwaite, above n 66 at 26.
[160] Borrie above n 83 at 101. Some of these issues will also be relevant to the exercise of the OFT's powers in relation to the Unfair Terms in Consumer Contracts Regulations 1999. See ch 6.

questioned whether even the risk of revocation is a sufficient tool, bearing in mind the sanctions for carrying on unlicensed business and the difficulty of discovering that unlicensed trading is being conducted. However, as has been pointed out, agreements entered into by unlicensed traders are unenforceable without a validating order from the Director General of Fair Trading. It may be that this is a significant threat. With the changes proposed by the White Paper in place, the regime should be stronger still.

CONCLUSIONS

Prior approval by licensing is in some ways the cornerstone of banking regulation. By screening out those who fail to meet minimum standards, the regulator is given considerable power to act in the public interest. In the words of Scott and Black '[t]he theory is that licensing permits beneficial activity but at the same time prevents its harmful consequences.'[161] It has a very strong preventive character and is probably the most interventionist form of regulation. That there are risks in the use of prior approval is not to be doubted, and those risks are considered at some length above. Indeed, it is important that those risks are considered by those influencing the regimes in question. However, it should not be concluded that these risks outweigh the benefits of prior approval in the areas examined here. It is submitted that a well-designed regime of authorisation and continued supervision can play a vital role in fulfilling the principal objective of banking regulation.

---

[161] Scott and Black, above n 88 at 447.

5

Self-Regulation and the Banking Code

INTRODUCTION

WHERE CONDUCT OF banking business is concerned, the principal example of regulation is that of the self-regulatory standards contained in the *Banking Code*.[1] This chapter examines the use of the *Banking Code*, and the role of self-regulation more generally in the control of the relationship between bank and consumer. It will be argued that self-regulation has brought advantages for the consumer, as well as allowing a degree of flexibility for the banking industry. The Government has shown its confidence in self-regulation through some of the provisions of the Enterprise Act 2002. The Office of Fair Trading (OFT), through its Consumer Codes Approval Scheme is now able to formally approve codes of practice that meet strict minimum criteria. The codes are drafted by their sponsors, who ensure that they meet the OFT's guidance on areas such as organisation, preparation, content, complaints handling, monitoring, enforcement and publicity.[2] The *Banking Code* has not been put forward by the sponsors for approval under this scheme, and there is no current intention for it to be so, although the possibility of seeking approval in the future has not been ruled out.[3]

SELF-REGULATION AND THE *BANKING CODE*

As regulation might be seen as containing 'the idea of control by a superior' and having 'a directive function',[4] it may be difficult to equate this with the concept of self-regulation. Indeed, self-regulation might be

---

[1] The *Banking Code* (March 2003).
[2] Office of Fair Trading, *Core Criteria for Consumer Codes of Practice* (OFT, May 2002). See also R Bragg, 'The Enterprise Act 2002' (paper to the Society of Legal Scholars Conference, 19 September 2003).
[3] Conversation with British Bankers' Association (BBA) and *Banking Code* Standards Board officials.
[4] A Ogus, *Regulation: Legal Form and Economic Theory* (Oxford, Clarendon Press, 1994) at 2.

perceived as merely 'the capacity and tendency of all individuals and organizations to regulate their own conduct.'[5] It could be argued that the term 'self-regulation' defies classification owing to the different meanings which can be attached to it.[6] However, for our purposes, a helpful definition is provided by Baldwin and Cave who refer to 'simple self-regulation' which 'usually involves an organisation or association (e.g. a trade association) developing a system of rules that it monitors and enforces against its own members or, in some cases, a larger community.'[7] Simple self-regulation is distinguished from 'enforced self-regulation' where the government has a role in structuring or overseeing the regime.[8]

Self-regulation, in its various forms, has long been an important part of the regulatory landscape in the UK. The principal example of the use of self-regulation to protect the consumer in banking is that of the *Banking Code.* The *Code* forms part of the self-regulatory process which has characterised the control of much of industry in the UK.[9] The *Banking Code* was created as a result of recommendations made by the Jack Committee which had been established to 'examine the statute and common law relating to the provision of banking services within the United Kingdom to personal and business customers.' One of its more specific functions was: 'if appropriate and after consultation to recommend the introduction of codes of good practice (on such matters as model contract terms, information for customers or new banking procedures).'[10] The Committee recommended that banks should develop a code of banking practice based on standards of best practice set out in the Committee's Report. It further recommended that the Government should assess whether this was an adequate response to the Report and, if it was not, that the Government should consider enacting enabling legislation to support a statutory Code of Banking Practice, and an associated duty to

---

[5] R Baldwin, C Scott and C Hood, 'Introduction' in Baldwin, Scott and Hood (eds), *A Reader on Regulation* (Oxford, Oxford University Press, 1998) 1 at 27. Indeed, the term is sometimes used in this way in the financial services field, for example, to refer to a firm's system of control over its employees. See J Black, 'Constitutionalising Self-regulation' (1996) 59 MLR 24.

[6] Black, *ibid* at 26–28.

[7] R Baldwin and M Cave, *Understanding Regulation* (Oxford, Oxford University Press, 1999) at 39. The Advertising Standards Authority is given as an example of a body whose jurisdiction covers a larger community. See also Baldwin, Scott and Hood, *Regulation* above n 5, ch 1.

[8] As was the case with the self-regulatory organisations operating under the Financial Services Act 1986. See Baldwin and Cave, *ibid* at 39–40; A Page and R Ferguson, *Investor Protection* (London, Weidenfeld and Nicolson, 1992).

[9] For discussion of self-regulatory codes of practice see G Borrie 'Law and Codes for Consumers' (1980) *Journal of Business Law* 315; W Richardson and D Morris, 'Towards More Effective Consumer Market-Place Interventions—A Model for the Improvement of OFT Codes of Practice' (1998) 11 *Journal of Consumer Policy* 315.

[10] *Banking Services Law and Practice: Report by the Review Committee* (the Jack Report) (Cm 622, 1989) Terms of Reference.

trade fairly with their customers. No doubt the spectre of statutory regulation was of some concern for the banks, and the first *Banking Code* followed soon after. Given the ideology of the Government of the time, it was not surprising that it favoured non-statutory self-regulation, and so saw no need to put the *Code* on a statutory footing. The first *Code* came into effect on 16 March 1992.

The role of the *Banking Code* was examined by the Banking Services Consumer Codes Review Group. The Review Group produced its report *Cracking the Codes for Banking Customers* in May 2001.[11] The Report concluded that the banking market was becoming more competitive and that it was appropriate to use codes of conduct to deal with services standards in banking. However, it identified four areas where it felt that codes could be improved cost-effectively: easier account switching; better customer information; clearer code review processes; and more information on compliance.

The use of codes offers some advantages over legislation. First, codes reduce many of the costs associated with legislation, in particular those associated with rule-making and parliamentary time.[12] Addressing detailed legislation at specific industries is frequently impractical, particularly for a reforming government with a tight parliamentary timetable. Secondly, codes are far more flexible than legislation and can be changed in the light of new judicial or statutory developments, or in the light of changes in business practice. The *Banking Code* provides good examples of this. For example, in relation to judicial developments, the *Code* has reflected, as well as influenced, decisions in the area of spouses giving a bank security over property, typically their share in the family home, to support their spouses' business debts.[13] In relation to statutory developments, the *Code* is able to reflect the introduction of the Financial Services and Markets Act 2000, and also looks to be central to the Government's implementation of aspects of the Distance Marketing Directive.[14] With regard to changes in business practice, the *Code* has been able to introduce provisions dealing with issues such as the development and use of electronic purses.[15] Indeed, the Review Group stated that codes 'should

---

[11] Banking Services Consumer Codes Review Group, *Cracking the Codes for Banking Customers* (hereafter, Cracking the Codes) (May 2001).
[12] See I Ramsay, *Consumer Protection: Text and Materials* (London, Weidenfeld and Nicolson, 1989) at 282.
[13] See for example *Barclays Bank v O'Brien* [1994] 1 AC 180, and *Royal Bank of Scotland v Etridge (no.2)* [2002] 2 AC 773, and the *Banking Code* s 13(4).
[14] Directive 2002/65/EC. The Directive, which must be implemented by 9 October 2004, aims to protect retail consumers when entering into contracts for financial services at a distance. It applies conduct of business rules to the distance marketing of deposit-based products.
[15] Sections 12.12–12.14.

continue to be updated to deal with new concerns as the competitive and regulatory environment changes' and argued that the *Banking Code* 'is something of an exemplar in this respect.'[16] However, concern has been expressed that the content of codes is only likely to bring benefits if there is a threat of legislation in the background. Writing in 1984 a former Director General of Fair Trading argued that:

> discussion of the value of codes of practice and self-regulation as opposed to regulation needs to take place against a background of political reality ... trade associations no longer perceive legislation as a realistic threat if no code of practice is concluded.[17]

The present regulatory environment might be conducive to such a threat, with the Government showing a willingness to use statute to control many areas of financial services.

The nature of codes means that they can contain provisions that would be difficult to incorporate meaningfully into legislation. However, this may reflect the fact that such provisions are relatively vague and difficult to assess.[18] They may be similarly difficult to test when challenged as part of a code. The Review Group recognised the difficulties that this raises. It argued that simple principle-based codes had advantages, chiefly that they allow flexibility in service delivery, thereby enabling firms to treat consumers as individuals and promoting competition through differentiation.[19] However, it recognised that judging compliance with them is difficult. An alternative to principle-based codes is to have detailed prescriptive rules. The Review Group was cautious about the use of such rules. First, the Group argued that they create inflexibility and threaten innovation.[20] To this extent they may have many of the disadvantages of legislation, with few of the advantages. The Group argued that participants find loopholes in the rules 'complying with the letter but not the spirit.'[21] As mentioned below, this raises the problem of 'creative compliance', where those regulated 'circumvent the scope of a rule while still breaching the spirit of the rule.'[22] The result of this may be to create even more detailed rules, reducing flexibility yet further. The first report

---

[16] *Cracking the Codes*, above n 11 at iv.
[17] G Borrie, *The Development of Consumer Law and Policy: Bold Spirits and Timorous Souls* (London, Sweet and Maxwell, 1984) at 196.
[18] For example, s 13.10 states 'we will consider cases of financial difficulty sympathetically and positively'. Although legislation can make use of relatively vague 'open texture rules', it would be surprising if such a standard found its way into a statute.
[19] *Cracking the Codes*, above n 11 para 1.14.
[20] *Ibid* para 1.15.
[21] *Ibid*.
[22] R Baldwin and M Cave, above n 7 at 102–3. See also D McBarnet and C Whelan, 'The Elusive Spirit of the Law: Formalism and the Struggle for Legal Control' (1991) 54 MLR 848.

of the *Banking Code*'s Independent Reviewer (Professor Elaine Kempson) concluded that the *Code* should continue to be principle-based, with the 'Guidance for Subscribers' (hereafter, 'Guidance') setting out how those principles should be interpreted in practice.[23]

CODES AND THE LAW

One difficulty with codes of practice is that their relationship with the law is not entirely clear. For example, it is not always obvious to what extent, if at all, breach of a provision of the *Banking Code* will give rise to civil liability. There will be some cases where the provisions of the *Banking Code* may be said to constitute trade usage, or otherwise constitute an implied term of the contract.[24] Ellinger, Lomnicka and Hooley argue that 'as subscribing banks advertise the fact that they adhere to the *Code* and make it available to customers, its provisions will no doubt be treated as implied terms in the banking contract.'[25] However, as the authors recognise, if an express term is at variance with the *Code*, the express term would apply.[26] Where such a provision is breached, the usual contractual remedies will apply. In other cases, and perhaps more commonly, the *Code* will have no effect upon the legal responsibilities owed by the bank to the consumer. The *Code* may be taken to represent good practice, but not necessarily to represent, nor even less to create, a legal duty. Cranston notes a third possibility. This is where the a code is used 'in a non formularly way in the enunciation of behavioural standards. The code is mined for appropriate conduct, which is then said to reflect legal policy.'[27] Similarly, but expressed as an alternative, Cranston notes that the standards in a code can be invoked to 'fortify conclusions said to follow as a matter of legal analysis.' In the two elements of this third example, the *Code* does not determine the legal standards, but has input into their formulation.[28] As we will see shortly, when banks subscribe to the *Banking Code*, they

[23] E Kempson, *Independent Review of the Banking and Business Codes* (November, 2002) para 2.3.
[24] R Cranston, *Principles of Banking Law*, 2nd edn (Oxford, Oxford University Press, 2002) at 202.
[25] E Ellinger, E Lomnicka and R Hooley, *Modern Banking Law*, 3rd edn (Oxford, Oxford University Press, 2002) at 61. The 'Guidance' states that the key commitments should be considered carefully as 'they may introduce obligations which could be implied into the subscriber/customer relationship' ('Guidance' s 2).
[26] *Ibid*. See also E Lomnicka, 'Unilateral Variation in Banking Contracts: An Unfair Term?' in P Cartwright (ed), *Consumer Protection in Financial Services* (London, Kluwer Law International, 1999) at 104–5.
[27] Cranston, above n 24 at 203.
[28] *Ibid*.

agree by contract to abide by its provisions. One consequence of seeing the provisions of the *Code* as evidence of usage is that the content of parts of the *Code* may, de facto, become binding on non-subscribers. This is important as one criticism commonly levelled at codes of practice is that they are not binding on non-subscribers. However, it is important not to push this point too far for two reasons. First, just because the *Code* contains a particular standard, this does not mean that the standard automatically represents the law. Secondly, in practice the vast majority of banks and building societies do subscribe to the *Banking Code*.[29] A further point to note is that the Financial Ombudsman Service (FOS) has compulsory jurisdiction over FSA-authorised firms, which includes banks.[30] The ombudsman takes 'best industry practice' into account when making decisions. This means that the provisions of the *Banking Code* may be taken into account, even when the bank in question does not subscribe to it.

DETAILS OF THE *BANKING CODE*

The *Banking Code* aims to set standards of good banking practice for financial institutions to follow when dealing with personal customers (hereafter consumers) in the UK.[31] The most recent version was published in March 2003. The *Code* is voluntary, but as noted above, the vast majority of banks subscribe to it.[32] The *Code* states that its voluntary character 'allows competition and market forces to work to encourage higher standards for the benefit of customers.'[33] Once a firm subscribes to the Code it is bound by contract to adhere to its standards as a minimum. It is not possible to analyse exhaustively all the *Code*'s provisions in this chapter. Instead, an overview of the main provisions will be given, with some key provisions considered in more detail. This will give a flavour of the content of the *Code*. The *Code* applies to: current accounts (including basic bank accounts); card products and services; loans and overdrafts; savings and deposit accounts (including mini cash and Tessa ISAs; and payment services (which includes foreign exchange services).[34]

---

[29] As of 31 March 2003 there were 121 subscribers (*Banking Code* Standards Board, *Annual Report 2002–03) at 16.*
[30] See ch 6.
[31] 'Personal customers' means private individuals and includes executors or trustees of private individuals. Small business customers are now covered by the *Business Banking Code.*
[32] It covers, for example, banks, building societies, credit card companies and National Savings and Investments. In keeping with the theme of the book, the chapter will concentrate on banks.
[33] Section 1.2.
[34] Section 1.1.

Key Commitments

The *Code* contains four 'key commitments', which are intended to 'under-pin the whole subscriber/customer relationship.'[35] Firms undertake to: act fairly and reasonably in all their dealings with the consumer; help consumers to understand how their financial products and services work; deal with things that go wrong quickly and sympathetically; and publicise and make the code available, training their staff to put it into practice. The 'Guidance' to the *Banking Code* specifically states that subscribers to the *Code* 'should ensure that they abide by the spirit, as encompassed by the key commitments, as well as the letter of the *Code*.'[36] This addresses the concept of 'creative compliance', where the regulated 'circumvent the scope of a rule while still breaching the spirit of the rule.'[37] The 'Guidance' provides that where there is doubt about a particular *Code* provision, the key commitments 'should provide clarification as to the spirit of the *Code*.'[38]

The *Code* is next divided into the following main subjects: information; account operations; protection; lending and further assistance.

Information

Sections 3 to 8 of the *Code* come under the heading 'information'. The role of information in protection of the consumer has been examined at length in chapter three. There are numerous reasons why an unregulated market may not provide consumers with the information they need to make informed choices and these will not be repeated here.[39] As has been explained in detail in previous chapters, the existence of information asymmetry, in particular between banks and consumers, is one of the principal justifications for banking regulation.[40] The Review Group identified information asymmetry as a reason for codes, and much of the *Code* is concerned with correcting this asymmetry.[41]

Section 3 is entitled 'helping you to choose products and services which meet your needs'. Under this heading, the *Code* requires banks to give consumers clear information which explains the 'key features' of the

---

[35] 'Guidance' at 7.
[36] *Ibid.*
[37] Baldwin and Cave, above n 7 at 102–3. See also D McBarnet and C Whelan, above n 22.
[38] 'Guidance' at 7. The *Code*'s independent reviewer commented that in some areas, notably superseded accounts, 'some subscribers are interpreting it to the letter rather than the spirit of its content'. Above n 23 para 4.1.3).
[39] See ch 3 and also Office of Fair Trading, *Consumer Detriment Under Conditions of Imperfect Information* (OFT Research Paper 11, prepared by London Economics, August 1997).
[40] See in particular chs 2 and 3.
[41] *Cracking the Codes* para 1.7.

services and products in which consumers say they are interested. Key features would include matters such as information on additional charges or loss of interest on early withdrawal or cancellation, and any restrictions on matters such as withdrawals.[42] One important part of this section is that banks undertake to provide the consumer with information on a basic bank account (if they offer one) and 'it would appear to meet' the consumer's needs. It has been suggested that banks have been less than enthusiastic in alerting consumers to the existence of basic bank accounts.[43] The section contains other undertakings, such as that banks will tell consumers of the different ways they offer products and services. There is a question about when it can be said that a basic bank account 'would appear to meet' the consumer's needs. The 'Guidance' suggests that such consumers might include those: who express an interest in opening a money transmission account which does not allow them to go overdrawn; whose main source of income appears to be state benefit; or who are 'content to accept the limited money transmission functionality of a basic accounts' (for example, to accept an account without a chequebook).[44]

Section 4 deals with the important issue of interest rates. The *Code* sets out how consumers can get information about interest rates, and what information will be provided, for example on becoming a customer. A major area of contention has concerned changes in interest rates.[45] A good deal has been said about the approach of some banks to changing interest rates, and the Financial Ombudsman Service (FOS) has stated that this part of the previous edition of the *Code* caused it 'vastly more difficulty in practice than any other'.[46] Where a loan operates on a standard variable rate, the lender is not required to vary rates according to any pre-set criteria. However, many consumers appear to be confused about this. Cruickshank's survey found that only 25 per cent of mortgage holders understood this. 53 per cent thought that the term 'variable rate' meant that the interest rate automatically changed with the base rate.[47] The *Code* states that banks will keep consumers informed about changes in interest rates on their accounts and will tell how they will do this.[48] There are different methods, depending on whether the account is one that is mainly run through branches. Details are found in sections 4.5 and 4.6 of the

---

[42] 'Guidance' at 9.
[43] See ch 8.
[44] 'Guidance' at 10.
[45] See E Lomnicka, above n 26. See also the submission of the Financial Ombudsman Service to the Independent Reviewer (summarised in *Ombudsman News* (March 2002)).
[46] FOS submission *ibid*.
[47] *Competition in UK Banking: A Report to the Chancellor of the Exchequer* (the Cruickshank Report) (20 March 2000) para 4.73.
[48] Section 4.4.

January 2001 version of the *Banking Code*. For both types of account the bank can tell the consumer personally within 30 days of the change.[49] For accounts run mainly through branches, the bank is entitled as an alternative to put notices in branches and newspapers within three working days of the change.[50] The FSA is due to issue guidance on interest rate variation terms for savings and current accounts, under the Unfair Terms in Consumer Contracts Regulations 1999. The 'Guidance' (and the *Code*) may have to be reviewed in the light of the FSA's approach.[51]

In relation to savings accounts, the *Code* sets out a variety of information that will be disclosed. For example, where a savings account has £500 or more in it, banks must send consumers annually: a summary of its savings accounts, details of the different interest rates that have applied to the account over the year, and any changes in the Bank of England base rate. There are additional obligations to give information where the consumer has a variable-rate savings account with £250 or more in it and the interest rate has fallen significantly compared with the Bank of England base rate. The Independent Reviewer recommended that this be monitored and reviewed, and the next review of the *Banking Code* will revisit the key issues.[52]

Section 5 of the *Code* deals with charges. It states first that when someone becomes a customer, they will be given details of any charges for the day to day running of the account they have chosen. The 'Guidance' states that the intention which underlies the requirements in this part is that consumers should not be surprised at any change they see appearing on their statement in connection with an account's basic operation. Where charges are increased, or new charges are introduced, banks will tell consumers personally at least 30 days before the change takes effect.[53] Where charges do not have to be notified to consumers upon the opening of an account, banks undertake to inform consumers of the charge for the service or product before it is provided and at any time the consumer asks.[54] Before banks deduct interest or charges for 'standard account services' they undertake to give the consumer at least 14 days' notice of how much will be deducted.[55]

---

[49] Personal notifications could include inter alia, post, email or secure internet messaging, depending on the circumstances. See the BBA/BSA *Code* of Conduct for the Advertising of Interest Bearing Accounts.

[50] The Independent Reviewer considered the distinction between branch-based accounts and others 'anachronistic' and suggested that the Code should be 'delivery channel neutral' (above n 23 para 4.1.1).

[51] 'Guidance' at 16

[52] Above n 23.

[53] 'Guidance' at 23.

[54] *Ibid.*

[55] Section 5(5). 'Standard account services' is defined as 'opening, maintaining and running accounts for transmitting money.'

One topical area that section five deals with is that of cash machine charges. First, banks undertake to give details of any charges they make for using cash machines when they issue the card. Secondly, the *Code* states that consumers will not be charged more than once for any transactions at a subscriber's cash machine. Next a distinction is drawn between cash cards and cards other than cash cards. The *Code* states that when a consumer uses a cash card at one of a bank's cash machines, they will be told, before they are committed to making a withdrawal, the amount, if any, that the consumer will be charged for the transaction and who is making the charge. The *Code* then states that when a consumer uses a card other than a cash card at a subscribing bank's cash machine, a message on the screen will tell the consumer, before they are committed to making the withdrawal, the amount they will be charged for the transaction. The message will also state that the card issuer may charge for the transaction. Cash machine charges will, under s 5.10, be shown on a statement of account. The provisions here are directed both at consumers of the subscribing bank and at those who might use the subscriber's machines. There has been a good deal of discussion about the problems raised by charges for using cash machines. A study by Sainsbury's Bank found that the number of cash machines that charge had grown 13 times over the previous three years.[56] The Nationwide Building Society claimed in July 2003 that one in four cash machines in the UK charged for withdrawals, but that the user was often not warned about this until the third or fourth screen.[57] Many of these appear to be what might be called 'convenience' cash machines, found at shops, petrol stations and the like. LINK announced on 31 July 2003 that from April 2004, customers would be informed before inserting a card into a fee-charging cash machine that a charge may be imposed for making cash withdrawals.[58] This followed a campaign by the Nationwide.

Section 6 of the *Code* deals with standard terms and conditions. Section 6.1 states that where a person becomes a customer or accepts a product for the first time, he or she will be given the relevant terms and conditions for the service in question. Section 6.2 then states that all written terms and conditions will be fair and will set out the consumer's rights and responsibilities clearly and in plain language.[59] Legal or technical

---

[56] BBC News On line 14 July 2003. LINK has pointed out that the number of free ATMs grew by 19% over the previous three years 'Link Members Accept Proposal for Pre-notification of Charges at Cash Machines' <http://www.link.co.uk/press> (30 July 2003).

[57] 'Cash Machine Charges Spark Link Row' <http://www.telegraph.co.uk/money> (21 July 2003).

[58] 'Cash Machines "Must Display Charges" says Link' (*The Guardian*, 31 July 2003). In practice, around 98% of cash machine transactions are not subject to any charge.

[59] This reflects the requirements of the Unfair Terms in Consumer Contracts Regulations 1999.

language will only be used 'where necessary.' The *Code* obliges banks to tell consumers how they will be informed about changes to terms and conditions. Where the change is to the consumer's disadvantage, the bank will tell that consumer about the change personally at least 30 days before it takes effect. At any time up to 60 days from the date of the notice the consumer may switch his or her account or close it without having to pay any extra charges or interest for so doing.[60] All other changes may be made immediately, but the consumer must be informed of it within 30 days.[61] Under s 6.6, where banks have made 'a major change or a lot of minor changes in any one year', they undertake to give the consumer a copy of the new terms and conditions or a summary of the changes. Changes in interest rates have already been considered above, and the provisions relating to notification of them are dealt with by s 4 of the *Code.*

Section 7 is entitled 'changing your account'. A considerable amount has been written about the importance of consumers being willing to switch from one supplier to another. In previous chapters it has been argued that market discipline only works effectively where consumers are able to exert that discipline by switching. However, it has long been recognised that there will frequently be barriers to switching, and there is evidence that consumers strongly perceive such barriers where financial products are concerned. A report for the Department of Trade and Industry (DTI) found that only six per cent of current account customers had switched their providers.[62] The Review Group argued that competition is inhibited by 'the real and perceived hassle involved in switching current accounts.'[63] It appears that one of the reasons why switching is uncommon for financial products is that many consumers believe that the financial market is so competitive that shopping around makes little difference.[64] It should be noted, however, that while it is clear that few consumers switch accounts, it is not clear that the practical barriers to so doing are as great as they are frequently perceived to be.[65] There is research to suggest that most consumers who have switched their account have found the experience to be positive. In particular, mystery shopping

---

[60] Section 6.4.
[61] Section 6.5.
[62] This contrasts with 37% of domestic gas customers and 53% of those with car insurance. Department of Trade and Industry, *Switching Suppliers* (London, October 2000).
[63] *Cracking the Codes*, above n 11 para 4.5.
[64] M Cook, F Earley, J Ketteringham and S Smith, *Losing Interest: How Much Can Consumers Save by Shopping Around for Financial Products?* (London, FSA, October 2002) at 4.
[65] It should also be noted that the perception of the difficulties of switching varies between products. For example, it is widely perceived to be easy to switch credit cards. At the other end of the scale, switching products such as mortgages or other loans may be difficult because of redemption penalties. Remortgaging also involves other costs such as property valuation and legal fees. See Cruickshank above n 47 para 4.74.

research undertaken by NOP (National Opinion Poll) for the *Banking Code* Standards Board found that 'the overwhelming majority of our sample found the process of transferring their current account to a new bank or building society smooth and easy.'[66] Only one of the 50 mystery shoppers involved stated that they would not recommend a friend to do so.[67] The high profile 'Switch with Which?' campaign undertaken by the Consumers' Association has helped to alert consumers of the benefits of switching. The Review Group recommended the introduction of new standards for account switching.[68]

Section 7 attempts to streamline the process of switching. First, under s 7(1), consumers are given a 14 day cooling-off period so that they can close an account without penalty and with interest. Cooling-off periods have an important role in consumer protection policy. It has been argued that '[a]s a matter of policy it is desirable to allow consumers some time for reflection with major credit agreements because of their onerous and complex nature'.[69] Cooling-off periods are sometimes justified on the basis of the risk that consumers will make rash decisions, perhaps because of high-pressure sales techniques or inadequate information. Secondly, s 7(2) states that where a consumer wants to move a current account to another institution, the 'old' bank will provide them with information on the consumer's standing orders and direct debits within three working days of receiving their request.[70] Where the consumer wants to move an account to a bank, that 'new' bank will give the consumer key information, such as how the process will work, and how long it will take. The *Code* also states: 'we will give you what you need to operate the account within 10 working days of approving your application'.[71] Under this section banks also undertake to cancel any charges which result from any mistake or unnecessary delay when the consumer transfers an account to them, and to give at least 30 days' notice before closing an account.[72] The provision that banks should waive charges that might otherwise have been incurred as a result of errors or delays was introduced

---

[66] *Banking Code* Standards Board, *Transfer of Account Survey* (June 2001) para 2.

[67] However, most mystery shoppers felt that the banks showed disinterest when informed that the customer wished to switch, and 16% felt that the old bank had been unhelpful in relation to the transfer. Nevertheless, the Report concluded that there was 'no evidence to suggest that the old banks/building societies are deliberately delaying or hindering the transfer process.' (Above n 66) para 2.

[68] *Cracking the Codes*, recommendation 1.

[69] C Scott and J Black, *Cranston's Consumers and the Law* (London, Butterworths, 2000) at 247–48. See ch 2 for the extent to which cooling off periods help to ensure distributive justice.

[70] The Review Group had originally suggested that the time scale should be 5 days, but the Independent Reviewer suggested that it should be five days 'moving towards three working days over the life of the next edition of the Code' (Above n 23 para 4.2.1).

[71] Section 7.3.

[72] Sections 7.4 and 7.5.

at the recommendation of the independent reviewer. The Review Group had suggested that consumers should be paid compensation in the event of a bank's failing to meet some of the time scales set out, justifying this in part on the basis that '[f]or the customer, the key concern is how long the end to end process to switch accounts will take.'[73] However, the independent reviewer doubted this, arguing that 'customers are more concerned about accuracy rather than speed and, in particular, about incurring extra charges as a direct result of errors made by the banks.'[74]

Section 7 also deals with branch closures. Section 7(6) states '[i]f we plan to close or move your branch, we will tell you at least eight weeks beforehand, and 12 weeks beforehand if yours is the last bank or building society branch within a five-mile radius.' The issue of branch closures is a topical and controversial one, and is considered elsewhere in this book.[75]

Section 8 deals with advertising and marketing. Section 8(1) states 'we will make sure that all advertising and promotional literature is clear, fair, reasonable and not misleading'. A wide variety of other codes, statutes and guidance will also be relevant here, including the British *Code* of Advertising, FSA Rules and Guidance, the Trade Descriptions Act 1968 and the Consumer Credit Act 1974. As previously mentioned, the role of information, including marketing and advertising is considered in chapter three. One issue that was considered in some detail concerns the standard by which potentially misleading information is judged. Perhaps the most obvious approach is to adopt an objective test, which focuses on how a reasonable consumer would interpret the advertising and promotional literature.[76] As Sunstein suggests, 'almost all substantive advertisements will deceive at least some of the people in the light of the exceptional heterogeneity of listeners and viewers'.[77] But there are alternative approaches, which depart from a totally objective standard. It was suggested in chapter three that the need to protect the most vulnerable might justify banks being required to consider how more credulous consumers might interpret information generally, and advertising and promotional material in particular. In particular, they should guard against ambiguity and exaggeration where this might lead to the misleading of more vulnerable consumers. It is particularly important that the law requires banks who target potentially vulnerable consumers, such as those on low income, to think about how their advertisements and promotional literature might be construed.[78]

---

[73] *Cracking the Codes*, above n 11 para 4.12.
[74] Above n 23 para 4.2.1.
[75] See ch 8.
[76] See the discussion in ch 3.
[77] C Sunstein, *Free Markets and Social Justice* (New York, Oxford University Press, 1999) at 284.
[78] See ch 3.

One interesting provision in this section is found in s 8.3 which states:

> Unless you specifically give your consent or ask us to, we will not pass your name and address to any company, including other companies in our group, for marketing purposes. We will not ask you to give your permission in return for standard account services.

This relates closely to the duty of confidentiality, as established in the case of *Tournier v National Provincial and Union Bank of England*.[79] The duty of confidentiality is a fundamental characteristic of the banker–customer relationship. The Jack Committee described the duty as 'a tradition which should be respected and, when under threat, emphasised the more strongly, because its roots go deeper than the business of banking: it has to do with the kind of society we want to live in.'[80] It is not proposed to go into detail on the duty here. However, it is worth noting that the *Tournier* case stated that one of the situations where a bank was entitled to disclose otherwise confidential information was 'where the interests of the bank require disclosure.' The paradigm of this exception will be where the bank has to disclose information in the course of an action to recover money from a customer.[81] However, there is an important question about how far beyond this it extends. Where a bank passes confidential information to a parent or subsidiary company in a banking group there will be breach of the duty.[82] There will not be breach of the *Code*, or the duty of confidentiality where consumers give their consent to the passing on of information. The duty of confidentiality is also relevant to section 11, which is considered below.

Another significant provision under this section is that banks will not insist that consumers buy an insurance product from them when agreeing to provide a lending product.[83] This prohibits the bundling of insurance and lending products. A couple of points are particularly noteworthy here. First, the provision does not (as the 'Guidance' makes clear) prevent banks from giving consumers an incentive to take out an insurance product which is linked to a lending product, provided the consumer is able to take the other product without the insurance. Secondly, subscribers are able to require the consumer to take out an insurance product in support of

---

[79] [1924] 1 KB 461. For discussion of the duty of confidentiality see Ellinger, Lomnicka and Hooley above n 25 at 135–66, and A Campbell 'Bank Confidentiality and the Consumer in the United Kingdom' in P Cartwright (ed) *Consumer Protection in Financial Services* (London, Kluwer Law International, 1999) 77.
[80] *Banking Services: Law and Practice* (the Jack Report) (Cm 622, 1989) para 5.26.
[81] Ellinger, above n 25 at 154.
[82] *Bank of Tokyo v Karoon* [1987] AC 45.
[83] Section 8.6.

their borrowing. The 'Guidance' states that '[t]he subscriber's terms for accepting such insurance should not be so disproportionately onerous that the subscriber's own insurance products appear more attractive.'[84]

Account Operations

The next part of the *Code* deals with account operations, and section 9 is entitled 'Running your account.' There is a lot of detail here. Like so much of the *Code*, the focus is on information that will be given to the consumer. The bank undertakes to give the consumer regular statements, tell them about the clearing cycle, and how direct debits, standing orders and recurring transactions work, as well as how to cancel them. In terms of other action, the banks undertake to keep original cheques or copies paid from the consumer's account for at least six years, unless these have already been returned to the consumer. Also, if the consumer informs the bank that a cheque book, passbook, card or electronic purse has been lost or stolen, or that someone else knows the PIN or other security information, the bank will take immediate steps to try to prevent these from being used.[85]

Section 10 deals fairly briefly with cards and PINs. In relation to cards, banks undertake to: only send a card if the consumer asks for it, or if it is a replacement; give consumers further information if they do not recognise a card transaction on their statement; show the rate of commission or charge for foreign currency card transactions; and warn consumers when an introductory promotional interest rate on their card is about to end. In relation to PINs, banks undertake to give consumers their PIN separately from the relevant card and not to reveal the PIN to anyone else. They will also inform consumers about how to change their PIN.

Protection

Sections 11 and 12 of the *Code* deal with protection.[86] In practice, this has been a very significant element of the *Code* and its predecessors. Section 11.1 reflects the decision on the banker's duty of confidentiality in *Tournier v National Provincial and Union Bank of England*, which is mentioned above.[87] It states that a bank will not reveal the consumer's name and address, or details of his or her account except where: it has to do so

---

[84] 'Guidance' at 33.
[85] Section 9.15.
[86] This also ties in with a new provision under s 9.14 where banks undertake to tell consumers what they can do to help to protect their accounts.
[87] [1924] 1 KB 461.

by law; there is a duty to the public to reveal the information; its interests require that the information be given; or the consumer gives consent. The third exception is considered above in relation to the discussion on disclosure for marketing purposes. The 'compulsion of law' exception is well established. Writing in 1999, Campbell suggested that at least 20 statutes provided for information to be disclosed, and the figure now is undoubtedly higher.[88] The 'duty to the public' exception was not elaborated upon in *Tournier*, and it remains unclear how far it might extend. In *Pharaon v Bank of Credit and Commerce International (SA) (in liquidation)* it was held that the public interest in the banker's duty of confidentiality could be overriden by the public interest in making a confidential document relating to fraud available to the parties to foreign proceedings for the purpose of uncovering the fraud.[89] In relation to the consent exception in *Tournier*, the case decided that where the customer expressly or impliedly consents, the bank may disclose the information. It was held in *Turner v Royal Bank of Scotland* that a consumer does not give implied consent to his bank providing confidential information in response to status enquiries merely by opening an account.[90] The Bank had argued that it was the general practice of banks to respond to such enquiries, and that this should be binding on the customer, even if he was unaware of it. However, the Court of Appeal held that to be so binding, the practice would have had to have been 'notorious, certain and reasonable and not contrary to law.'[91] The *Banking Code* now specifically provides in s 11.2: 'if we are asked to give a banker's reference about you, we will need your written permission before we give it.' It has been argued that this means that express consent must be given every time that a status enquiry is made.[92] Although this might be the most obvious reading of the provision, it could also be interpreted to mean that banks will have to ensure that they have consent before giving out information, and that this consent may be given in advance. Ensuring that such consent has been given, for example when an account is opened, appears to be banks' normal practice.

Section 12 also deals with important issues relating to cards, although its operation has been controversial. Some commentators have been keen to praise these provisions, arguing that 'one of the most important ways in which the *Code* has shown its value to bank customers is by extending a good deal of the protection provided by statute for card holders of certain

---

[88] Campbell, above n 79 at 87.
[89] [1998] 4 All ER 455. See Ellinger, above 25 at 154.
[90] [1999] 2 All ER 664.
[91] The test for terms implied through custom or usage. See *Cunliffe-Owen v Teather and Greenwood* [1967] 1 WLR 1421 at 1438–439.
[92] Ellinger, above n 25 at 158.

cards to those of any payments cards.'[93] Some parts of the *Code* appear to place obligations upon the consumer. For example, s 12.4 says 'do not keep your cheque book and cards together' and 'never write down or record your PIN, password, or other security information.' Section 12.6 also states: '[i]t is essential that you tell us as soon as you can if you discover that: your cheque book, passbook, card or electronic purse has been lost or stolen; or someone else knows your PIN, password or other security information.' The 'Guidance' describes the two examples given in 12.4 as 'advice', and that in 12.6 as a 'requirement'. The provisions will generally reflect the express terms contained in the agreement between the bank and the customer. The most significant part of s 12 is arguably that which deals with liability for losses. First, s 12.9 states: '[i]f you acted fraudulently, you will be responsible for all losses on your account. If you acted without reasonable care, and this causes losses, you may be responsible for them. (This may apply if you do not follow section 12.4).' So a consumer who acts fraudulently cannot have the advantage of the limits on liability considered below. The importance of tackling fraud has been considered elsewhere in this book. Cranston comments that markets cannot function effectively unless 'persons can deal with each other in the knowledge that fraud is an exceptional, rather than a regular, feature of the environment'.[94] The moral and social justifications for tackling fraud are obvious. More problematic is the part concerning consumers who act without reasonable care. Previous editions of the *Code* refers to consumers being potentially liable for losses if they acted with 'gross negligence'. The 'Guidance' suggests that the two standards can be equated with one another. It states:

> [p]revious editions of the *Code* referred to 'gross negligence' rather than 'without reasonable care'. The words have changed to make them more readily understandable to consumers, given that 'gross negligence' is not a phrase in common usage. However, subscribers should note that the standard has not changed, and that the old gross negligence standard is still that applied by the Financial Ombudsman Service.[95]

This must be criticised. To argue that the term 'gross negligence' is not in common usage is reasonable, but to argue that it is synonymous with the phrase 'without reasonable care' is surely wrong. Gross negligence implies a far higher degree of carelessness, and there must be many cases where a consumer can be said to have acted without reasonable care, but cannot

---

[93] J Wadsley and G Penn, *The Law Relating to Domestic Banking*, 2nd edn, London, Sweet and Maxwell, 2000) at 483.
[94] Cranston, above n 24 at 73.
[95] 'Guidance' at 44.

possibly be said to have demonstrated gross negligence. The Ombudsman has recognised that gross negligence must involve more than mere carelessness, whereas without reasonable care seems to be synonymous with carelessness.

Section 12.10 states:

> [u]nless we can show that you have acted fraudulently or without reasonable care, your liability for the misuse of your card will be limited as follows: if someone else uses your card before you tell us it has been lost or stolen or that someone else knows your PIN, the most you will have to pay is £50. If someone else uses your card details without your permission for a transaction where the cardholder does not need to be present, you will not have to pay anything. If your card is used before you have received it, you will not have to pay anything.

This is self-explanatory, and it is clear that the burden of proving fraud or lack of reasonable care is on the bank.

Lending

Section 13 deals with lending. Lending is subject to considerable statutory regulation, in particular under the Consumer Credit Act 1974. This section again is largely concerned with ensuring that consumers receive appropriate information. For example, banks undertake to give information about overdrafts and give reasons for decisions not to lend. In other ways, the *Code* reflects developments in the common law. For example, s 13.4 deals with guarantees and other security. It is worth setting out this section in full:

> If you want us to accept a guarantee or other security from someone for your liabilities, we may ask you for your permission to give confidential information about your finances to the person giving the guarantee or other security, or their legal advisor. We will also:
>
> — encourage them to take independent legal advice to make sure that they understand their commitment and the possible consequences of their decision (where appropriate, the documents we ask them to sign will contain this recommendation as a clear and obvious notice);
> — tell them that by giving the guarantee as well as other security they may become liable instead of, or as well as, you; and
> — tell them what their liability will be.
>
> We will not take an unlimited guarantee.

There have been several important cases in recent years that have examined the difficult area of the relationship between undue influence and the giving of guarantees. It is not proposed to go into detail on undue influence here, and the subject is considered in chapter six. The main difficulties for our purposes arise where one person (such as a wife) agrees to stand surety for another's (in this example her husband's) business debts. In a typical example, the security offered will be the wife's interest in the family home. Where the bank attempts to enforce the security, the wife may claim undue influence against the husband, and seek to have the transaction set aside on the grounds of the bank having constructive notice. The Guidelines for such a situation are set out in the cases of *Barclays Bank v O'Brien* and *Royal Bank of Scotland v Etridge (no 2)*.[96] In *O'Brien*, Lord Browne-Wilkinson held that the bank is put on notice by a mixture of two factors: first, that the transaction is on its face, not to the advantage of the wife; and secondly, that there is a risk in such cases that the husband will have committed a wrong that entitles the wife to have the transaction set aside.[97]

So what, in practical terms, should a bank do? Although in *O'Brien*, Lord Browne-Wilkinson suggested that banks should warn the wife of the risks of her decision in the absence of her husband and urge her to take legal advice, this does not appear to be common practice. Ellinger suggests that this is because of the risk that the surety might later claim that the bank has taken on the role of adviser.[98] In practice, banks usually require the surety to obtain independent legal advice, and insist on confirmation that such advice has been taken.[99] Cranston suggests that in essence, the bank 'must take reasonable steps to satisfy that … [the surety] has brought home, in a meaningful way, the practical implications of the proposed transaction.'[100]

Undue influence can arise in a number of different ways: in some cases because of the relationship between the parties, in others because of the existence of special trust and confidence placed in one party by another, in others because of the exercise of domination by one over the other. The provisions in s 13.4 of the *Banking Code* do not make a distinction on the basis of whether the parties are in a close relationship. In all cases when one person provides a guarantee or other security they will have their liability explained to them and be encouraged to take independent legal advice.

---

[96] Above n 13. See discussion in ch 6.

[97] [1994] 1 AC 180 at 196. It is not, however, limited to the relationship of husband and wife. Indeed, in *Etridge*, Lord Nicholls stated that the only practical way forward was to regard banks as being put on inquiry 'in every case where the relationship between the surety and the debtor is non commercial.' Above n 13 at 814.

[98] Ellinger, above n 25 at 117–18.

[99] *Ibid*.

[100] Cranston, above n 24 at 219.

The 'Guidance' suggests that some banks might insist that a potential guarantor who refuses to take independent legal advice signs a declaration to that effect.[101] The undertaking that banks will not take an unlimited guarantee appears to be more stringent than the guidelines under the common law.[102]

Other areas within this section concern credit reference agencies and financial difficulties. These will not be examined in great detail. It is, however, worth saying something about the approach of banks to borrowers in financial difficulty. At various points this book has made reference to the problem of overindebtedness. This has recently been considered by a number of reports, and remains a topical of great concern.[103] The *Code* states '[w]e will consider cases of financial difficulty sympathetically and positively. Our first step will be to try to contact you to discuss the matter'. Other obligations are to 'do all we can to help you overcome your difficulties ... develop a plan with you for dealing with your financial difficulties' and 'tell you where you can get free money advice.' The *Code* also contains advice about what consumers should do, such as contact the bank as soon as possible. The DTI intends to develop an 'overindebtedness' strategy by spring 2004. Part of this strategy will involve reform of the Consumer Credit Act 1974, which has been outlined in the White Paper *Fair Clear and Competitive: the Consumer Credit Market in the 21st Century*.[104] Although only 7 per cent of households fell into the criteria of overindebtedness set out in the DTI's Household Survey, 20 per cent of households approached for the survey admitted that they were having financial difficulties at the time of the survey. Overindebtedness is likely to be tackled in a number of ways. These include inter alia improving financial literacy and debt advice, encouraging the provision of affordable credit, and tackling irresponsible money lending. The issue of responsible lending is also likely to be of increasing importance. These issues are considered elsewhere in this book[105]

Further Assistance: Complaints Monitoring and Compliance

The final part of the *Code* is entitled 'Further Assistance'. Section 14 concerns complaints. Chapter six deals with this topic in some detail, and considers the provisions of the *Code* in this respect. Section 15 concerns

---

[101] 'Guidance' at 46.
[102] Cranston, above n 24 at 220.
[103] See, for example, E Kempson, *Overindebtedness in Britain: A Report for the Department of Trade and Industry* (Personal Finance Research Centre, September 2002); Task Force on Tackling Overindebtedness, *Second Report* (DTI, undated).
[104] Cm 6040 (London, HMSO, December 2003).
[105] See in particular chs 3 and 8.

monitoring, and contains brief details of the *Banking Code* Standards Board. One of the main criticisms of self-regulatory codes of practice is that their provisions for monitoring, compliance and discipline are inadequate. Because of the importance of these issues, they are dealt with in some detail now.

Monitoring, Compliance and Discipline

Under s 15.1, banks undertake to have a 'Code Compliance Officer', and that their internal auditing procedures ensure that they comply with the *Code*. Responsibility for ensuring that banks comply with the *Code* rests principally with the *Banking Code* Standards Board (BCSB). The BCSB does this through compliance inspections and mystery shopper visits. The BCSB is also responsible for the disciplining of banks that fail to comply with the *Code*.

In relation to ensuring compliance, the BCSB has a monitoring team, members of which carry out visits and assess the extent to which subscribers comply with the *Code*. Where an adverse report is made, this is followed up to ensure that corrective action has been taken. Banks have to complete a self-certification questionnaire, entitled the Annual Statement of Compliance, which is signed by the organisation's Chief Executive. In addition, banks' compliance is monitored through compliance visits. The BCSB states that these compliance visits: are tailored according to the size and complexity of the organisation; review high level compliance controls; check details of sales documentation; and include visits to a sample of sales outlets and administration departments.[106] In addition, market research activities are undertaken, including spot checks through mystery shopping, and banks are subject to monitoring through complaints to the BCSB helpdesk and media monitoring. This is a major improvement on the previous scheme of monitoring, undertaken by the *Code*'s Independent Review Body. Indeed, the new system of monitoring is cited by the National Consumer Council as an example of best practice.[107]

In relation to discipline, a bank that wishes to subscribe to the *Code* must agree to be bound by the *Code*, and the BCSB rules. The BCSB states that it seeks and expects an open and co-operative relationship with subscribers, and expects that many, and hopefully most, instances of non-compliance will be resolved 'through dialogue without resorting to formal enforcement or disciplinary action.'[108] The seriousness of breaches can vary dramatically, and the BCSB has set out the factors that

---

[106] <http://www.bankingcode.org.uk/the role>.
[107] National Consumer Council, *Better Business Practice* (January 2001) at 12.
[108] *Banking Code* Standards Board, *Compliance Policy* (May 2003) clause 1.2(c).

it will consider when assessing the seriousness of a breach. These will include: the extent of actual or potential customer harm; whether the problem was isolated or systemic; whether the breach was inadvertent, or represented a knowing act of commission or omission; the length of time over which the breach continued undetected or without effective remedial action being taken; whether there were any warning signals, such as concerns expressed in the media, customer complaints or guidance from the BCSB, and what heed was paid to such signals; the extent of damage to confidence in, or the reputation of, the banking industry at large; and the extent to which the subscriber sought to profit, or to avoid or mitigate a loss, by its actions or omissions.[109] Where the Board decides not to deal with matters in an informal manner, it may decide to impose disciplinary sanctions. The purposes of such sanctions are to raise public confidence, act as a deterrent, prevent subscribers from profiting from breaches, and exclude institutions which demonstrate 'unwillingness or serious inability to comply with *Code* obligations.'[110]

The Board has a variety of sanctions at its disposal. It can: publish details of the bank and the breach in the BCSB Annual Report; issue directions as to future conduct; issue recommendations on the remedy of past conduct; issue a warning or reprimand; cancel or suspend a subscriber's registration; and publicly censure the subscriber.[111] In relation to remedying past conduct, it is clear that the Board, and the BCSB, are keen not to usurp the role of the FOS. Indeed, the BCSB website states: 'we cannot deal with claims for compensation for bad treatment', and 'we cannot intervene in disputes between customers and their banks ...' However, there will be occasions when the Board will *recommend* that banks make restitution to consumers who are disadvantaged because of breach by a subscriber.

An important question concerns the extent to which the sanctions are adequate. The National Consumer Council has emphasised that '[t]o be taken seriously, self-regulation demands adequate, meaningful and commercially significant sanctions for non-compliance.'[112] The Cruickshank Committee argued that the 'failure of self-regulation' had been implicitly recognised by the Government's decision to put the Banking Ombudsman Scheme on a statutory basis, and showed a similar lack of enthusiasm for self-regulation under the *Banking Code*.[113] It quoted the comment of the then banking ombudsman that the lack of a wider policing and enforcement mechanism had undermined the effectiveness of

---

[109] *Ibid* cl 2.4.
[110] *Ibid* cl 3.1. The term 'Board' is used to refer to the board of directors of the BCSB, or any duly authorised sub-committee of the Board
[111] *Ibid* cl 3.2.
[112] National Consumer Council, *Better Business Practice* (NCC, 2001) para 12.
[113] Cruickshank, above n 47 para 4.79.

the *Code*.[114] The Committee also noted that the BCSB was negotiating with the British Bankers' Association to introduce new powers on disciplinary procedures and penalties. However the Committee stated that it 'doubts that such procedures will prove effective.'[115] It is difficult to judge the effectiveness of the BCSB's powers. What is clear is that there is no power to fine subscribers. This contrasts with codes in some other sectors, and other parts of the financial services sector.[116] The imposition of a fine of £105,000 under the ABTA (Association of British Travel Agents) Code on a tour company following changes that were made to consumers' holiday arrangements is in sharp contrast, although it is conceded that this appears to be an exceptional case.[117] The principal sanctions under the *Code* are cancellation or suspension of registration, or some form of adverse publicity. The extent to which even cancellation of a subscription is likely to act as a deterrent is difficult to judge. It is a feature of self-regulation that firms are entitled to continue trading outside the relevant scheme. This is one of their weaknesses. Where a firm operates outside a code, those enforcing the *Code* lose their influence over that firm. Very often, it is the traders operating outside recognised trade associations who pose the greatest threat to consumers.[118] It should also be noted that there may be incentives upon those enforcing a code not to expel members. There is a potential conflict between the role of code sponsors as representatives of a business and as regulators of the business when a consumer is in dispute with a member business. Many trade associations admit to a conflict here, in particular when faced with an errant member.[119] In particular, there is likely to be a reluctance to remove a source of funding.[120]

There has been support for the BCSB's position on sanctions from the Review Group. The Group stated: '[w]e agree with the BCSB's decision not to seek the power to fine its members on the grounds that reputational risk via "naming and shaming" presents a more powerful sanction

---

[114] The Banking Ombudsman, *The Banking Code and the Mortgage Code: Suggestions for Review* (May, 1999).

[115] Cruickshank, above n 47 para 4.81. A different view was taken by the Review Group who said "we believe that the resources and governance structures that have been put in place provide a framework for the BCSB to carry out its current monitoring and compliance functions effectively." *Cracking the Codes*, above n 11 para 3.13.

[116] For example, the Mortgage Code Compliance Board (MCCB) has the power to fine institutions for non-compliance under registration rule 8.1.3. See MCCB, *Disciplinary and Appeals Procedures Notes* (September 2002).

[117] (*The Times*, August 9, 1990).

[118] See G Borrie 'Trading Malpractices and Legislative Policy' (1991) 107 LQR 559 at 571.

[119] *Raising Standards of Consumer Care: Progressing Beyond Codes of Practice* (London, OFT, 1998) para 2.16.

[120] In relation to OFT approved codes, some trade associations admitted to the OFT that they were in business to gain membership and said that they would not expel their members. *Ibid*.

for its members.'[121] The main reason why cancellation is likely to have an impact upon the bank is because of the adverse publicity it would generate. It seems therefore that adverse publicity is, in practice, the principal effective sanction available to the Board. Adverse publicity can potentially be a significant sanction. Banks are motivated by the need to make profits, and to the extent that adverse publicity can reduce profit, it is likely to be effective. It is difficult to know how far negative publicity changes consumer decision-making, although in a competitive market it is not necessary for there to a huge shift for profits to be severely damaged. Furthermore, it has been argued that adverse publicity may be effective beyond its ability to reduce profits. Fisse and Braithwaite argue forcefully that 'adverse publicity orders would jeopardise what we have found to be a vital part of organizational being—corporate prestige.'[122] Although the authors are focusing on sanctions for criminal offences, it can be argued that publicising breaches of the *Code* can also be justified. It should be noted that adverse publicity may have benefits beyond that of bringing the bank in question to book. Such publicity may also serve a broader educational function, informing the public about the content of codes, so that they are better able to insist upon their rights in future. Indeed, such publicity may have the effect of improving confidence in the financial system, with consumers more assured in their decision making and more willing to engage with financial products. However, adverse publicity, and other significant sanctions, have to be treated with some care. First, it has been suggested that there may be a question mark about the extent to which trade associations should have the power to discipline traders, particularly when this may affect the trader's ability to earn a living.[123] Secondly, there is a risk that adverse publicity might not accurately reflect the wrong done by the bank. The publicity might lead consumers to believe that the bank had engaged in a serious wrong, when in practice its activities were little different from those of similar firms. In this way the sanction might be disproportionate to the wrong done.[124] In particular, the sanction is determined by 'the capricous jury of public opinion.'[125] A third and related point, is that the tougher the sanction, the more likely it is to generate negative spillovers. Where a bank is harmed financially, be it by a direct financial penalty or by the financial penalty generated indirectly by adverse publicity, the harm may extend far beyond those

---

[121] *Cracking the Codes*, above n 11 para 3.14.
[122] B Fisse and J Braithwaite, *The Impact of Publicity on Corporate Offenders* (Albany, State University of New York Press, 1983) at 287.
[123] Above n 119 para 2.17. See also *Thorne v Motor Trade Association* [1937] AC 797.
[124] See B Fisse 'Publicity as a Criminal Sanction against Business Corporations' at 139–41. Cited in Fisse and Braithwaite, above n 122 at 310.
[125] Fisse and Braithwaite, above n 122 at 310.

executives who sanctioned or failed to tackle the offending conduct. This may point towards placing greater emphasis on individual responsibility, rather than imposing sanctions on the bank as a whole. Literature on corporate crime has long advocated the need to recognise the responsibility of individuals within corporations, and has recognised that in some cases sanctions may call into question the viability of the corporation.[126] The problem is compounded where banks are concerned because of the potential for the insolvency of a bank to create systemic risk. Of course, it is unlikely that even if fines were available under the *Banking Code* they could affect the solvency of the bank, and lead to financial contagion. But it is not fanciful to think that adverse publicity could in exceptional cases call the viability of a bank into question, particularly if the media took up the case against an institution.

Another point to note in relation to enforcement, is that banks will be under other incentives to comply with the *Code*. There is the chance of private law enforcement, particularly if the *Code*'s provisions are likely to be treated as implied terms of the banking contract.[127] However, for the reasons considered elsewhere in this book, private law enforcement will frequently not produce adequate incentives.[128] The transaction costs involved mean that obtaining redress through private law is unlikely to operate as an effective regulator. Perhaps more importantly, the FSA will take compliance with the *Code* into account when exercising its powers. For example, the FSA *Principles for Businesses* (PRIN) state that 'a firm must pay due regard to the interests of its customers and treat them fairly' and the FSA has drawn attention to the close relationship between the Principles and the high level commitments in the *Banking Code*.[129] The Principles are a general statement of the fundamental obligation of firms under the regulatory system, and breach of them makes a firm liable to disciplinary sanctions.[130] More specifically, as examined in chapter four, a bank will only obtain authorisation if it satisfies the threshold conditions. The suitability condition requires the FSA to be satisfied that the bank is a fit and proper person having regard to all the circumstances. One element of this is that the bank must conduct business with integrity and in compliance with proper standards, and the *FSA Handbook* makes it clear that a factor in this is whether there has been contravention of codes of practice.[131]

---

[126] See, eg, C Wells, *Corporations and Criminal Responsibility*, 2nd edn (Oxford, Oxford University Press, 2001); J Gobert and M Punch, *Rethinking Corporate Crime* (London, Butterworths, 2003).
[127] See Ellinger, above n 25 at 61.
[128] See in particular ch 6.
[129] A Bradley, 'Speech to the Building Societies Association Conference' (8 May 2003), available at <http://www.fsa.gov.uk/pubs/speeches/sp130.html> (17/05/04).
[130] PRIN 1.1.7 G.
[131] *FSA Hankbook*, 'Threshold Conditions' 2.5.6.G.4.

SOME CONCERNS WITH THE USE OF CODES

The above discussion has involved some consideration of the strengths and weaknesses of the *Banking Code* as a form of regulation. It is worth considering some of the strengths and weaknesses of codes of practice more generally as a regulatory technique. Despite the undoubted strengths of codes of practice, and of the *Banking Code* specifically, there must be doubts about the extent to which such a form of control can be effective in protecting the consumer. In addition to the points emphasised above, there are three principal additional problems: lack of credibility, lack of visibility, and their potential for being anti-competitive.

In relation to credibility, it has been suggested that 'when traders elaborate and monitor the rules themselves, they are concerned primarily with the interests of trade and not with the interests of consumers'.[132] Although the Review Group did not go this far, it recognised that self-regulation is 'by definition, regulation agreed by the industry' and that 'a voluntary code is only viable if it is agreed by the practitioners that have to abide by it.'[133] Furthermore, as noted above, the Cruickshank Committee had serious misgivings about the role of self-regulation in banking. The *Banking Code* is drawn up by the relevant trade associations, the British Bankers' Association (BBA), the Building Societies Association (BSA), and Association of Payment Clearing Services (APACS), although there is consultation with stakeholders before the writing stage. Traditionally this was done through stakeholders being invited to make contributions through written submissions and bilateral meetings; representations being sought from the public through a press release; and a consultation workshop to consider the main themes. Although the Review Group described the consultation process for drawing up the *Code* as wide-ranging, it felt that the process could be improved. It noted three main concerns. First, the Group felt that consultees did not have a sufficiently clear idea of the structure of the review process, including the timetable for review. Secondly, it felt that there was a lack of systematic and transparent feedback from those conducting the reviews. Thirdly, it argued that decisions on the content of the final *Code* were not seen to have sufficient independent scrutiny. The Review Group looked at various ways of improving the *Code*'s review process.[134] It concluded that an independent person ('the *Code* Reviewer') should consult stakeholders and put forward proposals for the *Code*, which are then either accepted or rejected by the industry.[135] It also suggested that

---

[132] European Consumer Law Group 'Non-Legislative Means of Consumer Protection' (1983) 6 *Journal of Consumer Policy*, 209 at 211.
[133] Above n 11 para 1.16.
[134] *Ibid* paras 4.35–4.55.
[135] This bears some similarity to the process in Australia.

the *Code* should be reviewed every two years. Professor Elaine Kempson was appointed as the independent code reviewer and her first report contained a number of recommendations about how the *Code* could be improved. Most of these were accepted by the industry.[136]

Lack of credibility also seems to be a problem to the extent that codes are linked to provisions for the obtaining of redress. The OFT has recognised that the redress schemes provided for in some codes are viewed as neither consumer-friendly nor genuinely neutral, either by consumers themselves or their advisors.[137] There is evidence in relation to some codes that both trade associations and consumer advisors often steer consumers away from these procedures: the former because they are seen as neither impartial nor easy to use, and the latter because of the cost to the association.[138] The Review Group mentioned complaints handling arrangements as one of the areas of concern most frequently cited by consumer groups and the general public.[139]

In relation to lack of visibility, it seems that high profile codes are the exception rather than the rule. A number of respondents to the OFT's consultation document on voluntary codes of practice commented that codes suffered from a lack of visibility. In 1998 the OFT found that 63 per cent of consumers said that they were aware of trade association voluntary codes, and consumers generally believed that codes offer reassurance, help to resolve problems and are an indicator of a quality firm. However, knowledge of specific codes was rare. When unprompted, only 34 per cent of consumers mentioned at least one product or service for which there is a code. The only sectors which were identified by more than 10 per cent of consumers when unprompted were electrical/electronic goods and holidays/travel.[140] Of course, if the lack of visibility of codes has little impact on the buying decisions of consumers in the first place, this acts as a disincentive to firms' signing up.

A final problem with codes concerns their competition implications. If the standards that codes lay down are seen as normal rather than as minimum standards of conduct, there may be a tendency for firms not to raise their standards. This is particularly concerning where associations adopt what might be called 'lowest common denominator standards', which a number of respondents to the OFT's consultation paper felt were common.[141] The Review Group commented that codes, 'tend to provide

---

[136] See 'Response of the BBA, BSA and APACs to Professor Kempson's Report: Independent Review of Banking and Business Banking Codes (November 2002).
[137] Above n 119 para 2.18.
[138] *Ibid.*
[139] Above n 11 para 3.4.
[140] *Raising Standards of Consumer Care: Report on a Conference held at New Hall College Cambridge* (OFT, February 1999) Appendix C at 29.
[141] Above n 119 para 2.14.

a set of minimum standards rather than standards of excellence,' and felt that there might be a risk that compliance with codes is 'misinterpreted by consumers as a mark of service excellence when in reality codes represent a baseline below which subscribers will not fall.'[142] This is an important point. This book has at many points emphasised the importance of consumers' understanding the role and limitations of different types of regulation. The FSA, as has been noted, has principal responsibility for public awareness, and regulation will only perform its function appropriately where there is awareness of what codes of practice are seeking to do. Of course, it could be argued that the *Banking Code* goes beyond the imposition of lowest common denominator standards, and contains standards of excellence. While in some cases this argument might be made, in large part the demands are not particularly onerous.

CONCLUSIONS

There are two related issues to conclude upon here: first is the *Banking Code* effective, and secondly, is self-regulation (particularly that operated through codes of practice) effective as a technique of regulation? First, is the *Code* effective? One of the leading textbooks on banking law argues that '[t]he *Banking Code* ... has done much to equalise the terms of the relationship between bank and customer.'[143] However, that work also argues that 'there are still doubts whether all its provisions—for example those as to variation of interest rates and charges as to customer liability for unauthorised use of accounts and cards—are consistent with consumer protection legislation.'[144] The *Code* has earned some praise from consumer groups, the Consumers'Association, for example, describing the *Code* introduced in September 2000 as 'a meaningful and demanding code with good coverage'.[145]

In relation to the second point, the Chief Executive of the BCSB has enthusiastically stated that self-regulation is 'unbureaucratic, dynamic and cost-effective.'[146] To some extent, a judgment on the effectiveness of self-regulation in general, and codes in particular, can only be made if we decide against what we are comparing them. The principal comparison is between codes and legislation. As explained in this chapter, codes have both advantages and disadvantages when compared with legislation, or other formal rule-bound regulation. Although the Office of Fair Trading has argued that codes cannot be a substitute for regulation or effective

---

[142] Above n 11 para 1.6.
[143] Ellinger, above n 25 at 97.
[144] *Ibid* at 60–61. See also Lomnicka, above n 26.
[145] Cited in *Cracking the Codes*, above n 11 at 34.
[146] *Banking Code* Standards Board, *Annual Report 2002–03* at 7.

enforcement, this rather overstates the case. There will be cases where a code can operate as an alternative to more formal regulation, such as legislation, and others where it cannot. The first *banking code* was introduced as an alternative to legislation. However, the *Code* does not operate in isolation. Codes are merely part of the regulatory jigsaw. They have role, and an important one at that, to play in the protection of the consumer, but they should not be seen as a substitute for legislation in all areas. As the Review Group argued: '[c]odes cannot resolve all…[consumers'] problems— better financial education and a more pro-active approach by consumers are also needed—but codes can go some way further towards empowering consumers to act in their own best interests.'[147]

---

[147] *Cracking the Codes*, above n 11 para 3.28.

6

Complaints and Redress

INTRODUCTION

THIS CHAPTER EXAMINES the mechanisms for consumers to seek redress from a bank.[1] It is not feasible to examine in detail every way in which a consumer might pursue a remedy against a bank, but, it is helpful to say something about the principal means by which such a remedy might be sought.[2] The traditional paradigm of dispute resolution is litigation. As discussed in chapter two, the idea of the rational, utility-maximising consumer is premised upon the belief that such consumers will be able to discipline the market by switching to alternative suppliers when dissatisfied, and suing when entitled to a remedy. Switching demonstrates consumer sovereignty by providing suppliers with incentives to win and maintain custom. Private law ensures that where there is a legal wrong, corrective justice is achieved.[3] The difficulties presented by this model are obvious, particularly with regard to the obstacle of transaction costs. Where there is breach of a private law duty, it is likely that this will go uncorrected.

---

[1] The chapter provides some discussion of the role of private law, but concentrates primarily on alternative dispute resolution. See E Ferran, 'Dispute Resolution Mechanisms in the UK Financial Sector' (2002) 21 *Civil Justice Quarterly* 135; R James and P Morris, 'The Financial Ombudsman Service: A Brave New World in "Ombudsmanry"?' (2002) PL 640 (hereafter, 'Brave New World'); and 'The New Financial Ombudsman Service in the UK' in C Rickett and T Telfer (eds), *International Perspectives on Consumers' Access to Justice* (Cambridge, Cambridge University Press, 2003) 167 (hereafter 'The New FOS'). For discussion of the banking ombudsman scheme which was the predecessor of the FOS in the field of banking see R James, *Private Ombudsmen and Public Law* (Aldershot, Dartmouth, 1997) ch 3; P Morris, 'The Banking Ombudsman' (1987) *Journal of Business Law* 133 and 'The Banking Ombudsman—Five Years On' (1992) *Lloyds Maritime and Commercial Law Quarterly* 227 (hereafter 'Five Years On').

[2] For an overview of mechanisms for consumer dispute resolution see R Thomas, 'Consumer protection: strategies for dispute resolution' in KJ Mackie (ed), *A Handbook of Dispute Resolution: ADR in Action* (London, Sweet and Maxwell, 1991) 157.

[3] This might be achieved through bringing an action under statute or common law. It has been argued that common law rules operate 'in a manner comparable to a market'. See C Scott and J Black, *Cranston's Consumers and the Law*, 3rd edn (London, Butterworths, 2000) at 28.

Despite these barriers to justice, the emphasis placed upon this 'individual claims paradigm' remains strong.[4] To some extent, the common law has seen the development of principles that minimise the harshness of bargains between banks and consumers, and this chapter considers briefly the role of such common law doctrines in providing consumer redress. In addition, there have been many examples of statutory intervention that allow consumers to challenge, or have challenged, bargains that are in some way unfair. These are perhaps more easily described as 'consumer protection provisions' than those developed at common law, as they involve statutory intervention in the marketplace with the principal aim of protecting the consumer.[5] Provisions that allow consumers to take action on the basis of unfairness can generally be categorised as 'open texture rules'. According to Collins, the need to examine all the circumstances of the case 'drive[s] the legal form of regulation of contracts away from clear or bright-line rules towards open-ended standards'.[6] Examples include the extortionate credit provisions contained in ss 137–40 of the Consumer Credit Act 1974, and the provisions of the Unfair Terms in Consumer Contracts Regulations 1999. The chapter looks briefly at these as illustrations of Parliament's intervention in the private law to protect the consumer, and considers their implications for the consumer of banking services.

Consumer redress in the financial services sector has been transformed by the use of alternative dispute resolution methods, in particular financial ombudsmen. After a brief consideration of internal mechanisms for the handling of complaints, this chapter examines the Financial Ombudsman Service (FOS), which was established under the Financial Services and Markets Act 2000 (FSMA). The chapter ends with a brief examination of the ability of the Financial Services Authority (FSA) to obtain redress on behalf of consumers through the exercise of its powers to seek restitution and redress. Conclusions are then drawn.

INDIVIDUAL REDRESS, UNFAIRNESS AND TRANSACTION COSTS

In the perfect market, consumers are able to protect themselves with the need for only minimal intervention from the State. They are rational maximisers of their own utility and sovereign in the market.[7] Parties, including consumers, can use the law of contract to give effect to their wishes safe in

---

[4] T Wilhelmsson, 'Consumer Law and Social Justice' in I Ramsay (ed), *Consumer Law in the Global Economy* (Aldershot, Ashgate, 1997) 217 at 223.
[5] Although some consumer protection provisions also protect traders.
[6] H Collins, *Regulating Contracts* (Oxford, Clarendon Press, 1999) at 266.
[7] See ch 2.

the knowledge that those wishes will be respected by the law. The law of contract therefore provides the framework within which the market can function. Intervention in the relationship between contracting parties is treated with suspicion by advocates of what we might call 'free market economics' or 'laissez faire', because of its capacity to restrict individual choice and create uncertainty.[8] In the supposed heyday of laissez-faire, contracts could be challenged on the grounds of procedural unfairness, but overturning agreements on the basis of substantive unfairness was, arguably, perceived as beyond the legitimate power of the courts.[9] This is sometimes referred to as the classical theory of contract. Although the arguments against intervention are well trodden, it will be seen that they sometimes fail to convince.

There are several well-known objections to provisions which allow contracts to be challenged on the grounds of alleged unfairness. Collins sets these out as follows: that apparent unfairness is often illusory, that intervention makes it difficult to construct markets, that it tends to backfire, and that emphasis should instead be placed on remedying market failure.[10] He then provides a convincing critique of such assertions. First, while unfairness may in some cases be illusory, Collins argues that the courts can address this by avoiding jumping to conclusions and by engaging in a detailed examination of all the circumstances of the transaction. Secondly, although it could be argued that provisions which allow contracts to be challenged on the basis of substantive unfairness make it harder to construct markets, Collins makes two main points. First, he suggests that business people do not regard planning documents as central to transactions, and that uncertainty about enforceability will seldom affect entry into those transactions. Secondly, he argues that, bearing in mind the great emphasis that they place on factors such as long-term business relations and customs of the trade, most parties would 'expect the legal system to decline to enforce terms in the planning documents that impose extremely harsh bargains'.[11] In relation to the argument that attempts to regulate unfairness tend to backfire, Collins is again sceptical, arguing that the empirical evidence is frequently ambivalent. It should be noted that there is a risk that some types of regulation may backfire, and the

---

[8] See eg R Epstein, 'The Social Consequences of Common Law Rules' (1982) 95 *Harvard Law Review* 1717; R Posner, *Economic Analysis of Law*, 4th edn (Boston, Little Brown, 1992).

[9] Although some commentators have questioned whether the classical theory of contract was ever as influential as is sometimes assumed. See B Reiter, 'The Control of Contract Power' (1981) 1 OJLS 347 and P Atiyah, *The Rise and Fall of Freedom of Contract* (Oxford, Clarendon Press, 1979). For a contemporary view that the ability of the courts to challenge substantive unfairness should be tightly limited see Posner, above n 8.

[10] Collins, above n 6 at 275–79.

[11] Collins, above n 6 at 271 This hints at another issue. It is perhaps easiest to justify intervention when it is there to give effect to the parties' expectations. See M Furmston (ed), *The Law of Contract* (London, Butterworths, 1999) para 1.76.

example of interest rate ceilings is given elsewhere in this book as an example. Where open-texture rules are used there is more flexibility, and while this may create uncertainty and still have exclusionary effects, it at least allows the courts to take a wide variety of factors into account in deciding if the bargain should stand. This should ensure some degree of control over regulatory backfiring. On the final point, that it is better to tackle market failure, a couple of points should be made. First, it is not doubted that attempts to tackle market failure will play an important part in any regime for the regulation of banks. As chapter three has argued, looking creatively at information asymmetry should enable us to think about the many ways in which this asymmetry can be addressed. But attempts to correct market failure can only go so far. The perfect market is likely to remain elusive, and it is important that we consider how consumers might be protected, and banks regulated, in the imperfect markets in which they find themselves.[12]

An additional point to note is that while adherents to the classical theory of contract appear to draw something of a sharp distinction between procedural and substantive fairness, it is sometimes difficult to separate such matters in practice.[13] Kronman looks at the different advantages one party may enjoy over another and argues that any such advantage may consist of: 'his superior information, intellect, or judgment, in the monopoly he enjoys with regard to a particular resource, or in his possession of a powerful instrument of violence or a gift for deception'. He goes on to argue that '[i]n each of these cases, the fundamental question is whether the promisee should be permitted to exploit his advantage to the detriment of the other party'.[14] Where a consumer is the recipient of a substantively unfair bargain we can frequently identify a procedural factor which has made the resulting contract unfair, but some of these we accept (such as greater knowledge or skill in bargaining) while others we do not accept (such as deception or violence). The key is to distinguish which factors are legally relevant and which are not. Atiyah counsels caution about 'the belief that we can wholly separate our ideas of fair procedures from our ideas of fair results'.[15] Indeed, he concludes that 'when there is some gross imbalance, something serious enough to offend our sense of justice, it will usually be found that some remedy is available'.[16]

---

[12] See the discussion in ch 4 of the Cruickshank Report (*Competition in UK Banking: A Report to the Chancellor of the Exchequer* (20 March 2000)).

[13] For discussion of the distinction between procedural and substantive unfairness see A Leff, 'Unconscionability and the Code: the Emperor's New Clause' (1967) 115 *University of Pennsylvania Law Review* 485

[14] A Kronman, 'Contract Law and Distributive Justice' (1980) *Yale Law Journal* 472 at 480.

[15] P Atiyah, *Essays on Contract* (Oxford, Clarendon Press, 1986) 329 at 333.

[16] *Ibid* at 338.

In practice it seems that perfect markets are few and far between, and that markets may need the helping hand of regulation to function effectively and fairly. It is clear from the discussion in the previous chapters that the ability of consumers to regulate the market by their own purchasing decisions is limited. One reason for this is that consumers frequently face significant transaction costs. These may arise when trying to obtain information about which product to purchase, when negotiating with the supplier, and when trying to enforce rights after a problem has arisen.[17] The cost to consumers of obtaining redress from a bank will frequently be prohibitive, particularly if pursued by lawsuit. Chapter three has already examined why consumers might find it difficult to get the information they need to make informed choices. It was argued that one type of information that consumers need, but that the market may not supply, is information about how to get redress.[18] Even if consumers know how to seek redress in theory, this does not mean that they will pursue it in practice because of the transaction costs involved. Litigation is time-consuming, uncertain, and expensive, particularly as costs have traditionally been paid by the unsuccessful party. Consumers are typical examples of the 'one shotters', dealing with the 'repeat players' of the banking industry.[19] Even allowing for the overall benefits brought to the consumer body by the actions of the marginal consumer, relying on individuals as the principal form of regulation seems inadequate. As Leff observes: 'one cannot think of a more expensive and frustrating course than to seek to regulate goods or contract "quality" through repeated law suits against inventive "wrongdoers"'.[20]

Although emphasis is frequently paid to the supremacy of freedom of contract, it is clear that such freedom is often limited, as it was even in the heyday of the classical theory.[21] The movement from freedom of contract to widespread intervention may be more a change of degree than a change of kind.[22] What is clear is that the protection of potentially vulnerable parties such as consumers, will involve placing restrictions on contractual freedom. In many cases, this protection will be the result of statutory intervention, for example through control of exclusion clauses. The common law has also developed provisions which give the consumer some protection.

---

[17] These can be identified as search, bargaining and enforcement costs. See I Ramsay, *Rationales for Intervention in the Consumer Marketplace* (London, OFT, 1984) para 3.6.
[18] See the discussion of consumer education in H Beales, R Craswell and S Salop, 'The Efficient Regulation of Consumer Information' (1981) 24 *Journal of Law and Economics* 49.
[19] See M Galanter, 'Why the "Haves" Come Out Ahead: Speculations on the Limits of Legal Change' (1974) 9 *Law and Society Review* 95.
[20] A Leff, 'Unconscionability and the Crowd—Consumer and the Common Law Tradition' (1970) 31 *University of Pittsburgh Law Review* 349 at 356.
[21] P Atiyah, *The Rise and Fall of Freedom of Contract* (Oxford, Clarendon Press, 1979).
[22] M Furmston (ed) above n 11 para 1.45.

PROTECTION THROUGH COMMON LAW AND EQUITY

It has already been noted that the common law (in particular the law of contract) has potential to operate like a market in providing redress for consumers and so incentives for suppliers to improve their performance.[23] A number of doctrines provide a degree of protection to the consumer, although they will be invoked relatively infrequently.[24] Concepts such as 'the red hand rule' may be relevant, for example where terms are particularly onerous, and inadequate steps have been taken to bring them to the notice of the consumer.[25] Even where the terms of an agreement are relatively clear, the contract may be vitiated on grounds of 'unfairness' in a broad sense. Cranston comments that there are 'a range of discrete common law doctrines, of different historical derivation, which can be invoked in limited circumstances to vitiate contracts which are procedurally or substantively unfair'.[26] The principal doctrines here are duress, undue influence and unconscionability. They are not limited to the relationship between banks and consumers, but the discussion below will focus principally upon their operation within that relationship.

Duress

Where a bank induces a contract by unlawful or other illegitimate pressure or intimidation, the contract will be voidable on the basis of duress.[27] Duress may be physical (for example, a threat to a person or to goods) or economic. It has been stated that duress involves 'a coercion of the will so as to vitiate consent' and that 'commercial pressure is not enough'.[28] This means that duress 'must be distinguished from commercial pressure, which on any view is not alone enough to vitiate consent'.[29] The key seems to be that the pressure must be such that the court classifies it as 'illegitimate'.[30] It will be rare that a banking transaction will be vitiated on this basis, even where one party is a consumer. In many cases where pressure is applied by one party to another, it will be viewed as legitimate. For example, when a borrower faces financial problems, it may be legitimate

---

[23] See Scott and Black, above n 3 at 28.
[24] See R Cranston, *Principles of Banking Law*, 2nd edn (Oxford, Oxford University Press, 2002). The expression 'common law' is being used here in the sense of case law. Some of the doctrines in question, notably undue influence and unconscionability, are creations of equity.
[25] *Spurling (J) Ltd v Bradshaw* [1956] 1 WLR 461
[26] Cranston, above n 24 at 213.
[27] See eg *North Ocean Shipping Co Ltd v Hyundai Construction Co Ltd*, (*The Atlantic Baron*) [1979] QB 705.
[28] *Pao On v Lau Yiu Long* [1980] AC 614 at 635 (Lord Scarman).
[29] *Atlas Express Ltd v Kafco (Importers and Distributors Ltd)* [1989] QB 833 at 839 Tucker J.
[30] See A Phang, 'Economic Duress' (1997) 5 *Restitution Law Review* 53.

for the bank to press the borrower for repayment or better security if it is not to call default.[31]

Undue Influence

Undue influence has already been considered briefly in chapter five in the context of its relationship to the *Banking Code*, but demands a fuller explanation here. Undue influence is concerned with the situation where there is a close relationship of trust and confidence between two parties that is capable of being abused. Although it was traditional for undue influence to be divided into separate categories, the House of Lords has recently held that it represents a single doctrine that can be reached by separate paths.[32] Taking the first path, a claimant can argue that there has been actual undue influence. This occurs where 'one party exercised such domination over the mind and will of the other that the latter's independence of decision was substantially undermined, and this domination brought about the transaction'.[33] It bears much similarity to, and appears to overlap with, the doctrine of duress, considered above.

Secondly, the law has recognised what has become known as presumed undue influence. According to Lord Nicholls in *Royal Bank of Scotland v Etridge (no 2)*, where seeking to rely on this, the complainant needs to establish two factors. First he must show that he placed trust and confidence in the other party in relation to the management of his affairs, and secondly, that there followed a transaction which 'calls for an explanation'.[34] In the absence of satisfactory evidence from the defendant to the contrary, this will be sufficient to discharge the burden of proof. Put another way, where the complainant establishes these two factors, the court will regard there as being prima facie evidence that the defendant abused his influence. The defendant will then have to discharge the evidential burden that is consequently placed upon him. Whether the relationship is one of sufficient trust and confidence is a question of fact. On appropriate facts, this might apply to the relationship between a bank and its customer, although this will be rare.[35] In relation to the issue of when the transaction 'calls for an explanation', the courts have had some

---

[31] Cranston, above n 24 at 216. But note the provisions of the *Banking Code* ss 13.10-13.13 dealing with consumers in financial difficulty. Most of the cases on duress concern contracts between businesses. It is possible that the courts would be more likely to find duress where one party is a consumer.

[32] *Royal Bank of Scotland v Etridge (no 2)* [2002] 2 AC 773.

[33] J Beatson, *Anson's Law of Contract*, 28th edn (Oxford, OUP, 2002) at 286. See also the test set out in *Bank of Credit and Commerce International SA v Aboody* [1990] 1 QB 923 at 967.

[34] *Etridge*, above n 32 at 796.

[35] See *Lloyds Bank v Bundy* [1975] QB 326. See also *National Westminster Bank plc v Morgan* [1985] AC 686.

difficulty. For example, if a wife guarantees her husband's business debts, Lord Nicholls in *Etridge* recognised that such guarantees might be said to be disadvantageous to her in a narrow sense. However, he suggested that there may be good reasons for such a transaction, particularly as the fortunes of husband and wife will frequently be bound up together. He concluded that he did not think, that

> in the ordinary course, a guarantee of ... [that] character ... is to be regarded as a transaction which, failing proof to the contrary, is explicable only on the basis that it has been procured by the exercise of undue influence by the husband.[36]

The situation where one person (for the sake of our discussion a wife) has agreed to stand surety for another's (in our case her husband's) business debts is the major area of concern for banks in relation to undue influence. Typically, the security offered will be the wife's interest in the family home. If the bank attempts to enforce the security, the wife may claim wrongdoing (usually undue influence but also potentially misrepresentation) on the part of the husband, and seek to have the transaction set aside.

The policy issues raised by this area of the law are both interesting and challenging. On the one hand, it is important that home owners should be able to make economic use of their homes and that banks should feel confidence that such transactions will be enforced where necessary.[37] On the other hand, it is important that steps are taken in those few cases where undue influence may have been exercised, and the surety may not understand the nature and effect of the transaction.[38] The solution has been something of a compromise. If there is a valid claim against the husband, the question will be whether the bank had notice (usually constructive notice) of the wrongdoing (in our example, undue influence).[39] According to *Etridge*, the bank will be put on inquiry 'whenever a wife offers to stand surety for her husband's debts'.[40] In such situations, the bank will have constructive notice of her right unless it takes reasonable steps to ensure that her agreement has been obtained properly. *Etridge* considered in some detail what steps a bank should take. Lord Nicholls stated that, '[t]he furthest a bank can be expected to go is to take reasonable steps to

---

[36] *Etridge*, above n 32 at 799.
[37] *Ibid* at 800.
[38] *Ibid* at 793.
[39] The same would apply to other fault, such as misrepresentation.
[40] *Etridge*, above n 32 at 804. This follows the approach if Lord Browne-Wilkinson in *Barclays Bank plc v O'Brien* [1994] 1 AC 180 at 196. It is also clear that this extends far beyond the relationship of husband and wife. Indeed, Lord Nicholls concluded that 'the only practical way forward is to regard banks as "put on inquiry" in every case where the relationship between the surety and the debtor is non-commercial' (at 814).

satisfy itself that the wife has had brought home to her, in a meaningful way, the practical implications of the proposed transaction'.[41] It is not necessary for the bank to provide the information directly to the wife, and it will generally be reluctant to do so.[42] In practical terms, banks usually require the surety to obtain independent legal advice, and insist on confirmation that such advice has been taken.[43] In the vast majority of cases, neither the bank, nor the solicitor, can ascertain with confidence whether there has been undue influence. As Lord Bingham points out, all the law can do is 'indicate minimum requirements which, if met, will reduce the risk of error, misunderstanding or mishap to an acceptable level'.[44]

Unconscionability

English law has not seen the development of a doctrine of unconscionability in the way that some other common law jurisdictions have.[45] However, there have been cases where individuals have been found to benefit from protection through what might be appropriately described as such a doctrine. There appear to be three elements to unconscionability.[46] First, one person must be at a special disadvantage to the other. There is no exhaustive list of such disadvantages. In the Australian case of *Blomley v Ryan*, Fullagar J referred to there being a wide range of potential circumstances including 'poverty or need of any kind, sickness, age, sex, infirmity of body or mind, drunkenness, illiteracy or lack of education, lack of assistance or explanation where assistance or explanation is necessary'.[47] Secondly, the dominant party must have exploited this weakness in a morally culpable manner. It is therefore clear that the doctrine is concerned with the culpability or impropriety of the stronger party's conduct, and not just with the harshness of the resulting bargain.[48] Thirdly, the resulting transaction must be so unfair as to be unconscionable. It appears that this means that the result must be 'not merely hard or improvident, but

---

[41] *Etridge*, above n 32 at 805.

[42] In *Barclays Bank plc v O'Brien* (above n 40) their lordships focused on the idea of a meeting between creditor and surety, but banks have always avoided this, apparently fearing that this might lead to the argument that the bank had assumed a role of advisor to the surety. See *Etridge* at 805.

[43] It seems that this will usually be sufficient.

[44] *Etridge*, above n 32 at 793.

[45] See for example D Harland, 'Unconscionable and Unfair Contracts: An Australian Perspective' in R Brownsword, NJ Hird and G Howells (eds), *Good Faith in Contract: Concept and Context* (Aldershot, Dartmouth, 1999) 243; A Leff, above n 13.

[46] See *Alec Lobb (Garages) Ltd v Total Oil (Great Britain) Ltd* [1983] 1 WLR 87.

[47] (1956) 99 CLR 362 at 405. Cranston adds ethnic origin as a possible additional factor (Cranston, above n 24 at 295).

[48] *Boustany v Piggott* (1993) 69 P & CR 298 at 303 (Lord Templeman).

overreaching and oppressive'.[49] One way of putting this is that the resulting terms must shock 'the conscience of the court'.[50] There will frequently be an overlap between unconscionability and the doctrines of duress and undue influence mentioned above. Indeed, some cases that have been decided on the basis of unconscionability overseas might be classed as cases of undue influence in English Law.[51] Because of the relative lack of English case law it appears that the doctrine is likely to be used sparingly. Where the unfairness is based upon the terms of a standard form contract, it may be that statute will provide some relief.[52] With this in mind, it is to the statutory control of contracts that we now turn.

STATUTORY INTERVENTION IN CONTRACTING

A number of statutory provisions allow contracts to be challenged on the basis of different forms of 'unfairness'. Most attention has focused upon standard form contracts. Writing in 1971, Slawson commented that 'the contracting still imagined by courts and law teachers as typical, in which both parties participate in choosing the language of their entire agreement, is no longer of much more than historical importance'.[53] He estimated that standard form contracts accounted for around 99 per cent of all contracts made. Standard form contracts remain of paramount importance to the supplier–consumer relationship in most industries, and banking is no exception. Where onerous terms are concerned, some degree of protection for the consumer was provided through the common law approach to matters of incorporation and construction.[54] In relation to incorporation, a well-known example is the 'red hand rule'. Denning LJ once famously commented that in the case of a particularly onerous term it 'would need to be printed in red ink on the face of the document with a

---

[49] Above n 46 at 94–95.

[50] *Ibid.*

[51] It is clear that English Law regards the doctrines as separate. See *Portman Building Society v Dusangh* [2000] Lloyds Rep Bank 197. There has, however, been debate about whether undue influence could, and should, be subsumed within the doctrine of unconscionability. See A Phang 'Undue Influence—Methodology, Sources and Linkages' (1995) *Journal of Business Law* 552; P Birks and N Chin, 'On the Nature of Undue Influence' in J Beatson and D Friedmann (eds), *Good Faith and Fault in Contract Law* (Oxford, Oxford University Press, 1995) 57; D Capper, 'Undue Influence and Unconscionability: A Rationalisation' (1998) 114 LQR 479.

[52] There is some evidence that the doctrine of unconscionability played a role in the well-known decision of the House of Lords in *A Schroeder Music Publishing Co Ltd v Macaulay* [1974] 1 WLR 1308. See in particular the speech of Lord Diplock.

[53] D Slawson, 'Standard Form Contracts and Democratic Control of Lawmaking Power' (1971) 84 *Harvard Law Review* 529 at 531.

[54] See for example *Interfoto Picture Library Ltd v Stiletto Visual Programmes Ltd* [1989] QB 433.

red hand pointing to it before the notice could be held to be sufficient'.[55] In relation to construction, the *contra proferentem* rule provides that where there is doubt or ambiguity in relation to a provision such as an exemption clause, the words will be construed against the person seeking to rely on the clause.[56] These approaches were, according to Lord Denning, weapons with which the courts could stab the 'idol, freedom of contract' in the back.[57] However, the principal changes have come through statutory intervention.

Unfair Terms Regulation

Intervention to tackle unfairness in contracts, including standard terms in banking contracts, has come via legislation. In particular, banking contracts may be subjected to the tests under the Unfair Contract Terms Act 1977 (UCTA) and the Unfair Terms in Consumer Contracts Regulations 1999 (UTCCRs).[58] Despite the strong arguments that the two pieces of legislation should somehow be combined, this has not yet been done.[59] The result is an unfair terms regime of considerable complexity, which can only be touched upon here.

UCTA is concerned primarily with contractual terms that purport to exclude or restrict liability. The Act makes certain terms void, (for example, those which purport to exclude liability for death or personal injury caused by negligence). Others are subjected to a test of reasonableness. For example, under s 2(2), a bank cannot exclude loss or restrict liability for negligence except in so far as the term or notice satisfies the requirement of reasonableness. According to s 1(1), negligence here means the breach of any obligation, arising from the express or implied terms of a contract, to take reasonable care or exercise reasonable skill in the performance of a contract, or of any common law duty to take reasonable care or exercise reasonable skill. Section 3 of UCTA covers contracts made on standard terms (including with other businesses), and contracts made with consumers (whether or not on standard terms). It provides that, as against the other party, a bank cannot exclude or restrict any liability of his in respect of the breach, or, claim to be entitled to render a contractual performance substantially different from that which was reasonably expected of him, except in so far as the term

---

[55] *Spurling (J) Ltd v Bradshaw* [1956] 1 WLR 461 at 466.
[56] See eg *Lee (John) & Son (Grantham) Ltd v Railway Executive* [1949] 2 All ER 581.
[57] *George Mitchell (Chesterhall) Ltd v Finney Lock Seeds Ltd* [1983] 1 All ER 108 at 113.
[58] SI 1999 no 2083.
[59] Although the Law Commissions have addressed the issue of consolidation. See E MacDonald, 'Unifying Unfair Terms Legislation' (2004) 67(1) MLR 69.

satisfies the requirement of reasonableness. As Cranston observes, the focus is on the reasonable expectations of (in our discussion) the consumer. It is clear that the obligation is on the bank to demonstrate that the term was reasonable.[60] Some of the main cases on UCTA's reasonableness test have concerned business to business, rather than business to consumer disputes.[61] Adams and Brownsword argue that decisions about reasonableness are frequently based on the notion of inequality of bargaining power and conclude that 'we can expect to find the courts well-disposed towards exercising their reserve powers in favour of consumer contractors and relatively weak contractors'.[62] In addition to the bargaining power of the parties, which it seems will frequently be important, other factors may be taken into account in deciding if the term is reasonable. These might include, inter alia, whether the consumer received an inducement to accept the term, or had the opportunity to accept a similar contract with others without the term, whether the consumer knew or should have known about the term, and the length of the contract.[63] It has been suggested that the courts will also be influenced by the bank's resources, which are likely to be substantial, and by its ability to underwrite its losses by insurance.[64]

The Unfair Terms in Consumer Contracts Regulations 1999[65] implement the EC Directive on Unfair Terms in Consumer Contracts.[66] The Regulations cover any term in a contract concluded between a supplier and a consumer, which has not been individually negotiated.[67] A consumer for these purposes is a (natural) person acting for purposes that are outside his or her business.[68] This reflects the notion of the consumer adopted in this book. Deciding whether a term has been individually negotiated is of central importance. Regulation 5(2) states that a term is always to be regarded as not having been individually negotiated where it has been drafted in advance and the consumer has therefore not been able to influence the substance of the term. This applies even if the consumer is given a choice of pre-drafted terms. Furthermore, even if part of

---

[60] Section 11(5). Cranston, above n 24 at 148.
[61] See in particular *Photo Production Ltd v Securicor Transport Ltd* [1980] AC 827; and *George Mitchell (Chesterhall) Ltd v Finney Lock Seeds Ltd* above n 57. The other leading House of Lords decision, *Smith v Eric S Bush* [1989] 2 All ER 514, concerned a consumer.
[62] J Adams and R Brownsword, *Key Issues in Contract* (London, Butterworths, 1995) at 268–69.
[63] See UCTAs ch 2 which strictly speaking only applies to the sale of goods and analagous matters, but is likely to be taken into account. See Cranston, above n 24 at 148. See also *Smith v Eric Bush* above n 61.
[64] J Wadsley and G Penn, *The Law Relating to Domestic Banking* (London, Sweet and Maxwell, 2000) at 116. See also UCTA s 11(4). Insurance was a factor in *George Mitchell (Chesterhall) Ltd v Finney Lock Seeds Ltd* above n 57.
[65] SI 1999 no 2083.
[66] Directive 93/13/EEC.
[67] Regulation 5(1).
[68] Regulation 3(1).

the contract has been individually negotiated, the Regulations will still apply to the rest of the contract if an overall assessment of it suggests that it is a pre-formulated standard contract.[69]

The Regulations provide that provisions which relate to the definition of the main subject matter of the contract, or to the adequacy of the price or remuneration as against the goods or services supplied in exchange cannot be challenged, provided they are expressed in clear language. Such provisions can be referred to as the 'core terms' of the contract. The Office of Fair Trading has explained the rationale behind this, arguing that the exemption allows 'freedom of contract to prevail in relation to terms that are genuinely central to the bargain between consumer and supplier'. However, this is conditional upon 'such terms being expressed and presented in such a way to ensure that they are, or at least are capable of being, at the forefront of the consumer's mind in deciding to enter the contract'.[70] It seems that the interest rate in a loan will be a core term.[71]

Schedule 2 of the Regulations provides an indicative and non-exhaustive list of terms which may be regarded as unfair (a so-called 'grey list').[72] There may be areas of difficulty where contracts between banks and consumers are concerned, as some examples on the list might appear to call well-established terms in banking contracts into question. For example, paragraph 1(j) deals with unilateral variation. It refers to terms which have the object or effect of enabling the seller or supplier to alter the terms of the contract unilaterally without a valid reason which is specified in the contract.[73] Lomnicka suggests that the expression 'valid reason' is 'clearly seeking to outlaw variation clauses which enable capricious changes to be made', while accepting that it is hard to pin down what amounts to a valid reason.[74] The provision is clarified by paragraph 2(b) which states that the provision is:

> without hindrance to terms by which a supplier of financial services reserves the right to alter the rate of interest payable by the consumer or due to the latter, or the amount of other charges for financial services without notice where there is a valid reason, provided that the supplier is required to inform

---

[69] Regulation 5(3).

[70] Office of Fair Trading, *Unfair Contract Terms Guidance* (OFT 311, February 2001) para 19.13. See also Beatson, above n 33 at 302.

[71] By contrast, the House of Lords has held that a term which provides for default interest to be paid until the time that the borrower repays will not be a core term. See *Director General of Fair Trading v First National Bank plc* [2002] AC 481. Note that this may be challenged as extortionate under the Consumer Credit Act 1974 (see below).

[72] The status of the list has been described as 'relatively insignificant' (Furmston (ed) above n 11 para 3.11), although it at least provides a degree of guidance.

[73] See E Lomnicka, 'Unilateral Variation in Banking Contracts: An Unfair Term?' in P Cartwright (ed), *Consumer Protection in Financial Services* (London, Kluwer Law International, 1999) 97.

[74] *Ibid* at 112–13.

the other contracting party or parties thereof at the earliest opportunity and that the latter are free to dissolve the contract immediately.

Paragraph 1(j) is also without hindrance to terms

under which a seller or supplier reserves the right to alter unilaterally the conditions of a contract of indeterminate duration, provided that he is required to inform the consumer with reasonable notice and that the consumer is free to dissolve the contract.

This second derogation applies not only to suppliers of financial services, but deals with the unilateral variation of any term, provided the contract is of indeterminate derogation. It seems that it will apply to terms in the banking contract under which the bank may unilaterally alter the contract conditions, provided the bank gives reasonable notice and the consumer is permitted to terminate the contract.[75]

Paragraph 1(g) deals with unilateral termination of contracts. It refers to terms which have the object or effect of 'enabling a seller or supplier to terminate a contract of indeterminate duration without reasonable notice except where there are serious grounds for doing so'. This is subject to paragraph 2(a) which states that paragraph 1(g) is

without hindrance to terms by which a supplier of financial services reserves the right to terminate unilaterally a contract of indeterminate duration without notice where there is a valid reason provided that the supplier is required to inform the other contracting party or parties thereof immediately.

This seems to state that provided there is a valid reason to terminate the contract, and provided the bank informs the consumer immediately, the bank is unlikely to be in breach. The OFT Guidance states that such a term should 'not be drafted in such a way that it could in practice be used arbitrarily to suit the interests of the supplier'.[76] The Guidance further states that a reason can only be considered valid if its inclusion in the contract 'offers real protection to the consumer against encountering unexpected and unacceptable changes in his or her position'.[77]

The Regulations specifically state that terms which are incorporated in a contract in order to comply with statutory or regulatory provisions of the UK are excluded from the Regulations. This would, for example, include terms required by the Financial Services Authority or by the Consumer Credit Act 1974.

---

[75] *Ibid* at 120.
[76] Office of Fair Trading, above n 70 at para 7.5.
[77] *Ibid* para 11.5.

Regulation 5(1) states that:

> a contractual term which has not been individually negotiated shall be regarded as unfair if, contrary to the requirement of good faith, it causes a significant imbalance in the parties' rights and obligations arising under the contract, to the detriment of the consumer.

According to regulation 8, if the term is declared to be unfair, it will not bind the consumer. However, the contract will continue to bind the parties if it is capable of continuing without the unfair term. It is important to say something about the concepts of significant imbalance and good faith, as these lie at the heart of the test.

To fall foul of the Regulations, the term must be contrary to the requirement of good faith.[78] The 1994 Unfair Terms in Consumer Contracts Regulations had mentioned four factors to be considered when deciding if this was met. These were: the strength of the bargaining position of the parties; whether the consumer had an inducement to agree to the term; whether the goods or services were supplied to the special order of the consumer, and the extent to which the seller or supplier had dealt fairly and equitably with the consumer. Although the 1999 Regulations do not contain this list, it seems likely that the same factors will, where appropriate, be taken into account.[79] The meaning of good faith has caused some difficulty for common lawyers, and has produced a vast literature. Well before the advent of the Regulations, Bingham LJ famously equated the civil law concept of good faith with 'playing fair', 'coming clean' and 'putting one's cards face up on the table'.[80] In *Director General of Fair Trading v First National Bank plc*, Lord Bingham argued that openness required 'that the terms should be expressed fully, clearly and legibly, containing no concealed pitfalls or traps'.[81] This lead Beatson to suggest that the focus of the test is on procedural rather than substantive unfairness:[82]

> the absence of any absolutely prohibited terms and the fact that the indicative and non-exhaustive list of terms which may be regarded as unfair are couched in an open textured way … suggest that the Regulations are not primarily concerned with substantive unfairness but with the prevention of unfair surprise and the absence of real choice.

---

[78] See H Beale, 'Legislative Control of Fairness: The Directive on Unfair Terms in Consumer Contracts' in J Beatson and D Friedmann (eds), *Good Faith and Fault in Contract Law* (Oxford, Clarendon Press, 1995) 231.

[79] These factors are contained in Recital 16 of the Preamble to the Directive which can be taken into account.

[80] *Interfoto Picture Library Ltd v Stiletto Visual Programmes Ltd* [1989] QB 433 at 439.

[81] [2001] 3 WLR 1297 at 1308.

[82] J Beatson, above n 33 at 305.

Beale, by contrast, argues that good faith has what he refers to as a 'double operation'. In relation to its procedural aspect '[i]t will require the supplier to consider the consumer's interests'.[83] In relation to the substantive element 'some clauses may cause such an imbalance that they should always be treated as being contrary to good faith and therefore unfair'.[84] The distinction between procedural and substantive unfairness is one that has long taxed commentators, and, as mentioned above, it is submitted that it is not an entirely satisfactory distinction. Some of the objections to a good faith test are similar to the objections to intervention based on unfairness considered above, and can be refuted on some of the same bases.[85] Even to the extent that good faith is based upon issues of procedural unfairness there may be concern about how far there will be intervention in procedure, in particular in relation to issues of disclosure. However, these concerns arise primarily in the commercial context rather than in the context between banks and consumers.[86]

The extent to which the provisions of the *Banking Code* can be taken into account under the Regulations has been the subject of debate. Although terms which are incorporated in a contract in order to comply with statutory or regulatory provisions of the UK are excluded from the Regulations, it seems that this will not extend to provisions of the *Banking Code*. Instead, the *Code*'s provisions are likely to be taken into account in deciding whether a term is unfair. It seems likely that failure to comply with the *Code*'s requirements could be regarded as evidence of a lack of good faith. Bearing in mind the lack of statutory provision concerning conduct of business in retail banking, it is important that the courts are willing to look closely at the *Code*'s provisions. This is considered further in chapter five.

As mentioned above, the term in question must cause a significant imbalance in the parties' rights and obligations arising under the contract, to the detriment of the consumer. The meaning of 'significant imbalance' was considered by the House of Lords in *Director General of Fair Trading v First National Bank plc*.[87] In that case, Lord Bingham stated that the requirement of significant imbalance is met if a term

> is so weighted in favour of the supplier as to tilt the parties' rights and obligations under the contract significantly in his favour. This may be by the

---

[83] Above n 78 at 245. Recital 16 to the Directive states that where the trader 'deals fairly and equitably with the other party whose legitimate interests he also takes into account', the requirement of good faith will be satisfied.

[84] *Ibid*.

[85] Compare the approach by Collins mentioned above with that in M Furmson (ed), above n 11 para 1.85.

[86] See M Bridge 'Good Faith in Commercial Contracts' in R Brownsword, N Hird and G Howells (eds), *Good Faith in Contract: Concept and Context* (Aldershot, Dartmouth, 1999) 139.

[87] Above n 81.

granting to the supplier of a beneficial option or discretion or power, or by the imposing on the consumer of a disadvantageous burden or risk or duty.[88]

In this case, their Lordships upheld a term in the Bank's loan agreement which stated that in the event that a borrower defaulted on his repayments, interest would continue to be payable at the contractual rate until judgment was satisfied. Their Lordships argued that such unfairness as there was resulted from the fact that the judgment did not cover the whole of the indebtedness rather than from the term itself. Their Lordships' approach to the meaning of significant imbalance demonstrates that, looked at as a whole, the Regulations are to a degree concerned with substantive fairness. What is still unclear is what is meant by a 'significant' imbalance. Cranston suggests that possible synonyms are 'really serious or exceptional' on the one hand, or merely 'non-trivial' on the other. One argument he cites for the latter is that the indicative grey list appears to cover some matters which would not normally be described as involving a serious imbalance.[89]

The final issue to consider on unfair terms regulation concerns enforcement. Under Regulation 10 of the 1999 Regulations, the Director General of Fair Trading is under a duty to consider complaints made to him that a contract term which has been drawn up for general use is unfair. If the Director General considers it appropriate to do so, he may either accept undertakings about the use of the term in question, or seek an injunction to prevent the use of that term. Regulation 12(1) allows any 'qualifying body' to apply for an injunction, subject to notifying the Director General or having previously obtained his consent. This ensures that the Director General retains a co-ordinating function in relation to the enforcement of the Regulations.

The FSA is a qualifying body under the Regulations. The Office of Fair Trading (OFT) has agreed with the FSA that each will take on some responsibility for different areas of banking. For example, the FSA will consider the fairness of financial services contracts for carrying on any regulated activity, general insurance (including broking) and lending, administration, advising and arranging in respect of certain mortgages. The OFT will consider the fairness of other financial services contracts involving carrying on activities governed by the Consumer Credit Act 1974, including second charge mortgage loans, buy to let mortgages, and non-mortgage personal loans (including credit cards). The following discussion looks at the approach of the FSA, about which it has published some helpful guidance.[90]

---

[88] *Ibid* at 1307.
[89] Cranston, above n 24 at 156–57.
[90] *FSA Hardbook*, 'Enforcement' (hereafter, ENF) 20.

The FSA can consider the fairness of a contract following a complaint from a consumer, or some other person (such as the OFT or another qualifying body) or on its own initiative. The FSA has stated that the main way it would act on its own initiative would be to undertake a review of contracts in a particular area of business. 'This might involve investigating the contract terms used by several firms in a particular sector, rather than waiting for complaints regarding a particular firm'.[91] It is clear that before taking formal action, the FSA will contact the bank, expressing its concern and giving it the ability to make representations. If the FSA concludes that the term is unfair it will usually ask the bank to undertake to stop using the term in new contracts, and relying on the term in existing contracts. Failure to give or keep to an undertaking may lead to the FSA's applying for an injunction under regulation 12. When deciding whether to apply for an injunction, the FSA will consider all the circumstances. Examples that may be taken into account include: whether the term falls within the test of unfairness under the Regulations; the extent and nature of detriment or potential detriment to consumers; the extent to which the bank has co-operated with the FSA; the likelihood of success; and the costs and benefits of applying for an injunction. On the final point, it is clear that the FSA will be more likely to apply for an injunction where it would 'not only prevent the continued use of the particular contract term, but would also be likely to prevent the use or continued use of similar terms, or terms having the same effect, used or recommended by other firms concluding contracts with consumers'.[92] Although this means that the FSA will be more likely to take action where a large number of consumers will potentially benefit, they are able to act where a more limited number of consumers will gain. In many cases, the FSA will expect to achieve a positive result without formal action.

Despite the advantages for consumers in this procedure over one where they have to take action themselves, the FSA is not empowered under the Regulations to grant redress to consumers who have suffered loss as a result of an unfair term.[93] Consumers will frequently have to complain to the firm, take action under private law or seek redress from the FOS. Where the use of an unfair term means that there has been a rule breach that has caused loss to consumers, the FSA can apply to the court for restitution, or can require restitution. This is examined below.

Extortionate Credit

Where a consumer's complaint is that a credit bargain provided by a bank is extortionate, the provisions contained in ss 137–40 of the Consumer

---

[91] ENF 20 20.4.3.G.
[92] ENF 20.4.6 G.
[93] ENF 20.6.1 G.

Credit Act 1974 may apply. Under s 137, if the court finds a credit bargain to be extortionate it can re-open it so as to do justice between the parties. Under s 138(1) a credit bargain is extortionate if it: '(a) requires the debtor or a relative of his to make payments … which are grossly exorbitant, or (b) otherwise grossly contravenes ordinary principles of fair dealing'. In deciding whether or not a bargain is extortionate, the court is required to have regard to the following: interest rates prevailing at the time it was made; the factors mentioned in subsection (3) to (5); and any other relevant considerations. Under subsection (3), the relevant factors in relation to the debtor include: his age, experience, business capacity and state of health; and the degree to which, at the time of making the credit bargain, he was under financial pressure, and the nature of that pressure. Under subsection (4), the factors applicable in relation to the creditor include: the degree of risk accepted by him, having regard to the value of any security provided; his relationship to the debtor; and whether or not a colourable cash price was quoted for any goods or services included in the credit bargain. Where the transaction is linked, the court will consider how far the transaction was reasonably required for the protection of the debtor or creditor, or was in the interest of the debtor. The provisions have been considered in detail by a number of reports, and the Consumer Credit White Paper indicates that reform may be imminent.[94]

The provisions are an example of open-texture rules (mentioned above) which allow the courts to consider a wide variety of factors before deciding whether the terms offend the legal standard. Such tests have obvious strengths. In the words of Collins: '[t]he only solution to devising regulation that has the potential to conform to its policy objectives must be one that employs standards that permit the adjudicator to consider all the circumstances of the impugned transaction'.[95] However, there is evidence that the extortionate credit provisions are not meeting their policy objective for a number of reasons.[96]

Perhaps the principal weakness of the provisions concerns the unclear wording of the test itself. The few reported cases indicate that the courts have tended to focus on the cost of credit. The reason for this may be the use of the word 'extortionate,' which is likely to be seen as focusing on cost.[97] On a related point, the White Paper argues that one reason that so few cases have come to court is that the qualifying hurdles under the current law are too high. The word 'extortionate' suggests a high target.

---

[94] Department of Trade and Industry, *Fair, Clear and Competitive: the Consumer Credit Market in the 21st Century* (Cm 6040, December 2003). Hereafter 'the White Paper'.
[95] Collins above n 6 at 267.
[96] There have only been approximately 30 cases in 30 years, and only 10 of those were successful. See the White Paper above n 94 para 3.43.
[97] Indeed, the Crowther Committee recommended that the wording used in the Moneylenders Acts, that the transaction be 'harsh and unconscionable' should be retained. (*Report of the Committee on Consumer Credit*) (the Crowther Committee) (Cmnd 4596, 1971).

One issue to consider here is the extent to which the test aims to address substantive, or merely procedural unfairness. Howells argues that the original legislation had both aims, with the 'grossly exorbitant' limb addressing substantive unfairness and the 'fair dealing' limb procedural unfairness.[98] In practice, the emphasis appears to have been on substantive unfairness. *Unjust Credit Transactions* observed that '[t]he courts have … largely failed to consider whether practices engaged in by lenders (or brokers) have "grossly contravened the ordinary principles of fair dealing."'[99] Instead, the courts have focused largely on the cost of credit which may be only a limited indicator of an unjust credit transaction. The White Paper refers to other potentially unfair practices such as pressure selling or churning which can cause serious detriment. The White Paper states that 'the object of reform will be to target any unfair credit transaction, widening the scope of the current "extortionate" definition, to ensure account is taken of unfair practices as well as the cost of credit'.[100] One issue to consider here is that the current test focuses on factors prevailing at the time that the loan is taken out. This issue was highlighted by *Paragon Finance plc v Nash and Staunton* [101] where a lender failed to reduce its rates to borrowers in line with market rates.[102] The Court of Appeal found that variations in interest rates could not be taken into account when determining whether an agreement constituted an extortionate credit bargain. The White Paper states that 'in determining whether a transaction is unfair, consideration should be given not just to how the agreement was concluded, but also to any subsequent events that may have led to unfairness'.[103]

It is clear that the Government is keen to broaden the test. The White Paper considers certain factors that should be taken into account when deciding if an agreement is unfair. First, under the heading 'unfair practices' it refers to whether the lender has engaged in an unfair commercial practice such as 'misleading, harassing, coercing or otherwise unduly influencing the borrower in connection with the transaction'.[104] It gives examples such as product mis-selling, unacceptable high-pressure selling techniques or the churning of credit agreements and aggressive debt-collection practices. Secondly, under the heading 'unfair credit costs' the

---

[98] G Howells, 'Controlling Unjust Credit Transactions: Lessons from a Comparative Analysis' in G Howells, I Crow and M Moroney (eds), *Aspects of Credit and Debt* (London, Sweet and Maxwell, 1993) 92 at 93–94.
[99] Office of Fair Trading, *Unjust Credit Transactions* (September, 1991) para 4.9.
[100] White Paper para 3.33.
[101] [2001] 2 All ER 1025. See also *Broadwick Financial Services Ltd v Spencer and another* [2002] 1 All ER 446.
[102] Many of the borrowers were captive and so unable to re-mortgage with another lender.
[103] The White Paper para 3.36.
[104] *Ibid* 3.37.

court or other body will be able to consider whether credit payments substantially exceed market levels. In relation to this, regard will be had not only to the original cost of the credit, but also to the total sum repayable when the loan falls into arrears.[105] Some concern has been expressed here. The DTI states that it is well aware that costs 'are not high or low in the abstract, but must be considered in the light of the nature and type of the agreement and circumstances in which it was made and how the lender has acted subsequently'.[106] But there may be concern that the courts or ADR (alternative dispute resolution) body will be too willing to be swayed by the consumer. The Director General of the Finance and Leasing Association has expressed concern that the changes 'could lead to a trouble makers' charter where all agreements could potentially be challenged, causing lenders to become overly cautious about who they lend to'.[107] The issue of regulatory backfiring is one to which this book has alluded before, and the issue of access is considered in more detail in chapter eight. This should be viewed in conjunction with the other main factor to be taken into account when judging the fairness of the agreement, namely responsible lending. The White Paper states that regard should be had to 'the lender's care and responsibility in providing the credit—including taking reasonable steps to ensure a consumer's credit worthiness and ability to meet the full terms of the agreement at the time it was concluded'.[108] The Government recognises that different sectors will have different approaches to this topic, but concludes that 'creditors should be expected to undertake enquiries that are proportionate, having regard to the type of agreement, their relationship with the customer, and the costs and risks involved'.[109] There are risks to the introduction of such provisions. First they are liable to increase the lender's costs, and this cost will be passed on to the consumer. Secondly, there may be a risk that in practice lenders will refuse to lend, rather than lend when they are in doubt about whether the transaction will be found to be irresponsible and unfair. This raises an issue that runs throughout the book—that we need always to consider the effect that any regulation is likely to have in practice on the activities of consumers and suppliers. There is evidence that stricter standards may sometimes have an exclusionary effect, and that is a factor to be considered.[110] However, it is submitted that the duty does not appear to be unduly onerous.

---

[105] This would include the level of default interest, charges and costs. *Ibid*.
[106] *Ibid*.
[107] 'Shake-up May Harm Poor's Attempts to Borrow Money' *Financial Times* (December 9 2003).
[108] Para 3.37. See G Borrie, 'Lending to those in Need—The Responsibilities of Lenders, Borrowers and Regulators' in G Howells, I Crow and M Moroney, above n 98 at 52.
[109] White Paper para 3.37.
[110] See in particular D Cayne and M Trebilcock, 'Market Considerations in the Formulation of Consumer Protection Policy' (1973) 23 *University of Toronto Law Journal* 396.

A final problem with the provisions is that they rely on consumers taking action themselves through litigation. Citing two important reports on the use of the extortionate credit provisions, the DTI emphasises the 'practical, psychological and cultural barriers' that exist to bringing action before the courts.[111] This is exacerbated where consumers are potentially vulnerable and likely to feel intimidated by either the court process or the lender. The White Paper puts forward two solutions to this. The first is to introduce a system of alternative dispute resolution (probably the Financial Ombudsman Service) which 'should make it easier to resolve disputes in a speedy, fair and inexpensive manner'.[112] The roles of alternative dispute resolution in general, and the FOS in particular, are considered below. The second solution is 'to enable certain designated bodies to bring an action on behalf of the collective interests of consumers requiring a trader to refrain from engaging in conduct which constitutes an unfair credit practice'.[113] This would be achieved through the use of the powers under Part 8 of the Enterprise Act 2002. These initiatives would constitute major steps forward and, on balance, it is submitted that the approach set out in the White Paper (which is, inevitably, short on detail) will be a considerable improvement on the present provisions. Improvements in clarifying the meaning of the test, introducing a broader range of factors to be taken into account, and making it easier for the test to be enforced will bring significant benefits for consumers.

ALTERNATIVE DISPUTE RESOLUTION

The limitations of redress through the courts have been noted above, and in many cases consumers will be keen to try to settle a dispute without litigation. The Government has made clear its determination to encourage disputes to be settled through ADR wherever possible. As will be seen below, the principal example of ADR of relevance to this chapter is the Financial Ombudsman Service. However, before examining that scheme, it is important to say something about the resolution of consumer disputes by banks themselves.

Banks and Consumer Complaints

Many disputes between consumers and their banks will be settled internally, without the need for any further form of dispute resolution mechanism.

---

[111] Para 3.31. The reports were: Citizen's Advice Bureaux, *Daylight Robbery: The CAB Case for Effective Regulation of Extortionate Credit* (CAB, 2000) and E Kempson and C Whyley, *Report to the DTI* (1999).
[112] White Paper para 3.44.
[113] White Paper para 3.41.

Ramsay observes that 'the great majority of consumer disputes are resolved either through the market response of exit or voice to a retailer'.[114] The FSA has powers under FSMA to make rules relating to the handling of complaints by firms, and those subject to the jurisdiction of the FOS are obliged to have internal procedures for the handling of complaints.[115] Details of the rules relating to the internal handling of complaints by firms are found in the *FSA Handbook*.[116] These are issued 'to ensure that complaints are handled fairly, effectively and promptly, and resolved at the earliest possible opportunity, minimising the number of unresolved complaints referred to the Financial Ombudsman Service'.[117]

Research for the FSA on complaints handling procedures in the financial sector found widespread consumer dissatisfaction with the way their complaints were addressed. The research project *Understanding Why Consumers Complain to Financial Suppliers and Their Experiences of Complaining*, paints, in the words of the FSA, 'a bleak picture of the way that the [financial services] industry has handled consumer complaints in the past'.[118] This follows similar findings from a number of earlier studies.[119] The research found that 11 per cent of adults had complained to a financial services supplier in the previous three years. Although the report does not distinguish between types of firm, it is apparent that the majority of complaints relate to banking products. 34 per cent of those complaints related to current accounts, 9 per cent to savings accounts, 8 per cent to mortgages 9 per cent to other loans or credit, and 14 per cent to a general 'problem with service'. The report also notes that banks receive the vast majority of complaints.[120]

It is clear that the FSA's new regime for the handling of complaints addresses many of the concerns that the complainants identified. First, many consumers complained about the length of time that the problem-solving process took.[121] The FSA's complaints handling regime requires that, for example, an acknowledgement letter be issued within five days, and a final response letter or holding letter be issued within four weeks of receiving a complaint. Within eight weeks of receiving a complaint a final

---

[114] I Ramsay, *Consumer Protection: Text and Materials* (London, Weidenfeld and Nicolson, 1989) at 123. But it is clear that many examples of consumer detriment go uncorrected.
[115] *FSA Handbook*, 'Dispute Resolution' (hereafter, DISP) 1.2.1 R.
[116] See generally DISP 1.
[117] DISP 1 1.12 G.
[118] Financial Service Authority, *Understanding Why Consumers Complain to Financial Suppliers and their Experiences of Complaining* (FSA Consumer Research 13, July 2002) at 5. The research looked at complaints handling before the introduction of the FSA scheme.
[119] See for example, National Consumer Council, *Ombudsman Services: Consumers' Views of the Office of the Building Societies Ombudsman and the Insurance Ombudsman Bureau* (London, NCCC, 1993) and J Birds and C Graham, 'Complaints against Insurance Companies' (1993) *Consumer Law Journal* 92.
[120] Above n 118 para 1.2.
[121] *Ibid* para 4.1.

response letter must be issued. If the consumer is dissatisfied with the final response, he or she has six months from the receipt of the final response letter to complain to the FOS.[122]

A second area of common complaint concerned communication channels.[123] Consumers who complained by telephone were frequently forced to deal with call centres and found the process unsatisfactory. The main problems identified here were that staff had relatively little knowledge of the supplier's products and services, and possessed little or no authority. In addition, consumers complained that they had to deal with a different member of staff each time, frequently repeating information that they had already given. This raised the suspicion that earlier calls were not being internally logged. The Complaints Handling Regime addresses these concerns in a number of ways. First, it provides that relevant complaints be investigated by 'an employee of sufficient competence' and 'to have the authority to settle complaints, or to have ready access to someone who has the necessary authority'.[124] Secondly the regime states that a firm must make and retain a record of all relevant complaints for a minimum of three years from the date when the complaint is received.[125] Information contained in this would include the name of the complainant, the substance of the complaint and any correspondence. In relation to the form of the complaint, the regime states that firms must operate 'appropriate and effective internal complaint handling procedures for handling any expression of dissatisfaction, whether oral or written and whether justified or not'.[126] Consumers are entitled to complain by 'any reasonable means'.[127]

A final area of concern identified by the research concerned the involvement of those external to the firm. There was a perception on the part of some consumers that firms only resolved complaints in a satisfactory manner when third parties became involved (such as citizens advice bureaux) or were threatened (such as by the FOS).[128] The research demonstrates that few consumers knew about the process for going to the FOS, although some were aware of its existence. Under the FSA procedure, firms must display a note in each office open to the public confirming that it is covered by the FOS.[129] Also, when a firm sends a final response to the consumer, they must inform them of their right to go to the FOS if unhappy with the firm's decision.[130]

---

[122] *FSA Handbook*, 'Dispute Resolution' (hereafter, DISP) 1.4. The *Banking Code* also contains provisions about the handling of complaints. See ch 5.
[123] Above n 118 para 4.3.
[124] DISP 1.2.16 R.
[125] DISP 1.5.1 R.
[126] DISP 1.2.1 R.
[127] DISP 1.2.8 G.
[128] Above n 118 para 4.5.
[129] DISP 1.1.9 R.
[130] DISP 1.4.12 R.

The complaints regime is an important step forward. In particular, it is pleasing that because of the FSA's rules, and its powers under FSMA, there will be more rigorous control over the ways that banks carry out the procedures they have on paper. A weakness in the previous regimes was the discrepancy between the position in theory and the position in practice.[131] This was compounded by the absence of an effective external control over internal complaints systems. It remains to be seen how effective the new regime will be. The Chief Ombudsman recently commented that '[d]espite regulatory requirements, the way in which firms handle retail customer complaints is still very variable'.[132]

The Financial Ombudsman Service

Introduction

Ombudsman schemes have become a central part of the consumer protection process where financial services are concerned.[133] Originally conceived as an alternative to litigation, they are increasingly seen by consumers as the only effective means of redress when dealing with financial services firms.[134] Financial sector ombudsman schemes developed from the 1980s onwards as the principal method for consumer dispute resolution in their respective sectors.[135] The Banking Ombudsman Scheme was originally established in 1986, and Morris suggests that three key factors induced its creation.[136] First, there was the National Consumer Council's (NCC's) 1983 Report *Banking Services and the Consumer*, which championed the creation of an independent agency for the resolution of disputes between banks and their customers. Secondly, banks saw the Scheme as a useful marketing

---

[131] See for example R James, M Seneviratne and C Graham, 'Building Societies, Customer Complaints and the Ombudsman' (1994) 23 *Anglo-American Law Review* 214; C Graham, M Seneviratne and R James, 'Publicising the Bank and Building Societies Ombudsman Schemes' (1993) *Consumer Policy Review* 85.

[132] 'Chief Ombudsman's Report' in Financial Ombudsman Service, *Annual Report 2003* (FOS, 2003).

[133] There is a vast literature on the various financial services ombudsman schemes that were replaced by the FOS. See for example P Morris, 'The Banking Ombudsman' (1987) *Journal of Business Law* 131 and 199; P Morris and G Little, 'The Ombudsmen and Consumer Protection' in P Cartwright (ed), Consumer Protection in Financial Services (Dordrecht, Kluwer Law International, 1999) ch 2; R James, *Private Ombudsmen and Public Law* (Aldershot, Dartmouth, 1997).

[134] See R James 'The Application of the EC Recommendations on the Principles Applicable to Out of Court Procedures to the New Arrangements for the settlement of Consumer Complaints in the UK Financial Sector' (1999) *Consumer Law Journal* 443.

[135] The first scheme was that of the Insurance Ombudsman Bureau, established in 1981.Subsequent ombudsmen took a variety of forms, including statutory (such as the Building Societies Ombudsman) and self-regulatory (such as the Banking Ombudsman).

[136] P Morris, 'The Banking Ombudsman' above n 1.

tool, both from the perspective of public relations and, originally, to enable them to distance themselves from non-bank competitors. The advantages for banks had been noted by the NCC, who argued that a banking ombudsman scheme 'would be an effective means of improving and maintaining public confidence'. They continued, 'it could provide banks with valuable information about the causes of dissatisfaction amongst their customers. It could enable them to improve their services'.[137] Thirdly, the Scheme was established as a means for avoiding the imposition of a less flexible statutory scheme, such as that subsequently imposed on building societies.[138]

When introduced, most of these schemes were examples of self-regulation, a concept considered in more detail in chapter five. At first glance, the introduction of a statutory scheme under FSMA may appear a highly significant development.[139] However, the move from self-regulation to statutory regulation may not be as significant as it first appears. Ferran suggests that '[i]t is the reduction in the fragmentation of regulation rather than the move away from self-regulation that is the really significant change brought about by FSMA'.[140] Certainly, the reduction in fragmentation is a major change, and should bring several advantages. First, it will reduce consumer confusion. Although James and Morris argue that the empirical evidence to support the conclusion that consumers are confused by the multiplicity of regulators is 'conspicuous by its absence', the new arrangements can only introduce clarity from the consumer perspective.[141] Indeed, it seems that both authors recognise the existence of such confusion. Writing of the state of the various financial sector ombudsmen in 1992, Morris argued that '[i]ncreasingly, consumer grievances arise and it is by no means clear which ombudsman has jurisdiction'.[142] Furthermore, writing in 1998, James argued that the FOS

> will deal with some practical issues which have given cause for concern, including the confusion caused to complainants when faced with a plethora of schemes which between them managed to combine areas of overlap with areas where no ombudsman's writ ran.[143]

---

[137] National Consumer Council, *Banking Services and the Consumer* (London, NCC, 1983) at 108.
[138] The Building Societies Ombudsman was introduced by sch 12 of the Building Societies Act 1986. The introduction of an ombudsman scheme had been vigorously opposed by the Building Societies Association. See Building Societies Association, *The Future Constitution and Powers of Building Societies* (London, BSA, 1983).
[139] Although the FOS only assumed its formal powers under FSMA on 1 December 2001 it had existed in a 'shadow form' since early 2000.
[140] Ferran, above n 1 at 137.
[141] James and Morris, 'The New FOS', above n 1 at 167.
[142] Morris, 'Five Years On', above n 1 at 228.
[143] R James, *'Reform of the Complaints Process in Financial Services—The Public and the Private'* (1998) PL 201.

Secondly, the FOS should ensure that decisions are made in a more consistent manner, with the scheme organised on the basis of product rather than provider.[144] Thirdly, by bringing together those with experience of different sectors, there should be synergies gained from the effective utilisation of expertise. In short a single body 'should, in principle, avoid problems of competitive inequality, inconsistencies, duplication, overlap and gaps all of which can arise in a regime based upon several regulatory agencies'.[145] Finally, a single ombudsman scheme should bring economies of scale by sharing resources and lowering institutional costs.

On the issue of the move to statutory regulation, it is possible to argue that the change of form will make significant differences. First, the FOS is given a good deal of independence from the financial services industry. Under the Banking Ombudsman Scheme, concern was sometimes expressed about the extent to which the ombudsman was truly independent of the industry.[146] There may still be limited concerns. The industry provides the funding for the FOS, through an annual general levy and individual case fees. However, there are now clear arrangements for independence. Under the previous schemes, a body was set up to act as a 'buffer' between the industry and the ombudsman.[147] The equivalent body under the new regime, FOS Ltd, is a company created by the FSA. Its chairman and board are appointed by the FSA, with the appointment of the chairman requiring the approval of HM Treasury. The FSA is responsible for approving the annual budget, deciding on the scope of the voluntary jurisdiction, defining which complainants have access to the compulsory jurisdiction, deciding the overall monetary limit on awards and approving the scheme rules put forward by FOS Ltd.[148] Concern may therefore be more about the extent to which the FOS has independence from the FSA than the extent to which it has independence from the industry. In the words of James and Morris

> while the FOS enjoys virtually unfettered operational autonomy in grievance resolution and a considerable degree of room for manoeuvre on policy

[144] James and Morris, 'The New FOS', above n 1 at 172.

[145] C Goodhart *et al*, *Financial Regulation: Why, How and Where Now?* (London, Routledge, 1998) at 152. Although the authors were considering the structure of a financial regulator rather than an ombudsman scheme, it is submitted that the same principles apply. See also W Merricks, 'Lessons From Merging the Financial Ombudsman Schemes' address to the annual conference of the British and Irish Ombudsman Association 25 May 2001.

[146] See eg *Banking Services: Law and Practice* the Jack Committee; (1989 Cmnd 622) National Consumer Council, *Ombudsman Services*, above n 119; R James, *Private Ombudsmen and Public Law* (Aldershot, Dartmouth, 1997). The same criticism was levelled at other financial services ombudsmen schemes. The Jack Committee recommended that the Banking Ombudsman Scheme be replaced with a statutory scheme with additional powers passing to the Bank of England (then the UK's banking regulator) (the Jack Committee ch 15).

[147] James and Morris, 'Brave New World', above n 1 at 643.

[148] *Ibid* at 644.

matters, the FSA retains significant 'ownership' of crucial aspects of the scheme with the result that the FOS cannot claim to be wholly independent of the FSA.[149]

However, while emphasising these concerns, the authors recognise that there are advantages to having close links between the ombudsman and the regulator. In some cases, a complaint may reveal the need for action to be taken by the regulator, and one of the criticisms levelled at the previous schemes was that there appeared to be relatively little contact between ombudsmen and regulators. Indeed, the FSA has recognised the synergies that may emerge from closer contact, stating that: 'complaints are an important source of regulatory information … They may indicate the existence of a more widespread, systemic problem which requires the FSA's attention'.[150]

Who Can Complain?

For a complaint to be dealt with by the FOS it must be brought by, or on behalf of, an 'eligible complainant'. A person is an eligible complainant if he or she comes within the list in the *FSA Handbook*.[151] A private individual is mentioned as the first example.[152] The term 'eligible complainant' does not include those who were intermediate customers or market counterparties in relation to the firm in question in relation to the matter which gives rise to the complaint. Nor does it cover firms or voluntary jurisdiction (vj) participants whose complaint relates to an activity which the firm has permission to carry on, or which the vj participant conducts, and which is subject to the compulsory or voluntary jurisdiction of the FOS.[153] This is designed to prevent authorised firms from using the Scheme to complain about other authorised firms who conduct similar business.[154]

   As well as private individuals, small businesses and charities are able to use the Scheme. There are good reasons for their inclusion. It has long been recognised that small businesses are frequently in a very similar

---

[149] James and Morris 'The New FOS', above n 1 at 173.
[150] Financial Services Authority, *Consumer Complaints* (FSA, December, 1997) at 24.
[151] DISP 2.4.3 R.
[152] Other eligible complainants are: (b) a business, which has a group turnover of less than £1million at the time the complainant refers the complaint to the firm or VJ participant; or (c) a charity which has an annual income of less than £1million at the time the complainant refers the complaint to the firm or VJ participant; or (d) a trustee of a trust which has a net asset value of £1million at the time the complainant refers the complaint to the firm or VJ participant.
[153] The concept of the voluntary jurisdiction is explained below.
[154] See Financial Services Authority/Financial Services Ombudsman Scheme, *Consumer Complaints and the New Single Ombudsman Scheme* (FSA, November 1999) para 3.14.

position to a private consumer when seeking redress from banks. Indeed, before the establishment of the FOS, the only financial services ombudsman scheme which excluded small businesses was the Insurance Ombudsman Bureau. Although the ability for small businesses to use the scheme is supported, this chapter focuses on use of the scheme by private individuals, which reflects the concept of the consumer used throughout the book.

About Which Activities Can Consumers Complain?

A distinction is drawn between compulsory and voluntary jurisdiction, and these terms demand some explanation. The Ombudsman can only consider a complaint under the compulsory jurisdiction if it relates to a firm's act or omission in carrying on one of a number of specified activities. They are: regulated activities;[155] lending money secured by a charge on land; lending money (other than restricted credit); paying money by a plastic card (other than a store card); the provision of ancillary banking services or activities ancillary to them.[156] In practice, this means that all the areas covered by the previous schemes are covered by the FOS jurisdiction, and this was the principal rationale for such an approach.[157] The voluntary jurisdiction is a contractual arrangement between the FOS and what are known as 'vj participants'. For example, mortgage and insurance intermediaries have, since April 2003, been able to join the voluntary jurisdiction in anticipation of their being covered by the compulsory jurisdiction in 2004, when they become FSA regulated.[158] There is potentially very wide jurisdiction here, although the FOS has made it clear that the voluntary jurisdiction will be expanded gradually on the basis of the FOS's ability to deal with the potential workload. Although voluntary jurisdiction only applies if the firm in question chooses to join the scheme, Blair suggests that 'market competitiveness and transparency … will create some commercial pressure to join up'.[159] As the FSA has recognised 'there is a tension between the desire to offer consumers as comprehensive a service as possible and the need to guard against the danger that the … [FOS] could be overwhelmed'.[160] Certainly, the suggestion that the

---

[155] The principal one for the purpose of banks being accepting deposits.

[156] DISP 2.6.1 R. Ancillary activities would include advice provided by the firm in connection with those activities. Ancillary banking services includes matters such as the provision and operation of cash machines and safe deposit boxes. They also cover the provision of general insurance.

[157] Above n 154.

[158] See Financial Ombudsman Service *Feedback on our consultation about extending our jurisdiction* (FOS, undated)

[159] M Blair *et al, Blackstone's Guide to the Financial Services and Markets Act 2000* (London, Blackstone Press, 2001) at 197.

[160] Financial Services Authority, above n 154 at para 3.51.

FOS might take on some responsibility for complaints about consumer credit companies would mean a significant increase in the organisation's responsibilities.[161] James and Morris sum up the situation thus:[162]

> Consumers will encounter no gaps in coverage compared with the status quo ante and there is an in built provision for controlled expansion in FOS jurisdiction, albeit on a voluntary basis, which takes into account the FOS's complaints handling capacity and the dynamics of the financial services industry.

As was the case with the previous schemes, there are certain limitations on the matters about which consumers can complain. For example, the ombudsman may dismiss a complaint without considering its merits in certain circumstances. Examples of such circumstances include: that the ombudsman is satisfied that the complainant has not suffered, or is unlikely to suffer, financial loss, material distress or material inconvenience; that he considers the complaint to be frivolous or vexatious; and that he considers that the complaint clearly does not have any reasonable prospect of success. In addition, he can dismiss a complaint without further investigation if he is satisfied that 'the firm has already made an offer of compensation which is fair and reasonable in relation to the circumstances alleged by the complainant and which is still open for acceptance'.[163]

A further reason for dismissing a complaint without further investigation of the merits is if the ombudsman is satisfied that 'it is a complaint about the legitimate exercise of a firm's commercial judgment'. The 'commercial judgment' exception is an interesting one. Under the Banking Ombudsman Scheme, the Banking Ombudsman was forbidden from investigating a complaint 'to the extent that the complaint relates to a bank's commercial judgment about lending or security', although this did not prevent him from considering complaints about maladministration in lending matters.[164] The commercial judgment exception received some support, one commentator arguing that 'it would be illegitimate for the Ombudsman to assume the mantle of an appellate body on commercial judgments reached in good faith by expert bank officials'.[165] The maladministration proviso, only added in 1988, was important because, in its original form, the exclusion was 'sufficiently wide to preclude the intervention of the ombudsman even if the decision … [was] clearly

---

[161] See the White Paper above n 94 para 3.45.
[162] James and Morris, 'The New FOS' above n 1 at 183.
[163] DISP 3.3.1 R.
[164] The 'maladministration proviso' was added in 1988.
[165] Morris, 'Five Years On' above n 1 at 235.

tainted with gross maladministration'.[166] DISP 3.3.6 G states that the ombudsman may decide to proceed with a complaint which would otherwise be dismissed under DISP 3.3.1 R(13), (14) or (15) if he considers that the complaint involves an allegation of negligence or maladministration. However, the commercial judgment provision is found in 3.3.1 R (11). This suggests that the exception in 3.3.6 G does not apply. However, the key seems to be the expression 'legitimate' exercise of commercial judgment. Where the allegation is that there has been some form of maladministration, it seems likely that the ombudsman would not hold that there has been a legitimate exercise of commercial judgment.

Decision-Making

The FOS adopts an inquisitorial rather than an adversarial approach, and this is reflected in the procedure adopted. As Blair notes, 'the ombudsman is in charge of the process, and he can require answers to questions and the delivery to him of files, correspondence and other records to help him deal with the issues before him'.[167] When it comes to decision making, the ombudsman's discretion is considerable. James and Morris argue that:

> [o]ne of the key advantages of the Ombudsman technique as a consumer redress mechanism is the capacity to transcend strict legal rules and draw upon a range of extra-legal standards in a manner which usually operates to the benefit of the consumer'.[168]

This ability to transcend legal rules is of great significance in the settlement of disputes between banks and consumers. The *FSA Handbook* states that: '[t]he Ombudsman will determine a complaint by reference to what is, in his opinion, fair and reasonable in all the circumstances of the case'. It continues by saying that in considering what is fair and reasonable in all the circumstances of the case, the Ombudsman will: 'take into account the relevant law, regulations, regulators' rules and guidance and standards, relevant codes of practice and, where appropriate, what he considers to have been good industry practice at the relevant time'.[169]

This test is extremely broad. It is subjective, as it is based upon what the Ombudsman believes to be fair and reasonable. The test is a good

---

[166] Morris, *Ibid* at 203.

[167] Blair *et al*, above n 159 at 188. See also FSMA s 231.

[168] James and Morris, 'The New FOS' above n 1 at 184.

[169] DISP 3.8.1 R. For a discussion of the role of the FOS in interpreting the *Banking Code* see *Norwich and Peterborough Building Society v the Financial Ombudsman Service* [2003] 1 All ER 65 and the analysis of this case in R Nobles 'Rules, Principles and Ombudsman: *Norwich and Peterborough Building Society v the Financial Ombudsman Service*' (2003) 66(5) MLR 781.

illustration of open-texture rules considered elsewhere in this chapter. It has been suggested that '[f]airness represents the essence of the ombudsman function—the requirement to do justice in the individual case, free from the constraints of formal precedent and taking a common sense approach'.[170] The discretion allows the ombudsman to look beyond the individual case to its wider ramifications. The Chief Ombudsman has argued that the test 'can encompass considerations of wider public policy or the general public good'.[171] There might be risks attached to allowing such a broad discretion to operate. Lord Ackner commented that such a test made the industry 'the hostage to fortune of uncertain and therefore unpredictable liability which may result from the Ombudsman acting as the embodiment of the conscience of the industry'.[172] Certainly, the purpose of such a broad test is to ensure that the Ombudsman is able to consider all the circumstances in deciding what is a fair and reasonable determination. This will, inevitably, lead to a degree of uncertainty for both banks and consumers. However, it is debatable whether the risks are as great as Lord Ackner opined.[173] Although the ombudsman is 'free from the constraints of formal precedent' in the sense of not being legally bound to follow previous decisions, is seems likely that he will pay extremely close attention to how previous cases have been decided. In particular, it is clear that a body of decisions are built up over time, which act as persuasive precedents. This is illustrated by the Chief Ombudsman's observation that, '[w]e are not bound by the doctrine of precedent, but we do aim for consistency'.[174] The FOS will endeavour to ensure certainty by the use of publicity tools such as bulletins, reports, and its publication *Ombudsman News*. It also provides briefing notes, explaining how it deals with specific cases or issues.[175] The FOS also uses lead cases to try to ensure consistency as well as efficiency in decision-making. Although it does decide each case on its own circumstances, the FOS has stated the following:

> if we receive lots of cases about the same financial product, we may choose one or more apparently typical cases as lead cases … Once a lead case has been decided … we contact whichever party (firm or customer) would lose

[170] James, above n 143 at 206.
[171] W Merricks, above n 145.
[172] Lord Ackner, *Report on a Unified Complaints Procedure* (London, PIA, 1993) para 93. Cited in James and Morris, 'The New FOS' n 1 at 185.
[173] In any event, the comments were made before the thrust towards alternative remedies provided by the civil justice reforms. However, there is still concern at the width of the discretion. Lightman J recently commenting that ideas of justice 'may vary with the length of each ombudsman's foot'. See Lightman J, 'The Pensions Ombudsman and the Courts' (2001) 88 *Pensions Lawyer* 1 at 8.
[174] W Merricks, above n 145.
[175] For example, there are briefing notes on the Abbey National dual variable interest rate case and on making awards for non-financial loss.

if we followed the lead case in the particular follow on case, and ask them to tell us how the circumstances of the particular case differ from the lead case.[176]

By taking this approach, the FOS is able to ensure that full consideration is given to the individual circumstances of the follow on case. A further point to emphasise is that where a particular issue is dealt with by a code of practice or some form of regulatory guidance (for example from the FSA), it seems likely that this will be extremely influential. Although the ombudsman is not bound to decide cases on the basis of FSA regulatory guidance, it is expected that this will frequently resolve the matter: 'FSA guidance is proliferating at a rapid pace and in practice will provide the level of detail, clarity and precision to resolve many complaints reaching the FOS without the need to refer to sectoral codes or the fair and reasonable standard'.[177] Furthermore, to the extent that the test does introduce a degree of uncertainty, that may be appropriate in industries such as banking. The banking sector is a particularly fast-moving part of the fast-moving financial services industry. A broad test such as that contained in the FOS ensures that the Ombudsman is able to keep abreast of industry developments where appropriate, without waiting for their implications to be considered by codes of practice etc. As Nobles argues 'while considerations of justice and the need for good administration point to the need for ombudsmen to decide matters on a consistent basis, they also need the ability to depart from usual practice where appropriate'.[178] The FOS will frequently consult on what its approach should be on difficult policy questions, and this consultation will inform that approach.

The Role of the Ombudsman in Raising Industry Standards

One area of debate concerns the extent to which the Ombudsman has the role of raising standards of industry practice. Some ombudsmen under the previous schemes appear to have focused very much on their role as judge of individual cases, and it may be that this approach will be continued under the FOS. There is a debate about whether it is appropriate for ombudsmen to be closely involved in raising standards of good practice in the industry. The contrasting positions can be described as the codification school and the reform school.[179] The codification school sees the role of the ombudsman as applying industry-determined concepts of good practice, while the reform school emphasises the role of the ombudsman

---

[176] 'A Briefing Note from the Financial Ombudsman Service: Abbey National Dual Variable Rate Lead Case' (12 September 2002).
[177] James and Morris, 'The New FOS' above n 1 at 187.
[178] Nobles, above n 169 at 789.
[179] James and Morris, 'The New FOS' above n 1 at 187.

in establishing standards of good practice which may go beyond those currently found in the industry.[180] James and Morris suggest that 'the wording and underlying spirit of the FOS strongly suggest a licence to reappraise and revamp even established practices in the various sectors where the fair treatment of consumers warrants it'.[181] However, some concern has been expressed about the extent to which the ombudsman should be involved in setting standards. The Banking Services Consumer Codes Review Group argued that while the FOS should be consulted about the content of the *Banking Code* (as well as other relevant codes), it should be cautious about stepping beyond a dispute resolution function. The Group argued that there was a danger that the dispute resolution function 'would be undermined if the FOS were asked to take too pro-active a role in standard-setting, as it could neither guarantee industry commitment nor does it face the checks and balances of a regulator'.[182] The Review Group noted the Ombudsman's issuing of guidance notes where a large number of cases appear to be emerging. These notes set out how the FOS is likely to treat cases before it. The Review Group stated that it felt such notes performed a worthwhile function but warned that 'it is important that they do not turn into "back door" regulation'.[183]

Remedies under the FOS

Where the ombudsman makes a determination against a bank, he may make such a money award as he considers fair compensation for financial loss, pain and suffering, damage to reputation and distress or inconvenience up to a maximum of £100,000. If he considers that a larger amount is necessary to amount to fair compensation, the ombudsman may recommend to the bank that it pays the balance. In relation to costs, where the ombudsman finds in the consumer's favour, he can make an award to cover some or all of the costs that were reasonably incurred by the complainant. However, it is envisaged that the award of costs will not be common as the Scheme is designed to encourage consumers to bring complaints without the services of professional advisors. It is clear that the ombudsman's powers are quite wide in respect of the circumstances for which compensation can be awarded. In *Watts v Morrow*, Bingham J stated

---

[180] *Ibid.*

[181] James and Morris, 'The New FOS', above n 1 at 188.

[182] Banking Services Consumer Codes Review Group, *Cracking the Codes for Banking Customers* (May 2001) para 4.54.

[183] *Ibid* para 4.55. This should also be viewed in the light of the discussion of the role of the ombudsman in interpreting the provisions of the *Banking Code* in *Norwich and Peterborough Building Society v Financial Ombudsman Service* above n 169. The Court emphasised in that case that interpretation of the banking code is purely a matter for the courts. See the discussion in Nobles above n 169.

that 'a contract breaker is not in general liable for any distress, frustration, anxiety, displeasure, vexation, tension or aggravation which his breach of contract has caused'.[184] It has been argued that the rationale for this is that '[t]he reparation of such non-pecuniary, non-physical harm poses problems of incommensurability and subjectivity, and difficulties of proof'.[185] However, the ombudsman is not so limited, and a perusal of the cases reported in *Ombudsman News* reveals that compensation is frequently awarded for matters such as distress and inconvenience.

THE FSA AND CONSUMER REDRESS

There can be little doubt that the creation of mechanisms for alternative dispute resolution such as ombudsmen have contributed considerably towards obviating some of the barriers to consumers' obtaining access to justice. Nevertheless, barriers remain, and there will be occasions where undesirable conduct will go uncorrected because of the inability, or unwillingness, of consumers to take action. A partial solution to this is to make it easier for a public body to seek redress on behalf of the consumer. It has already been noted that there is provision under the Unfair Terms in Consumer Contracts Regulations 1999 for bodies, including the OFT and the FSA, to take action against unfair terms following complaints from consumers. In addition, there is the possibility of prosecutions being brought, for example by trading standards officers under the Consumer Credit Act 1974, which may lead to compensation orders being payable to consumers. There is also the possibility of court orders being obtained by enforcement bodies under Part 8 of the Enterprise Act 2002.

In addition, an important part of the FSA's armoury relates to its ability to seek restitution and redress on behalf of consumers. Under s 382(1) of FSMA, the FSA is empowered to apply to the court for an order for restitution. The court may make an order if it is satisfied that a person has contravened a relevant requirement or been knowingly concerned in the contravention of such a requirement, and: '(a) that profits have accrued to him as a result of the contravention; or (b) that one or more persons have suffered loss or been otherwise adversely affected as a result of the contravention'. The court can award such sum as appears to it to be just having regard, as appropriate, to the profits accrued, or the loss or adverse effect that has been suffered.[186] The sum that the court orders to be paid

---

[184] [1991] 4 All ER 937. There are exceptions where the distress is consequential on physical loss, and when the purpose of the contract is to provide enjoyment or peace of mind. See *Perry v Sydney Phillips and Son* [1982] 1 WLR 1297, and *Jarvis v Swan Tours Ltd* [1973] QB 233.
[185] Beatson, above n 33 at 593.
[186] Section 382(2).

will be paid to the FSA and distributed as the court directs.[187] There are additional powers in relation to market abuse.[188]

Section 384(1) of FSMA also permits the FSA to require restitution from a firm which has breached a relevant requirement. The FSA may exercise this power if it is satisfied that a firm has contravened a relevant requirement or has been knowingly concerned in contravention of such a requirement, and (a) that profits have accrued to him as a result of the contravention; or (b) that one or more persons have suffered loss or been adversely affected in any other way as a result of the contravention. The FSA can require the person concerned to pay to the appropriate person, or share between appropriate persons identified by the FSA, an amount which the FSA regards as fair, having regard to profits, losses and adverse effects. This is subject to procedural safeguards, including the giving of warning and decision notices.[189]

In the Handbook, the FSA identifies the factors it will consider when deciding whether to exercise its powers to seek or obtain restitution under ss 382, 383 or 384 of FSMA. These include: whether the profits are quantifiable; whether the losses are identifiable; the number of persons affected; the costs to the FSA of securing redress; whether redress is available elsewhere, including through another regulator; whether persons can bring their own proceedings; whether the firm is solvent; the other powers available to the FSA; and the behaviour of the persons suffering loss.[190] This demonstrates the extent of the FSA's discretion in relation to enforcement.[191]

CONCLUSIONS

This chapter has examined how consumers can obtain redress from banks. By necessity, the approach taken has been selective in some ways, but broad in others. The limitations of redress through the private law, and in particular the existence of transaction costs, have demonstrated the necessity for other mechanisms for consumer redress. In the words of Ramsay, '[s]ince the transaction costs … of enforcing individual consumer claims may often outweigh the expected recovery, the private law system may fail either to deter socially wasteful activity or to compensate for violation of rights'.[192] In some cases these difficulties will be addressed by

---

[187] Section 382(3). There are similar powers in s 383 relating to market abuse which are beyond the scope of this work.
[188] See ss 383.
[189] See ENF 9.5.7 G and 9.5.8 G.
[190] See ENF 9.6.
[191] See the discussion in ch 4 .
[192] Ramsay, above n 17 para 3.9.

public enforcement, and the ability of public bodies to seek redress on behalf of consumers is welcome. However, the most significant development has been the move towards alternative dispute resolution and, in particular, the creation of the FOS.

Ombudsmen schemes have brought considerable benefits to consumers, and constitute an important way of overcoming transaction costs. Financial ombudsmen have even found support among commentators sceptical of the need for regulation to protect consumers. Benston, one of the best known critics of traditional justifications for financial regulation, sees a role for an ombudsman. He argues that given that there will be a desire on the part of legislators to take action to protect consumers from unfair treatment, 'the best procedure would be to establish an independent agency that would serve as an ombudsman for consumers who believe they have been mistreated by a financial service firm or salesperson'.[193] Despite some concern that the FOS might play the part of quasi regulator, there now appears to be widespread support for the FOS, and it looks set to continue to play a major role in helping consumers to obtain redress from banks.

---

[193] G Benston, *Regulating Financial Markets* (London, Institute of Economic Affairs, 1998) at 120.

7

Financial Compensation and Deposit Protection

INTRODUCTION

MECHANISMS FOR PROVIDING compensation when a bank faces insolvency are an important element in the UK's financial regulatory regime. Financial compensation schemes, of which deposit protection schemes are an example, provide obvious benefits to consumers by providing a payout in the event of a firm no longer being able to meet its liabilities.[1] However, as will become apparent, they also bring other benefits. Chief among these is the promotion of confidence in the financial system as a whole, something that plays a vital role in the avoidance of systemic risk. Consumer protection and market confidence are both objectives of the FSA, and compensation schemes therefore play an important role in helping the Authority to meet its statutory objectives.

Before FSMA 2000 came into force there was a plethora of compensation schemes operating in different sectors of the financial services industry.[2] The various schemes had their strengths and weaknesses, but the very existence of such diversity could generate confusion among consumers. There has been general acceptance for some time that rationalisation would bring benefits, and some degree of rationalisation has taken place. However, although the Financial Services and Markets Act 2000 (FSMA) has created a unified Financial Services Compensation Scheme (FSCS), the decision was taken to divide this into three separate sub-schemes. A number of reasons can be put forward in favour of this division. Different sectors involve different products, behaviour by consumers and levels of risk, and have different abilities to fund compensation.[3] This chapter will

[1] Deposit protection schemes are sometimes referred to as deposit guarantee schemes, or deposit insurance schemes.
[2] The Financial Services Compensation Scheme replaces the Building Societies Investor Protection Scheme, the Deposit Protection Scheme, the Friendly Societies Protection Scheme, the Investors Protection Scheme, the PIA Indemnity Scheme, the Policyholders Protection Scheme and the Section 43 Scheme.
[3] Financial Service Authority, *Consumer Compensation: A Further Consultation* (FSA Consultation Paper 24, June 1999) para 2.1.

concentrate on deposit protection which, it is argued, raises some issues that are different to those posed by the other sub-schemes.

The chapter begins by explaining the objectives of deposit protection schemes, and follows this with an explanation of the operation of the deposit protection sub-scheme of the Financial Services Compensation Scheme in the UK. The chapter then looks critically at the operation of such schemes, questioning some of the premises upon which they are founded. It will be argued that while the new regime brings advantages over the previous schemes, improvements are necessary before deposit protection in the UK meets its prime objectives.

DEPOSIT PROTECTION SCHEMES: OBJECTIVES AND CONTEXT

There are two principal objectives of deposit protection schemes. The first is to protect the individual consumer from losses that would otherwise be suffered in the event of a bank becoming insolvent. The second is to avoid systemic risk by maintaining confidence in the financial system. In addition, we might identify a third objective, which is to aid the functioning of a single market in financial services. This was a major factor behind the Deposit Guarantees Directive, the provisions of which still underpin the UK scheme.[4]

Depositor Protection and Consumer Protection

Deposit protection schemes play an important role in protecting consumers by providing compensation should a firm find itself unable to meet its obligations to them. It has been argued that consumer protection was the main motivation behind the creation of the original deposit protection scheme in the UK.[5] Such protection can be justified on an economic and social basis.[6]

From an economic point of view, the consumer protection element of depositor protection can be explained on the basis of information asymmetry.[7] Consumers are unable to judge how safe an institution is, and the market is unable, or unwilling, to provide this information.[8]

---

[4] See generally A Campbell and P Cartwright, 'Banks and Consumer Protection: the Deposit Protection Scheme in the UK' (1998) *Lloyds Maritime and Commercial Law Quarterly* 128.
[5] See M Hall, 'The Deposit Protection Scheme: The Case for Reform' (1987) *National Westminster Bank Quarterly Review* 45.
[6] For a discussion of economic and social rationales for regulation see ch 2.
[7] See generally ch 2. There are also economic justifications for deposit protection in relation to its role in avoiding systemic risk. These are considered below.
[8] For an examination of the reasons why consumers may not get optimal information from the market see Office of Fair Trading Consumer Detriment Under Conditions of Imperfect

Indeed, the consumer will be concerned that the bank should continue to be solvent as long as a deposit is maintained, but this will depend upon the subsequent behaviour of bank management. The existence of information asymmetry does not automatically lead to the conclusion that regulation is necessary, nor that deposit protection schemes are a necessary response. Another less interventionist, and more market-friendly, response might be for the regulator to insist that certain information be disclosed by the industry, or for the regulator to provide comparative information to this effect.[9] However, it is unlikely that even with detailed information about the financial condition of firms, consumers would be equipped fully to understand the risks that such firms pose. Indeed, it may be that because of the nature of fractional reserve banking, a well-run and well-capitalised bank could find itself in unexpected and unavoidable financial difficulty.[10] Deposit protection schemes ensure that choice of firms becomes less significant than it would be were no scheme in place.[11] As will be seen later, this raises some concerns in relation to the possible creation of moral hazard.

From a social perspective, deposit protection schemes can be justified on the basis of the significant harm that would be suffered by depositors in the event of a firm becoming insolvent. Consumers frequently have a large proportion of their assets in the form of deposits, and this proportion is likely to be particularly high for the less sophisticated.[12] The need to provide some form of safety net for consumers therefore forms part of the justification for deposit protection. Furthermore, the least sophisticated consumers are also likely to be the least able to judge the soundness of an institution, making it particularly important to address their needs.

The social role of deposit protection is also reflected by the fact that not all consumers are protected to the same extent. The UK's Financial Services Compensation Scheme protects 100 per cent of the first £2,000 deposited, and 90 per cent of the next £33,000. This means that those with the smallest deposits receive the highest degree of protection. The covering of 90 per cent rather than 100 per cent of a deposit up to a set sum is

---

Information (Office of Fair Trading Research Paper 11, prepared by London Economics, August 1997) para 3.2 and ch 3.

[9] The supply of comparative information is an important element of the FSA's consumer protection policy, but this does not extend to the provision of comparative information about a firm's soundness. For discussion of an approach based on disclosure and market discipline see D Mayes, *A More Market Based Approach to Maintaining Systemic Stability* (FSA Occasional Paper 1, August 2000).
[10] See ch 2.
[11] As will be seen later, it is important that deposit protection schemes are not viewed in isolation. They work most effectively when part of a well-designed regulatory system.
[12] See R Cranston, *Principles of Banking Law*, 2nd edn (Oxford, Clarendon Press, 2002) at 78–80.

generally referred to as co-insurance. Although supported by many for attempting to introduce an element of market discipline, co-insurance presents difficulties and forms part of deposit protection schemes in only a minority of jurisdictions.[13] The issues raised by co-insurance are considered later.

Deposit Protection and Systemic Risk

Deposit protection schemes play an important role in the avoidance of systemic risk, and some jurisdictions appear to view such schemes as concerned primarily with this objective.[14] As explained in chapter two, systemic risk refers to the risk that the failure of one firm may have a knock-on effect, leading to the collapse of the financial system as a whole. This may occur because depositors lose confidence in firms and decide to withdraw their deposits in fear of those firms becoming insolvent: 'banks could collapse not because they are weak, but because some depositors think that other depositors think that a collapse is possible'.[15] Deposit protection schemes address this by providing a guarantee to depositors that should their firms become insolvent, they will receive some compensation. Knowing that the deposit is protected, at least in part, consumers are provided with less incentive to withdraw the deposit and initiate a run. As will be seen later, there are weaknesses with this analysis, particularly because of the imposition of a co-insurance element in many deposit protection schemes.[16]

Deposit Protection and the Single Market

For the European Single Market in financial services to function effectively, it was seen as important to form agreement on deposit protection at a European level. The result was the Deposit Guarantees Directive, which requires Member States to have certain minimum provisions on

---

[13] Co-insurance exists in 20 of the 67 countries to have explicit, limited coverage depositor protection systems. See Gillian G H Garcia, *Deposit Insurance: Actual and Good Practice* (IMF Occasional Paper 197, 2001) Table 11.

[14] See J R Macey and G P Miller, *Banking Law and Regulation*, 2nd edn, (New York, Aspen Law and Business, 1997) at 22–23; E White, *Deposit Insurance* (World Bank Policy Research Paper 1541) (November 1995)).

[15] C Ford and J Kay, 'Why Regulate Financial Services?' in F Oditah (ed), *The Future of the Global Securities Market: Legal and Regulatory Aspects* (Oxford, Clarendon Press, 1996) 145 at 147.

[16] For an argument that depositor protection may be detrimental to bank stability see A Dermirguc-Kunt and E Detragiache, *Does Deposit Insurance Increase Banking System Stability?* (IMF Working Paper, January 2000 (WP/00/3)).

depositor protection.[17] A key feature of the Directive is the provision for 'topping up', which limits the extent to which depositor protection schemes can be a vehicle for competitive advantage.[18] Under the Directive, if a Member State sets up a scheme for its own firms the scheme will cover depositors at branches set up by those firms in other member states. In these circumstances the cover in the home state must not exceed that usually provided by the host state. Where the host state's laws provide better protection than the home state's, the Directive requires that the incoming firm be allowed to join the scheme to supplement the cover that the home state provides. This 'topping up' provision was designed to avoid disparities in compensation and unequal conditions of competition between national firms and branches of firms from other Member States.[19]

The Politics of Deposit Protection

An additional reason for having depositor protection, although perhaps not one of its explicit rationales, is that it is politically attractive. Banks have a special place in the public psyche, and a special trust attaches to them. Recent events, for example the closure of uneconomic bank branches, have demonstrated an inclination on the part of the public to oppose decisions made on purely economic grounds where banks are concerned. The relationship between bank management, the public and the regulators has long been a difficult one, and there is room for debate about the extent to which each should impinge on the territory traditionally occupied by the others.[20] Certainly, loss on the part of depositors is likely to be viewed as a political issue, at least in part.[21] *The Economist* has pointed to the political backlash that the failure of a large bank could cause, arguing that 'ensuring that … [depositors] have somewhere safe to invest their savings is widely considered to be the government's responsibility'.[22] There may also be practical advantages to having deposit protection which are attractive to regulators and politicians.

---

[17] Directive 1994/19/EEC.
[18] See Campbell and Cartwright, above n 4, at 131–32.
[19] *Ibid*; M Andenas, 'Deposit Guarantee Schemes and Home Country Control' in R Cranston (ed) *The Single Market and the Law of Banking*, 2nd edn (London, Lloyds of London Press, 1995) at 105.
[20] For an interesting discussion about the relationship between the Government and the banking industry see T Sweeney, 'The Death of Banking' (26 March 2001) available at <http://www.bba.org.uk>. See also the discussion in ch 2 and 8.
[21] Even in the absence of explicit deposit protection schemes, it is likely that many governments will intervene to protect depositors in the event of bank failure.
[22] 'International Banking: Coping with the Ups and Downs', *The Economist* (27 April 1994) at 6.

Hall argues, for example, that deposit protection 'makes it easier for regulators to close down banks expeditiously by reducing political opposition to such moves'.[23] It is important that the political reasons for having deposit protection are not overlooked.

Deposit Protection and Moral Hazard

One of the main concerns with deposit protection schemes is that they may generate a moral hazard.[24] 'Moral hazard' refers to the risk that if people are insured against an event occurring, they are less likely to take adequate precautions to protect themselves in the event of that occurrence. Deposit protection acts as a form of insurance, protecting consumers regardless of the care they take in choosing where to place their investments, and providing an incentive for bankers to take excessive risks.[25] This is considered in more detail below.

DEPOSIT PROTECTION IN THE UK AND THE FINANCIAL SERVICES COMPENSATION SCHEME: GENERAL ISSUES

FSMA recognises that traditional barriers in the financial services industry have become eroded. As the Chancellor of the Exchequer commented:[26]

> There is a strong case in principle for bringing the regulation of banking, securities and insurance together under one roof. Firms organise and manage their businesses on a group wide basis. Regulators need to look at them in a consistent way. This would bring the regulatory structure into line with the day's increasingly integrated financial markets.

This is reflected in the approach that has been taken to financial compensation. Whereas previously there were separate compensation schemes for deposits, investments and insurance policies, there is now a single compensation scheme, managed by the Financial Services Compensation Scheme Ltd (hereafter FSCS).[27] This brings obvious advantages from the

---

[23] MJB Hall, 'Incentive Compatibility and the Optimal Design of Deposit Protection Schemes: An Assessment of UK Arrangements' 2002 10(2) *Journal of Financial Regulation and Compliance* 115.

[24] See P Cartwright and A Campbell, 'Deposit Insurance: Consumer Protection, Bank Safety and Moral Hazard' (1999) 10 *European Business Law Review* 96.

[25] See FSA Consultation Paper 24, above n 3 para 4.7. As mentioned above, deposit protection is frequently referred to as deposit insurance.

[26] Chancellor of the Exchequer, Speech of 20 May 1997, available at <http://www.hm-treasury.gov.uk./newsroom_and_speeches> (17 May 2004).

[27] See Hall, above n 23 at 115. For details see COMP (Compersation) in the *FSA Handbook*.

point of view of consumers, as there is now a single point of contact in the event of a firm being unable to meet its obligations.

One issue upon which the FSA consulted was whether there should be a single scheme, with a single set of rules, or whether it would be preferable to divide up the scheme into a number of sub sets. The decision was made to create a single body, the FSCS, but to divide the scheme into deposit, investment business and insurance sub-schemes. It is recognised that there are differences between these sectors regarding the products involved, the behaviour of consumers, the risks faced by consumers, the ability of each sector to fund compensation and the differences in scope and practice. These differences were seen as justifying separate sub-schemes under the umbrella of the FSCS.[28] This chapter focuses on the deposit protection sub-scheme, although reference will be made to the scheme as a whole where appropriate.[29]

In order to investigate how effective the new scheme is, it is important to examine some broad policy questions that are raised. An initial point to note is that there are some limitations upon what the FSA can do. FSMA gives the FSA the responsibility for establishing a compensation scheme where firms are unable, or unlikely to be able, to meet claims against them.[30] Part XV of FSMA ensures that the UK continues to comply with the relevant consumer compensation directives as well as providing protection in relation to general insurance.[31] However, beyond these confines, considerable discretion is available. There are several general policy issues to investigate. First is the question of what type of scheme should be created.

Explicit and Implicit Schemes

A number of important issues emerge when deciding on the most appropriate type of scheme. Perhaps the most significant question is whether the scheme should be explicit or implicit. Explicit schemes are those that set out clearly in advance the circumstances in which compensation will be paid, and the levels of such compensation. There are many strengths to explicit schemes, most of which are based upon the certainty they provide. Explicit schemes reduce the likelihood of systemic risk by providing a high degree of confidence for the depositor. Knowing that protection is

---

[28] Financial Services Authority, *Consumer Compensation,* above n 3 para. 2.1.
[29] For discussion about the role of deposit protection and the strengths and weaknesses of different types of scheme see Financial Stability Forum, *Guidance for Developing Effective Deposit Insurance Systems* (September 2001); George Hanc, 'Deposit Insurance Reform: State of the Debate' 1999 12(3) *FDIC Banking Review 1;*
[30] FSMA 2000 Part XV.
[31] Directives 94/19 EC and 97/9 EC.

provided as a matter of law, depositors will be provided with an incentive not to initiate a bank run.[32] Explicit schemes also provide a specific degree of consumer protection, although the precise level of protection will vary depending on the particular limits set out in the scheme. Explicit schemes will also be funded in advance, which brings the advantage of having a fund in place should the scheme be activated. However, it should be recognised that on occasions the scheme will be insufficient to pay all depositors, and in those circumstances there are strong arguments that there should be a mechanism in place to make up any shortfall.

Implicit schemes exist where there is an assumption that deposits will be protected by governmental intervention in the event of bank failure.[33] There are various ways in which this may be carried out. For example, the government might make a payment directly to depositors, might arrange the transfer of deposits to a healthy bank, might promote the merger of the failing bank with a successful institution, or might inject public funds into the failing bank.[34] The main advantage of implicit schemes over explicit schemes is the flexibility that they offer. Governments can decide on a case by case basis whether to intervene. In addition, because there is no formal infrastructure in place, there are neither establishment nor operational costs *ex ante*. Despite these advantages, it is submitted that implicit schemes should be treated with some caution. While some costs are avoided by implicit schemes, funds will have to be raised at short notice. Furthermore, while an implicit scheme raises the expectation that depositors will be reimbursed, it remains only an expectation.[35] For example, the South African Reserve Bank states that in all cases where depositors' funds were either lost or likely to be lost, the Reserve Bank stepped in with the support of the Government to protect 'a substantial part' of the deposits. The Bank concludes by saying that: '[i]f recent history is anything to go by, this means that, to all intents and purposes, South Africa already has a form of implicit deposit insurance'.[36] The uncertainty that is created may lead depositors to withdraw their funds in fear that a decision will be made not to protect deposits. This will significantly reduce the effectiveness of an implicit scheme in maintaining confidence and avoiding systemic risk. Alternatively, the vagueness might lead consumers to believe that the Government was likely to protect even those with extremely large deposits. This could lead to moral hazard, with even substantial and sophisticated depositors being under little incentive to

---

[32] Provided that the protection is sufficiently high.

[33] See R MacDonald, *Deposit Insurance* (Handbooks in Central Banking, no 9) (Centre for Central Banking Studies, 1996) at 8.

[34] *Ibid* at 8–9.

[35] To that extent, there must be a question about whether it is correct to talk about this being a scheme at all. However, it is customary to use such terminology.

[36] 'The Bank Supervision Department' available at <http://www.reserve bank.co.za>.

take care. The FSCS is an explicit scheme. It sets out clearly in advance when a consumer will be able to make a claim on the fund. As such, it provides a high degree of certainty. It is suggested that this is an appropriate form of scheme.

Methods of Funding

A second question relating to the type of scheme is whether the scheme should be publicly or privately administered and funded. One possibility is for the government to set up an unconditional guarantee that all deposits will be repaid in full. This type of scheme provides significant confidence for the depositor and it has been argued that it might be beneficial where the commercial banking system is seriously under-capitalised.[37] However, 100 per cent guarantees raise the spectre of moral hazard, providing an incentive for risk taking by both depositors and management. Although it is argued that the moral hazard argument is sometimes over stated, it may counsel against 100 per cent protection for all depositors. At the other extreme, it would be possible for banks to organise private insurance without any input from the government. There are obvious advantages to private insurance.[38] First, the provider of the insurance would charge a premium based on the risk that the bank was deemed to present. As a result, high-risk activity would not be subsidised by careful activity, a charge that can be levelled where there is no form of risk-related premium. Secondly, any payout would be funded by the provider, for example an insurance company, rather than by the Government (thus saving public funds), or the banks (who may not be in a position to make a judgment about the failed institution in the same way as the insurer can). However, it is doubtful that private deposit protection is likely to be acceptable to stakeholders. *The Economist* has argued that 'the thought of underwriting banks' deposits fills most insurers with horror', and there may be doubts about the extent to which the insurance industry is willing, or even able, to take on this role.[39] There are several reasons for this. First, in many countries, the insurance industry will be less developed than the banking industry. Given the nature of bank runs, which are low probability but high cost, Goodhart concludes that 'the size of reserves necessary among private insurance agencies to provide a credible promise to meet all bank failures would be enormous and therefore extremely expensive to maintain'.[40] Secondly, in their attempts to relate premiums to risk

---

[37] MacDonald, above n 33, at 11.
[38] See Hall, above n 23 at 119.
[39] 'International Banking: Coping with the Ups and Downs' *The Economist* (27 April 1996) at 37.
[40] C Goodhart, 'Bank Insolvency and Deposit Insurance: A Proposal' in C Goodhart, *The Central Bank and the Financial System* (Basingstoke, MacMillan Press, 1995) at 86.

in an accurate manner, insurance companies would want full access to banks' books and to have control over the risks that banks assume. These are unlikely to be granted.[41] As is explained below, it may be possible to build some characteristics of private insurance into a deposit protection scheme, although that too raises considerable practical difficulties.

Most countries with deposit protection schemes avoid the two ends of the spectrum considered above. A common scheme is one that is publicly owned, established by the government, but administered by a special organisation which has been set up for this particular purpose and which is funded by the banks, with the possibility of further funding where necessary. This approach is taken in the UK and the USA. The organisation is public, but the funding is private. There is general support for the view that funding should be from the industry wherever possible. According to Hall: 'a fully privately funded scheme is to be preferred because it encourages bankers to keep their institutions sound and lays the costs on those (*i.e.* the banks) who benefit most from the scheme'.[42] The Financial Stability Forum (FSF) came to a similar view, arguing that banks should pay the cost of deposit insurance as they and their clients directly benefit from having such a system.[43] One difficulty presented by the creation of a single financial compensation scheme is that it must be carefully designed if there is not to be cross subsidy from one sector of the industry to another. The Deposit Guarantees Directive requires that funding must be provided by the credit institutions themselves and that the level of financing be proportionate to the liabilities of the scheme.[44] Under the Funding Rules, the FSCS is split into three sub-schemes, as discussed above, although there are contribution groups within those sub-schemes.[45] Firms carrying on different activities are allocated to different contribution groups. It is beyond the scope of this chapter to examine this in detail.[46] Suffice it to say that efforts have been made to avoid cross-subsidy where possible.

A further issue concerns the basis upon which funding is provided. It is possible to provide funding on an *ex ante* basis, where a fund is accumulated over time. Although this has the advantage that a fund is built up, there are concerns that this might lead to a reduction of capital from the banking system.[47] An alternative is to have a system of *ex post* funding,

---

[41] *Ibid*, at 85.
[42] Hall, above n 23, at 119.
[43] Financial Stability Forum, *Guidance for Developing Effective Deposit Insurance System* (September 2001). See also R Helfer, 'What Deposit Insurance Can and Cannot Do' (1999) (March) *Finance and Development* 22 at 22.
[44] See Deposit Guarantees Directive, above n 17, Recital 23.
[45] The Accepting Deposits sub-scheme covers only one contribution group.
[46] See COMP 13.

where banks make contributions after failures have occurred. Although this may improve market discipline by encouraging banks to monitor each other closely, it has the disadvantage that failed banks will not have contributed to the fund that tackles their failure. Moreover, as failures often occur where there is an economic downturn, this is liable to create difficulties for the banks that are asked to make a contribution.

An additional matter is whether deposit protection should be funded by risk adjusted, or flat rate, premiums. Flat rate premiums have the advantage of simplicity. However, they may lead to a form of cross subsidy, with low-risk banks subsidising high-risk banks. This is liable to generate moral hazard. Risk adjusted premiums address this by trying to ensure that the level of premium charged reflects the risk that the bank poses. In practice, however, determining the appropriate premium is generally a difficult and resource intensive task. As was considered above, this is one of the barriers to the provision of private deposit insurance. Although many commentators prefer the idea of risk-based premiums in theory, some argue that they are extremely difficult to set accurately in practice.[48] Goodhart argues that '[i]t is practically impossible to calculate banking risk *ex ante*, so deposit insurance premiums cannot be objectively related to risk'.[49] Indeed, as sources of risk take time to emerge, there is a lag before they are incorporated into the calculation of premiums. Goodman and Shaffer conclude therefore that this creates an incentive for banks to move towards new forms of potentially risky investments: '[l]ike a dog chasing its own tail, a risk-based premium would find itself always playing catch-up, in the process driving its goal ever more swiftly beyond its reach'.[50] Even if an accurate premium can be set, there is a reluctance to charge high premiums to high-risk banks as this has the potential to lead to their insolvency.[51]

Powers of the Scheme

A further question is that of how far the scheme's powers should extend. FSCS is an example of a relatively narrow scheme, responsible merely for the management of the fund and the payment of compensation. In other

---

[47] As contributions cannot be used for other purposes. See Financial Stability Forum, above n 43, at 26.

[48] Hall, above n 23, at 133. See also F Black and M Scholes, 'The Pricing of Options and Corporate Liabilities' (1973) 81 *Journal of Political Economy* 637, and RC Merton, 'An Analytical Derivation of the Cost of Deposit Insurance and Loan Guarantees: An Application of Modern Option Pricing Theory' (1977) 1 *Journal of Banking and Finance* 3.

[49] C Goodhart, above n 40, at 75

[50] LS Goodman and S Shaffer, 'The Economics of Deposit Insurance: A Critical Evaluation of Proposed Reforms' (Federal Reserve Bank of New York, Research Paper no 8308, 1983)

[51] Alternative approaches can be taken to such problem banks through the supervisory process. See Hanc, above n 29 at 12.

jurisdictions, powers include being a receiver of banks that have their licences withdrawn, and re-capitalising, liquidating, and selling failed banks.[52] For example, the Federal Deposit Insurance Corporation (FDIC) in the USA has a much wider role than the FSCS in the UK. There are concerns where deposit insurers are given wide-ranging powers, for example to act as an administrator or receiver. Where a deposit insurer acts as administrator of a bank, it may face conflicts of interest, for example between its own short-term financial interests, and the longer-term interests of the banking system.[53] Asser suggests that deposit insurance agencies with wide powers are unlikely to be trusted to the same extent as the judiciary to treat other creditors impartially.[54]

It is important that the powers of the deposit insurer are set out clearly, particularly *vis-a-vis* the regulator. In the UK there is a Memorandum of Understanding between the FSA and the FSCS. It is clear from this document that while the two bodies are operationally independent they 'need to co-operate and communicate constructively with each other in order to carry out their functions effectively'.[55] For example, the two bodies will share information, meet regularly, consult each other on draft statements, rules etc, and give each other warning of relevant issues.

Coverage of the Scheme

When deciding which types of deposits should be included or excluded, a number of policy issues arise. First, schemes will often try to exclude the deposits of those who are thought to be able to exert market discipline by ascertaining a bank's condition. Secondly, schemes will generally exclude deposits of those who bear some responsibility for a bank's failure. Under FSCS, deposits by banks and building societies, and deposits by large companies are excluded.[56] In addition, deposits of those connected with a criminal conviction for money laundering are excluded, as is required by the Directive.[57] Also excluded are deposits of a number of other persons, including directors and managers of defaulting firms, close relatives of such directors and managers, and persons who, in the opinion of the FSCS, have been responsible for, or have

---

[52] Similar wide powers are found in a number of jurisdictions including the USA and Japan. See Hall, above n 23 at 121.
[53] See T Asser, *Legal Aspects of Regulatory Treatment of Banks in Distress* (Washington, IMF, 2001) at 108–9.
[54] *Ibid*.
[55] FSCS and FSA Memorandum of Understanding, para 1.
[56] COMP 4.2.2 R.
[57] Directive 94/19/EC Art 2.

contributed to, the firm's default.[58] Deposits denominated in non-EEA currencies are now protected on the basis that the depositors making them are no more likely to be sophisticated than depositors holding sterling or other EEA currencies.[59]

Difficulties arise when deciding which deposits should be protected. In order to avoid a run, it is important that coverage is relatively generous. Although this might be thought of as increasing the potential for moral hazard, it can be justified on the basis of the need to ensure confidence in the financial system and avoid systemic risk. This is considered in detail below.

Levels of Compensation

Different limitations are placed on the amount of compensation payable depending on the type of business involved. For the purposes of this chapter, the main type of business is deposit-taking. Under the Rules, 100 per cent of the first £2,000 is protected, as is 90 per cent of the next £33,000. This means that the maximum payment is £31,700. The appropriateness of this is considered below.

DEPOSIT PROTECTION IN THE UK AND THE FINANCIAL SERVICES COMPENSATION SCHEME: A CRITIQUE

It is difficult to judge precisely how successful deposit protection has been in the UK, and to predict how successful the new regime is likely to be. If judged on the basis of how many banks have become insolvent, then its success would be high, as relatively few deposit-taking institutions have failed, and the UK's only systemic crisis since the introducing of deposit protection was minor, and was one about which depositor protection could do little.[60] Of course, it is difficult to know what impact the scheme has had in preventing potential failures, as banks might have continued in business even in the absence of deposit protection. It is perhaps easier to consider how effective depositor protection schemes are as a consumer protection measure.

---

[58] Directors and managers will be included if the defaulting firm is a mutual association, not a large firm or large partnership, and the directors and managers do not receive a salary or other remuneration performed by them for the defaulting firm.

[59] An approach previously taken to investments but not deposits.

[60] This followed the collapse of BCCI. See Hall, above n 23, at 130, and D Maude and W Perraudin, 'Pricing Deposit Insurance in the United Kingdom' Bank of England Working Paper 29, (1995). There have been far more failures in relation to investment business.

Deposit Protection and Market Discipline

It will be apparent from the above discussion that deposit protection schemes present difficulties for policy makers. Chief among these is the problem of providing sufficient protection to compensate the consumer adequately and avoid systemic risk, while at the same time limiting the likelihood of moral hazard. Perhaps inevitably, the result of this has been something of a compromise. In the European Union, this compromise has been reached in part through the creation of a co-insurance requirement. In this context, co-insurance means that consumers bear some of the cost of bank failure, by receiving only a proportion of their deposits from the fund. The current regime in the UK marks a departure from the previous approach by removing co-insurance, in part. Prior to FSMA, 90 per cent of the first £20,000 was protected, with no protection thereafter. This was subject to criticism, in particular because all consumers were subject to an element of co-insurance.[61] Now the Act protects 100 per cent of the first £2,000 and 90 per cent of the next £33,000. The move away from co-insurance is to be welcomed, but the level at which 100 per cent protection has been set must be questioned as too low. Indeed, it is possible to take issue with the whole notion of co-insurance. The Financial Services Consumer Panel comment that they dislike the term, as 'it assumes that consumers choose not to take care, or check the safety and soundness of a firm, because of the availability of compensation. We have seen no evidence of this'.[62]

The main justification for co-insurance is that it encourages consumers to take care by ensuring that they bear the cost of bank failure, at least in part. It is true that consumers who are fully protected will be under relatively little incentive to take care about where they place their savings, and will be under an incentive to look for the highest return.[63] By contrast, those liable to lose out in the event of a bank failing have incentives to choose institutions carefully and monitor their performance.[64] However, it is doubtful that consumers can be expected to take a great deal of care when deciding where to place their deposits. For consumers to make informed decisions about the risk posed by a bank, they need to have reliable information about that bank. They may be able to form a preliminary view of the bank's safety by its reputation, although this may

---

[61] See inter alia A Campbell and P Cartwright, above n 4; M Hall, above n 5; Financial Services Consumer Panel, *Response to FSA Consultation Paper 24* (September 1999).
[62] Financial Services Consumer Panel, *ibid* para 16. The Committee describes the notion of co-insurance as a 'misleading euphemism' and suggests that it be referred to as 'non-recoverable loss', para 4.
[63] Although they will face the transaction costs of establishing a claim should the firm become insolvent.
[64] Financial Stability Forum, above n 29 at 8–10.

not be a reliable indicator.[65] When it comes to more specific information, consumers are unlikely to have access to that information.[66] To make an informed choice, the consumer would need to know not only quantitative data such as the levels of capital held by the firm, but also qualitative data, such as the competence of the firm's management. Much information cannot be gleaned at all, and much that might be helpful to this end is not in the public domain for policy reasons. As the Financial Services Consumer Panel points out, this places consumers in an invidious position. 'On the one hand it is argued that they should act responsibly by assessing the risk posed by a financial institution, yet on the other hand they are denied information by the FSA on the basis that they might use it to act'.[67] Furthermore, many bank failures have resulted, not from incompetent management, but from dishonest management. As fraud tends to be clandestine by its very nature, no amount of disclosure will bring this to the attention of the consumer. So the first difficulty for the consumer is one of obtaining the information upon which to make an informed judgment.

Even if consumers were given access to the sort of information that is necessary in theory to make an informed decision about the risk that a firm poses, it is doubtful that many could act upon this in any meaningful way. From an economic perspective, it is understandable that we should want as much relevant information as possible to be in the marketplace. In the words of Mayes '[t]he public availability of meaningful information sufficient for people to make informed decisions about the likely standing of banks both individually and relatively is the keystone of market discipline'.[68] However, the information in question is likely to be both voluminous and complex, if it is available at all. Some jurisdictions have attempted to address the problems raised by information overload by endeavouring to disclose information in a user-friendly manner. For example, New Zealand requires banks to display a Key Information Summary prominently in every branch. This contains information which aims to be accessible to the average bank customer, but it is questionable whether it achieves this aim. In reality, few customers read the KIS, and it is doubtful to what extent those who do read it are capable of acting upon it in an informed manner.[69]

---

[65] Barings, for example, was widely regarded as a firm of the highest integrity and competence.
[66] Some of the economic literature concedes this point. According to Demirguc-Kunt and Detragiache 'it is very costly (and perhaps impossible) for depositors, especially small ones, to be effective monitors of banks', see *Does Deposit Insurance Increase Banking System Stability?* above n 16 at 25.
[67] Financial Services Consumer Panel, above n 62, para 17.
[68] D Mayes, above n 9 at 33.
[69] See ch 3.

Another difficulty for consumers is that if they are to take full responsibility for holding a bank to account through the mechanism of market discipline, they need not only to make a judgment about the bank at the time they open an account or place an investment, but also to continue to monitor its performance so long as they continue in a relationship with it. It is difficult enough for regulators to obtain the information they need to judge a bank's standing, let alone for consumers to do the same. One answer to this is to say that if there is a demand for user-friendly information, which it is assumed there would be in the absence of deposit protection, then it will be supplied by the market through ratings. Of course such firms have a role in rating banks, but the New Zealand experience shows how difficult it is to present that information in a user-friendly manner. The economies of scale present in charging the regulator with supervising banks is a major argument in favour of a formal regulatory regime which, it is submitted, it is rational for consumers to demand.[70]

A further difficulty with expecting consumers to take responsibility is that acting upon their discoveries is not cost-free. Even if we assume that consumers can discover the risks their banks pose at an early stage and decide to switch as a result, this may be costly. In relation to investment products, costs include front loading of charges, for mortgages there may be redemption penalties, and even for savings accounts there will be a loss of interest.[71] This is in addition to the transaction costs of switching. It seems likely that there are disincentives to consumers' taking action, and therefore limits to the extent that consumers are likely to be able to exert market discipline.[72]

As already mentioned, the second main justification for depositor protection is that it discourages consumers from withdrawing their funds at the first sign of an institution being in trouble. Herein lies an inherent difficulty. If consumers are to take responsibility for their actions, then that must mean taking responsibility by withdrawing their funds in the event that circumstances change for the worse. If enough customers identify the risk posed by the institution then the bank rapidly becomes illiquid and then insolvent. The consumers are acting precisely as the market suggests that they should. Indeed, the perfect market only functions where sufficient consumers express their disapproval with suppliers by withdrawing their custom.[73] But in so doing, they risk creating an externality—the collapse

---

[70] See D Llewellyn, The Economic Rationale for Financial Regulation (FSA Occasional Paper 1, April 1999) at 30–32.

[71] See Financial Services Consumer Panel, above n 62 para 20.

[72] Although it should be pointed out that it is not necessary for all consumers to act for markets to function efficiently.

[73] See ch 2.

of other banks whose position, or confidence, is adversely affected by the failure of the first bank. So long as this systemic failure remains a possibility, there will be an incentive upon states to have measures in place which deter it from taking effect. Financial regulation and measures of intervention such as lenders of last resort are examples of such measures, and deposit protection schemes are a third.

As mentioned in chapter two, not all commentators agree about the extent to which financial markets are subject to systemic risk in the sense that this term is traditionally understood. Benston and Kaufmann, for example, doubt the assumptions frequently made about the nature of systemic risk and financial contagion.[74] However, there can be little doubt that the fear of systemic risk will continue to provide a persuasive argument in favour of deposit protection. Greenspan argues that 'there is always a remote possibility of a chain reaction, a cascading sequence of defaults that will culminate in financial implosion if it is allowed to proceed unchecked'.[75] Indeed, the remoteness of the possibility of systemic risk is not necessarily an argument against deposit protection. Goodhart *et al* suggest that we should see regulation to avoid systemic risk (of which depositor protection forms a part) as 'an insurance premium against a low probability occurrence'.[76]

Deposit Protection and Public Awareness

One difficulty with the argument that deposit protection schemes work to increase confidence and therefore reduce the likelihood of systemic risk is that awareness of such schemes seems to be low. Although there are no data on the extent to which consumers are aware of deposit protection schemes, the Personal Investment Authority (PIA) found a low level of awareness of the investor compensation scheme.[77] Consumers will only be encouraged to leave their deposits in place if they are aware that they will receive compensation, and if that compensation is substantial (perhaps as high as 100 per cent).[78] Neither element appears to be present in

---

[74] See, for example, G Benston and G Kaufmann, 'The Appropriate Role of Bank Regulation' (1996) 106 *Economic Journal* 688. See also K Dowd, *Laissez-faire Banking* (London, Routledge, 1993).

[75] A Greenspan, 'Remarks at the VIIIth Frankfurt International Banking Evening' (Frankfurt, 1996), cited in C Goodhart *et al, Financial Regulation Regulation: Why, How and Where Now?* (London, Routledge, 1998) at 9.

[76] Goodhart *et al, ibid.*

[77] According to the Personal Investment Authority Consumer Panel, *Annual Report of 1996,* only 18% of consumers were aware that a compensation scheme for investors existed.

[78] Goodhart argued that 75% protection (that offered by the UK at the time of his writing) was too low, but that 100% protection was not necessary. C Goodhart, 'Bank Insolvency and Deposit Insurance', above n 40 at 91–92.

the UK. Consumers who are unaware of such schemes might assume that there is no protection.[79] This might be argued to reduce the likelihood of moral hazard, with depositors feeling a need to at least try to take care, but equally raises the possibility of systemic risk. The lack of awareness of deposit protection is a matter for concern. One of the FSA's statutory objectives is to promote public awareness and understanding of the financial system, and it is important that their attention is directed towards promoting understanding and awareness of the Financial Services Compensation Scheme.[80] However, it is submitted that even if consumers were aware of the protection provided by a deposit protection sub-scheme, this might not be sufficient to avoid systemic risk. Those consumers with £2,000 or less deposited will be refunded in full, and will be under little incentive to withdraw their funds, but many consumers have considerably larger deposits. For all those with deposits in excess of £2,000 the existence of co-insurance will provide them with some incentive to withdraw their deposits as soon as they can in order to protect the full amount. Otherwise they will have to bear some of the cost themselves. If sufficient consumers act in this way the bank will quickly become insolvent, and, depending on the effect that this has on confidence elsewhere, this may have systemic consequences.

Deposit Protection and Social Justice

If consumers cannot be expected to make informed decisions about the soundness of a bank, then arguments in favour of a higher level of protection may be strengthened. If consumers are unaware of the protection offered then this too must be addressed, particularly if this ignorance might lead consumers to initiate a run. These arguments can be justified on economic concepts of the need to avoid externalities and the need to recognise the existence of asymmetric information. But there are also social arguments in favour of providing a high degree of protection. The protection of 100 per cent of the first £2,000 in the current scheme is a step forward from the previous system where all consumers were subject to an element of co-insurance. However, it is submitted that £2,000 is too low a limit. If consumers are unable to make informed choices (as has been argued) then the question is whether, for policy reasons, we think they should receive protection. The role of deposit protection in the

---

[79] It is interesting that the FSCP argues that consumers who use a regulated firm are likely to assume that 100% of their money is protected. This must be questionable. It seems more likely that they will assume that even if a firm is regulated, this does not guarantee the firm's success, and that if the firm fails, their money is lost.
[80] See Financial Stability Forum, above n 29 at 29.

avoidance of systemic risk has already been discussed, but there are also social arguments in favour of a high level of compensation. Some of these are founded on the concept of distributive justice.

One argument in favour of depositor protection is that it is socially just to provide compensation for depositors, not just because they are unable to assess the safety of a firm, and therefore play their role in market discipline, but because bank deposits are special. Deposits are likely to be chosen by cautious, risk-averse consumers precisely because they are perceived to be the safest of investments. Whether this means that the Government should guarantee 100 per cent of deposits is questionable. Certainly, it is argued that governments should not guarantee the survival of a bank that is badly run, in the absence of evidence that it might cause a disruption to the financial system. Even where there is intervention, it is hoped that it will be in a form that ensures that the bank and its management take responsibility for their mistakes. But requiring depositors to bear the price of failure is questionable. They are internal to the bank, but given the problems that have been identified in their ability to monitor the bank's actions, there seems an argument for placing them in a special position.

Does Depositor Protection Induce Adverse Incentives for Bankers?

So far, we have examined the argument that deposit protection provides an incentive for consumers to take unwarranted risks and have questioned the assumptions upon which that argument is based. A further argument that is sometimes advanced is that deposit protection schemes provide an incentive for bankers to take such risks.[81] The rationale behind this contention is that management and shareholders will benefit if these risks prove fruitful, but will not bear the loss should they fail, as the deposit protection scheme will bear much of the loss. However, there are weaknesses to this line of thinking. First, deposit protection will generally not provide 100 per cent cover, and so most depositors will lose out to some extent should the bank fail. Secondly, most countries with deposit protection schemes exclude from those schemes certain depositors, including bank employees and those who were at fault in the bank's collapse. To the extent that they hold deposits, therefore, they will not be reimbursed. Thirdly, unlike lender of last resort facilities, deposit protection schemes do not act so as to save the bank should a crisis emerge. Therefore, if the risky strategies are not successful, the shareholders and employees of the

---

[81] For discussion see G Benston, 'Safety Nets and Moral Hazards in Banking' in K Sawamoto, Z Nakajima and H Taguchi (eds), *Financial Stability in a Changing Environment* (Bank of Japan, 1995) at 329.

banks will suffer in terms of losing their investments and their jobs. Furthermore, some regimes have the ability to hold decision-makers to account for losses incurred following wrongful or fraudulent trading, and this may even lead to disqualification from being able to hold the position of director. There will generally be incentives upon managers and directors to exercise some control. For example, they may be personally liable in some instances, and in any case face damage to their professional reputations where their judgment has contributed to a bank's failure. The combination of these factors should be enough to minimise the risk of moral hazard in the vast majority of cases.

CONCLUSIONS

Deposit protection schemes play an important role in banking regulation. First, they help to avoid systemic risk by reducing the incentive for consumers to initiate runs. Secondly, they provide a degree of consumer protection by guaranteeing a proportion of the consumer's deposit should the bank become insolvent. Such schemes can also aid the creation and functioning of trade areas such as the Single Market in Financial Services. The main risk that such schemes create is said to be that of moral hazard, and the principal mechanism for dealing with this is the imposition of co-insurance. Unfortunately, some of the arguments in favour of co-insurance make assumptions about the extent to which it is possible for consumers to make informed choices which cannot be justified in practice. If deposit protection schemes are to play an effective role in the avoidance of systemic risk and the protection of the consumer, it is important that they are appropriately designed and appropriately publicised. Only then will they meet their objectives fully.

8

Access to Banking Services

INTRODUCTION

R ECENT YEARS HAVE seen considerable debate about the extent
to which firms should be required to provide banking services at a
loss in the name of social justice, or financial inclusion.[1] In 1997 the
UK Government established the Social Exclusion Unit, which interpreted
social exclusion as involving 'what can happen when people or areas suffer from a combination of linked problems such as unemployment, poor
skills, low incomes, poor housing, high crime environments, bad health,
poverty and family breakdown'.[2] One element of social exclusion is financial exclusion, where consumers are excluded, in practice, from mainstream financial services. Several recent initiatives have considered the
subject of financial exclusion. HM Treasury set up a Policy Action Team
whose report (hereafter PAT 14), focused on access to financial services.[3]
Prior to this, the Director General of Fair Trading's inquiry *Vulnerable
Consumers and Financial Services* had issues relating to access and exclusion
close to its heart.[4] Other initiatives, such as the Cruickshank Committee's
investigation into the competitiveness of the banking industry, and the
Sandler Committee on the competitiveness of the retail savings industry
also paid attention to the topic.[5] A considerable quantity of helpful

---

[1] There is now a wealth of literature on this topic. The literature is drawn together skilfully
in Financial Services Authority, *In or Out? Financial Exclusion: A Literature and Research Review*
(London, FSA, July, 2000) (hereafter *In or Out?*).
[2] <http://www.socialexclusionunit.gov.uk>.
[3] Policy Action Task Force, *Access to Financial Services*, (HM Treasury, November 1999) (hereafter PAT 14).
[4] Director General of Fair Trading, *Vulnerable Consumers and Financial Services* (OFT,
January 1999).
[5] The terms of reference of Cruickshank were: to examine the banking industry in the UK
(excluding investment banking); to examine levels of innovation, competition and efficiency
in various sub-markets, including relationships with small and medium sized businesses; to
look at how these compare with international standards; and to consider options for change.
The Committee saw part of its role as considering whether increased competition would
'ensure an adequate supply of basic banking services to low income customers'
HM Treasury, *Competition in UK Banking: A Report to the Chancellor of the Exchequer* (the
Cruickshank Report), 20 March 2000 (hereafter 'the Cruickshank Report'), (Executive
Summary para 63). The Sandler Committee was given a remit to 'identify the competitive

research has also emerged from the work of the Personal Finance Research Group at the University of Bristol.[6] Access to financial services is one topic upon which there is no paucity of literature.

This chapter examines how the problem of lack of access to banking services can be tackled. It considers the types of such services that are most essential to consumers, and looks at whether the industry is under sufficient incentives to provide them. It also examines whether the special position of banks in society could justify the state putting obligations upon banks to provide services or products to consumers which they would not provide on a simple economic basis. The issues of access and inclusion have implications for many academic disciplines. The Office of Fair Trading's Head of Consumer Economics, has recognised that 'too often, attention has been focused on those who currently consume, and those who are excluded have been forgotten'.[7] This is an area where social, economic and legal perspectives all have a role in setting the debate, as well as trying to resolve it.

THE DIMENSIONS OF FINANCIAL EXCLUSION

Much of the literature on financial exclusion concentrates on geographical and similar physical factors.[8] The most conspicuous, and most investigated, example of such exclusion has been the movement away from branch banking, caused in part by branch closures. By the end of 1998 there were 14,904 branches of banks and building societies in Britain, 5679 fewer than 10 years previously.[9] Poorer communities appear to have suffered disproportionately here. Access may also be limited in a physical sense because of consumers' inability to shop around, for example because they lack a computer, car or telephone, or because they suffer from a physical disability. Kempson and Whyley take the topic further by

---

forces that drive the industries concerned [those concerned with retail savings], in particular in relation to their approaches to investment and, where necessary, to suggest policy responses to ensure that consumers are well served.' (Press Release 18 June 2001).

[6] See <http://www.ggy.bris.ac.uk/research/pfrc>.

[7] Quoted in M Hewitt, 'Left Out in the Cold' (1999) 22 *Fair Trading*, 12 at 13–14.

[8] See in particular the work of Andrew Leyshon and Nigel Thrift. Their publications in this area include: 'Access to Financial Services and Financial Infrastructure Withdrawal—Problems and Policies' (1994) 26 *Area* 268; 'Financial Exclusion and the Shifting Boundaries of the Financial System' (1996) 28 *Environment and Planning A* 1150 and *Money/Space* (London, Routledge, 1997).

[9] E Kempson and T Jones, *Banking Without Branches* (London, BBA, 2000). Similar developments have taken place in other jurisdictions. Avery *et al* found that the number of bank branches in low-income communities fell by 21% from 1975 to 1995 while the number of branches increased overall by 29%. See R A Avery, R W Bostic, P S Calem and G B Canner, 'Changes in the Distribution of Banking Offices' (1997) 83 *Federal Reserve Bulletin* 707.

identifying five other 'dimensions' of financial exclusion.[10] First, there is access exclusion, where consumers have their access to financial services restricted through the process of risk assessment, something that firms can measure more accurately than ever before. Secondly there is condition exclusion, where conditions are attached to products which make them inappropriate for the needs of some people. This is a particular problem where savings products are concerned. Third is price exclusion, where consumers cannot afford the prices charged for financial products.[11] One result of improved risk assessment mentioned above has been an increasing ability to offer consumers tailor-made financial products and to reflect risk in the price demanded. High-value customers have increasingly been cherry-picked and offered products on better terms than their less profitable counterparts. This may lead to consumers having access to a product, but on terms less favourable than those offered to high-value consumers. This has always been the case in relation to insurance, and leads to the unfortunate social outcome that, in the words of Burchardt and Hills '[t]hose most in need of insurance and least able to self-insure are likely to be those least able to afford highly differentiated premiums'.[12] Fourth is marketing exclusion where targeted marketing and sales exclude certain consumers. Some consumers therefore do not get access to information about financial services because providers do not see it as worthwhile to court their custom.[13] Although consumers complain frequently about receiving too much information by way of marketing, it can play an important role in bringing information to the attention of consumers. Finally, the authors point to self-exclusion, where people do not apply for financial products because they believe that they will be refused.

Having considered the dimensions of financial exclusion, it is also important to consider the effects of such exclusion. In extreme cases, exclusion may mean no choice. More likely it will mean limited choice, in particular a choice of inappropriate products. Where bank accounts are not available, money may be kept in a vulnerable position in the home, cash may be the only means of payment, and cheque cashers may be called upon to provide payment services. There will also be difficulties

---

[10] E Kempson and C Whyley, *Kept Out or Opted Out? Understanding and Combating Financial Exclusion* (Bristol, Policy Press, 1999). E Kempson and C Whyley, 'Understanding and Combating Financial Exclusion' (1999) 21 *Insurance Trends* 18. Financial Services Authority, *In or Out?* above n 1, para 1.17.

[11] See R Vaughan, Distributional Issues in Welfare Assessment and Consumer Affairs Policy (London, OFT, 1999).

[12] T Burchardt and J Hills, 'Financial Services and Social Exclusion' (1998) 18 *Insurance Trends* 1, cited in *In or Out?* above n 1, para 2.48.

[13] N Thrift and A Leyshon, 'Financial Desertification' in J Rossiter (ed), *Financial Exclusion: Can Mutuality Fill the Gap?* (London, New Policy Institute, 1997).

where consumers have access to bank accounts with limited facilities, for example those accounts that do not allow direct debits to be made. Where credit is concerned, exclusion from mainstream providers means in practice a choice of high-cost credit from alternative providers. In relation to credit, financial exclusion unquestionably leads to the poor paying more.

SOCIAL RESPONSIBILITIES AND BANKING SERVICES

One important issue to consider is whether the special nature and importance of banking justifies the imposition of an obligation to provide certain suitable banking services and products to consumers.[14]

In some cases absence of choice may raise questions about fair competition, and it might be appropriate for competition authorities to take action.[15] Where absence of choice results, not from inadequate competition, but from a competitive financial services industry taking an economic decision only to offer more profitable products, there are difficult issues to address about the respective obligations of the industry and the state. The extent to which financial services providers should be obliged to take on loss-making business in order to fulfil social justice objectives is a matter for fierce debate. In April 2000 the Economic Secretary to the Treasury made it clear that she regarded banks as having 'a responsibility to ensure that everyone has access to their services'.[16] Others commentators too have made reference to banks' 'social obligation to the public, as well as whatever they owe to their shareholders'.[17] A contrasting approach has been taken by Tim Sweeney, a former Director General of the British Bankers' Association. He bemoaned the lack of debate about what social responsibility means for banks, and has suggested that 'there is no shared language or shared view of the world' between the UK government and banks.[18] Certainly, it appears that the Government has put pressure upon the banks to offer 'basic accounts', for which the banks have argued that they will receive little economic benefit. As Sweeney puts it: 'banks are not public utilities, they are rational economic units, and can only be

---

[14] I refer to these obligations as social responsibilities. As will become apparent, social responsibilities involve more than merely ensuring access.

[15] Not that competition law will necessarily provide a solution. PricewaterhouseCoopers has argued that '[a] very aggressive competition policy and social exclusion are mutually exclusive'. PWC 'The Breaking Wave' February 2000, cited in British Bankers' Association, 'Promoting Financial Inclusion—the Work of the Banking Industry' (April, 2000) at 1.

[16] M Johnson, 'Speech by the Economic Secretary to the Treasury to the Conference on Tackling Financial Exclusion' 12 April 2000.

[17] Sir Peter Kemp, 'Why Don't the Banks Like the Universal Bank?' 2000 *Source Public Management Journal* available at <http://www.sourceuk.net/articles>.

[18] T Sweeney, 'The Death of Banking', 26 March 2001, (BBA) available at <http://www.bba.org.uk>.

drawn seamlessly and easily into an approach which somehow meshes with their underlying business instincts'.[19] This reflects the traditional free market orthodoxy on the duties of corporations. Milton Friedman's famous observation that the social responsibility of business is to increase its profits is often cited.[20] There may even be a legal basis for this approach. Gower is quoted as having argued that 'directors who subordinate the long term interest of shareholders to those of the consumers, the nation and the employees, are likely to fall foul of the law'.[21] However, it seems that company law has moved some way from that approach, and it may also be that further movements will take place. Schedule 2 of the White Paper *Modernising Company Law* provides that a director must act is a way he decides, in good faith, would be most likely to promote the success of the company for the benefit of its members as a whole.[22] In deciding what would be most likely to promote that success, the director must take account, in good faith, of all the material factors that it is practicable in the circumstances for him to identify. Those material factors include, inter alia, (a) the company's need to foster its business relationships, including those with its employees and suppliers and the customers for its products and services; (b) its need to have regard to the impact of its operations on the communities affected and on the environment; and (c) its need to maintain a reputation for high standards of business conduct. This, in the language of the Company Law Review, is the 'enlightened shareholder value' approach.[23] However, when it comes to enforcement, it is difficult to see what impact the proposed changes are likely to have. The primary duty is still to act in the best interests of the company, but in so doing to take other interests into account. As Davies observes: '[t]he theory is that it is in the interests of the members that the interests of stakeholder groups should be taken into account, and the duty to do so, accordingly, is owed to the company'.[24] The stakeholders themselves will have no right to redress, and it seems unlikely that the members will be keen to litigate. In any event, it is likely to be difficult in practice for members to prove that no consideration was given to a relevant matter.[25] When a bank takes a decision which adversely affects groups of consumers, communities or

---

[19] *Ibid.*

[20] M Friedman, *Capitalism and Freedom* (Chicago, Chicago University Press, 1962).

[21] LCB Gower quoted in G Goyder, *The Responsible Company* (Oxford, Blackwell, 1961) at 20. However, this does not truly reflect the legal position. See J Parkinson, 'The Socially Responsible Company' in MK Addo (ed), *Human Rights and the Responsibility of Transanational Corporations* (Dordrecht, Kluwer Law International, 1999) 49.

[22] Department of Trade and Industry, *Modernising Company Law* (Cm 5553–1, July 2002) sch 2.

[23] Company Law Review, *Modern Company Law for a Competitive Economy: The Strategic Framework* (February 1999) ch 5.1.

[24] PL Davies, *Gower and Davies' Principles of Modern Company Law*, 7th edn (London, Sweet and Maxwell, 2003) at 378.

[25] See also the proposals for disclosure under the operating and financial review discussed below.

employees, but in the judgment of the directors is in the commercial interests of the bank, it is unrealistic to expect it to be challenged.

Attempts have been made to persuade banks that it is in their long-term business interests to take on apparently uneconomic business, but this has been treated with some scepticism.[26] However, it should be noted that the Government has not given out an entirely unambiguous message. PAT 14 argued that one of the principles that underpinned the Government's vision was non-compulsion. This means not only that people should not be compelled to have bank accounts if they do not want them, but that 'banks' selection of which sections of the market to serve should be left to their commercial judgement'.[27] In practice there appears to be some pressure upon banks to offer basic bank accounts, and there is certainly pressure upon consumers to have accounts which enable them to receive payments.[28]

A justification for the imposition of duties upon banks to provide services when they deem it not in their commercial interests to do so can be found in work of Wilhelmsson. In an important essay, Wilhelmsson examines justifications for imposing duties on corporations that provide services of general interest.[29] It has been argued that there are certain services that 'are considered to be necessary for a "decent life" in modern society'.[30] Wilhelmsson argues that such services have the following features: the service fulfils a basic need for its users; there is often not any reasonable alternative to the service; there are few producers of the service; and the service is based on a long-term relationship. Where such a service is provided by the private sector, Wilhelmsson suggests that there are strong arguments why it is acceptable to put special obligations on the providers of such services, and suggests ways in which this might be done. It is worth considering these issues in more detail. First, however, it is helpful to consider whether banking services fall within this categorisation.

Wilhelmsson accepts that financial services generally differ from those services normally thought of as 'essential' because citizens have not normally expected the state to provide them. In this way, they contrast with public utilities such as fuel, water and telephone services. In those cases there is recognition of a right to access, which Graham

---

[26] T Sweeney, above n 18. It could be said that the rationale behind the White Paper's approach to enlightened shareholder value is that it is in the interests of the company that directors have regard to the stakeholder interests set out.

[27] PAT 14, above n 3 para 4.2.

[28] In particular because of the Government's policy that benefits should be paid by automated credit transfer.

[29] T Wilhelmsson,'Services of General Interest and European Private Law' in C Rickett and T Telfer (eds) *International Perspectives on Consumers' Access to Justice* (Cambridge, Cambridge University Press, 2003) 149.

[30] *Ibid* at 153. See also C Scott, 'Services of General Interest in EC Law: Matching Values to Regulatory Technique in the Public and Privatised Sectors' (2000) 6(4) *European Law Journal* 310.

describes as 'a freedom to claim a supply without discrimination'.[31] However, Wilhelmsson argues that some financial services, such as payment services operated through accounts and credit cards can be treated as 'social rights' in same way as services provided by traditional public utilities.[32] Domont-Naert argues similarly that '[f]inancial services should be considered as an essential requirement in order to live in a decent way, recognised by international texts'.[33] At several points in his work, Wilhelmsson makes it clear that he regards (some) banking services as falling within the category of services of general interest, and so relevant to this obligation.

Next it is helpful to consider the basis upon which the imposition of social obligations can be justified. The principal bases identified by Wilhelmsson are legitimate expectations and corporate responsibility. Wilhelmsson argues that because large corporations have significant economic power, and generate trust on the part of the consumer, this can be used to justify a call for greater responsibility. In a slightly different context, Ramsay has noted the great emphasis that some corporations place on the issue of trust:

> many financial institutions stress the importance of the relationship of trust and confidence which they wish to develop with consumers and this is part of their advertising image ... It does not seem far fetched to argue that these images and stories may raise consumer expectations that they will be treated fairly.[34]

Just as their stressing of trust and confidence may allow us to impose stringent duties on financial institutions not to mislead so, we might argue, does it justify our requiring duties to provide fair access. Secondly, Wilhelmsson points out that corporations can arrange for loss to be borne by a large number of consumers through the price mechanism. As he puts it: '[t]he losses caused by the responsibility to take into account the special needs of some consumers can be borne by the consumer collective through (usually modest) price increases'.[35] This is an element of distributive justice, a well-known non-economic rationale for regulation which is discussed in chapter two. A final element to the corporate responsibility justification is the principle that corporations should bear responsibility for the problems that they cause. For example, Wilhelmsson argues that if

---

[31] C Graham, *Regulating Public Utilities: A Constitutional Approach* (Oxford, Hart Publishing, 2000) 100. In telecommunications it is customary to refer to this as a universal service obligations.
[32] Wilhelmsson, above n 29 at 154.
[33] F Domont-Naert, 'The Right to Basic Financial Services: Opening the Discussion' (2000) *Consumer Law Journal* 63 at 66.
[34] I Ramsay, *Advertising, Culture and the Law* (London, Sweet and Maxwell, 1996) at 18.
[35] Wilhelmsson, above n 29 at 157.

the credit card society causes problems for those excluded then 'the finance companies, which have made this development possible, should take some responsibility for solving the problems'. This echoes the principle of trying to internalise externalities.[36]

There is an important additional argument, which is not considered by Wilhelmsson. This is that banks command a privileged position, and that the *quid pro quo* for that privilege is social responsibility.[37] This may be most obvious in relation to large banks who can be said to be operating under a state guarantee as they are 'too big to fail.' This means that banks will not be allowed to become insolvent where that might lead to the insolvency of other banks and, potentially, the collapse of the banking system. There is certainly a widespread feeling that states will not allow their national banks to be liquidated.[38] It is difficult to say with any degree of certainty which banks are too big to fail, although the major high street banks will undoubtedly be included. The Financial Services Authority (FSA) emphasises that a zero failure regime is neither possible nor desirable, but this does not mean that failing banks will never be saved. If a bank is so influential in the markets that its failure is likely to lead to a collapse in market confidence then the regulator is likely to step in.[39] However, given that smaller banks are not subject to this implied guarantee, there could be seen to be less justification for imposing social obligations on them.

In relation to legitimate expectations, Wilhelmsson argues that consumers might have a legitimate expectation that certain needs will be met. However, it is submitted that the notion of legitimate expectations as it relates to consumer law was developed in a different context.[40] As Howells and Wilhelmsson say:

> [t]he idea that lies behind this [the concept of legitimate expectations] is that consumers purchasing anywhere in the Community should expect goods and services to be of a quality and safety which they are entitled to expect and contract terms should not surprise them.[41]

This is different from arguing that consumers should have access to such services. It might be argued that consumers have legitimate expectations

---

[36] This approach is well known in environmental law through the 'polluter pays' principle.
[37] I am grateful to Professor Andrew Leyshon for discussions on this matter.
[38] Indeed, the Federal Deposit Insurance Corporation (FDIC) in the USA has explicitly recognised that large banks will not be allowed to fail. See C Goodhart, *The Central Bank and the Financial System* (Basingstoke, MacMillan, 1995) ch 17.
[39] Financial Services Authority, *A New Regulator for the New Millennium* (FSA, January 2000).
[40] The concept was developed in particular by Hans Micklitz. See H-W Micklitz, 'Principles of Justice Within the European Union' in E Paasivirta and K Rissanen (eds), *Principles of Justice and the Law of the European Union* (Helsinki, Helsinki University Institute of International Economic Law, 1995).
[41] G Howells and T Wilhelmsson, *EC Consumer Law* (Aldershot: Dartmouth, 1997) at 320.

that certain services will be provided for them. However, while this might cover public utilities it is questionable that this would extend to banking products.

Having identified the justifications for imposing social responsibilities on certain corporations, Wilhelmsson looks at two principles that illustrate how this might work in practice. First he refers to the principle of non-discrimination and access to service. This is, of course central to our discussion. Referring to banks as 'private actors with social functions', Wilhelmsson argues that 'weak consumers should receive services equally as easily as those who are better off'.[42] He sees this as an element of principles against discrimination, and gives examples of how discrimination can be evidence of unfair practices that give the courts the power to adjust the contract.[43] However, Wilhelmsson recognises that this would not extend to what might be called 'the poor pay more syndrome' because different treatment based only on variations in risk or costs seems to be accepted. This is crucial. It is clear that there are areas of essential services where the poor pay more. One obvious example is in relation to fuel bills, where, rather than disconnect consumers, firms will supply them with pre-payment meters which, as well as being more expensive than other forms of supply, are calibrated to recover debts accrued.[44] In relation to banking this is also an issue. The most obvious example is in relation to credit, which is discussed below. Because there are genuine financial reasons for charging poorer consumers more, it might appear difficult to see how this can be challenged. However, there are areas where this is done for reasons of public policy. It is most obvious in relation to services such as waste disposal, telecommunications etc where charges are not directly related to cost. However, the same logic has been applied in relation to financial services. Recent discussion about forbidding gender discrimination in relation to insurance is perhaps the best example. Although there appear to be legitimate actuarial data to explain the differential payments made to men and women on retirement, this has been argued not to be sufficient to justify those differentials.[45]

Secondly, Wilhelmsson looks at arguments for giving special treatment to the more weak or vulnerable. He argues that 'financial institutions, as well as other actors performing services of general interest to the

---

[42] Wilhelmsson, above n 29 at 163.
[43] *Ibid.*
[44] C Graham, above n 31 at 101.
[45] The Sex Discrimination Act 1975 s 45 provides that insurance companies can discriminate on grounds of sex if the discrimination is based upon actuarial data upon which it is reasonable to rely. Bodies such as the Equal Opportunities Commission have recommended that this should be changed and replaced by unisex actuarial factors. See <http://www.eoc.org.uk>. This is particularly topical following the European Commission's proposals for a directive implementing the principle of equal treatment between men and women in access to and supply of goods and services.

consumers may, to some extent, be made responsible for the economic welfare of their clients'. He gives the example of consumer bankruptcy schemes which, he argues, 'could be described as the kind of (partial) private responsibility of the creditor(s) for the social security of the debtor'.[46] More specifically, he examines social *force majeure* schemes. Such schemes in Nordic law provide protection for those consumers who, through no fault of their own, find themselves unable to meet their liabilities.[47] The two examples mentioned here are closely related. What is being proposed is essentially a redistribution from one group to another, whether the policy is expressed as non-discrimination or giving special treatment to the more vulnerable. Of course, a good deal of regulation involves such redistribution, and the question is normally one of when and to what extent redistribution is justified. Given that redistribution is inevitable in regulation, the question becomes primarily one of policy.[48] It is perhaps most appropriate to ask the simple question: as a matter of policy, is it desirable for banks to be under an obligation to provide appropriate services to all consumers? Strong arguments have been made that it is important for regulators to take social factors more fully into account. When discussions were taking place about the scope of consumer protection in the statutory objectives in FSMA, there was some support for more explicit social objectives to be included. This came from the House of Commons Treasury Select Committee, and also the National Consumer Council, who suggested that reference be made to: 'the need for reasonable access to financial services for those who have difficulty in getting access to products appropriate to their needs'.[49] Ultimately it was decided that this would create too many difficulties for the regulator, particularly when considering the other statutory objectives contained within FSMA.[50]

It will be apparent from the above discussion that it is possible to argue that it is legitimate to put social obligations on banks although the precise justification for such an imposition is a matter for debate. If we accept in principle that it may be appropriate to impose such an obligation, the next

---

[46] Wilhelmsson, above n 29 at 164.

[47] See T Wilhelmsson, ' "Social Force Majeure"—A New Concept in Nordic Consumer Law' (1990) 13 *Journal of Consumer Policy* 1.

[48] Although it is accepted that it is possible to talk about the topic on the basis of socio-economic rights. See inter alia the works of A Gewirth such as *Human Rights* (Chicago, Chicago University Press, 1982), and 'Economic Rights' in G R Lucas (ed) *Poverty, Justice and the Law* (London, University Press of America, 1986). These are discussed in Graham, above n 31 at 134–36. An excellent discussion of the literature can be found in M Seneviratne, 'The Case for Economic and Social Rights' in D Campbell and N Douglas Lewis, *Promoting Participation: Law or Politics?* (London, Cavendish, 1999) 267.

[49] Cited in M Taylor 'Accountability and Objectives of the FSA' in M Blair *et al*, *Blackstone's Guide to the Financial Services and Markets Act 2000* (London, Blackstone Press, 2001) at 33.

[50] Those objectives are market confidence, consumer protection, public awareness and the reduction of financial crime. See FSMA s 2(2).

question to consider is how far as matter of policy this should extend. It seems both unrealistic and undesirable to expect banks to offer all services to all consumers. Nevertheless, we may be able to identify certain services that are so important to consumers that it is appropriate to oblige banks to provide them regardless of their own economic judgment. It is to this issue of 'essential' financial services that we now turn. As will be seen, while there has been pressure on banks to provide some essential services, this has been relatively limited.

THE SCOPE OF ESSENTIAL BANKING SERVICES

To some extent, limited choice will be inevitable. Indeed, it is desirable that banks do not attempt to sell inappropriate products to consumers. There has recently been an increasing recognition of the importance of responsible lending, where providers are encouraged, or required, to take steps to ensure that borrowers are likely to be able to repay the loan in question.[51] However, there may be some circumstances where financial products can be seen as necessities, and where consumers' exclusion from those products is a matter for considerable concern. The Director General of Fair Trading has argued that there are four financial services that most consumers are likely to regard as essential: cash transmission and banking; insurance; short-term consumer credit and long-term savings.[52] It is recognised that there may be an overlap between these. For example, money transmission services are difficult to undertake without a bank account, and such an account may be a gateway to other financial services.[53] As the Financial Services Consumer Panel has correctly noted, financial exclusion is a complex issue and has a number of possible dimensions, including not only access to products and services, but also awareness of what is available, and the suitability of such products and services for the most vulnerable.[54] The following section looks at the principal essential financial services identified by the Director General of Fair Trading's

---

[51] See *Report by the Task Force on Tackling Overindebtedness* (London, DTI, July 2001) paras 4.17–4.25, which examines the extent to which there are core principles of good lending practice. The concept is also mentioned in the proposed new consumer credit directive (2002/0222 COM 2002 443, 11 September 2002).

[52] Above n 4, para 302. Domont-Naert suggested that essential financial services were: banks accounts; payment means; credit; insurance and protection against overindebtedness. It is difficult to see the final example as being a financial service, although protection is certainly important to consumers. F Domont-Naert, above n 32 at 67–69. A former President of the British Bankers Association suggested that mortgages might also be viewed as 'essential requirements'. Andrew Buxton, 'Financial Services: Serving the Community?' speech to the Chartered Institute of Bankers 19 January 1999.

[53] Above n 4 para 302.

[54] Financial Services Consumer Panel, *Response to HM Treasury's Financial Services Policy Action Team Consultation on Financial Exclusion,* (24, March 1999) para 3.

Report, and considers how problems of access and exclusion might best be tackled. The section concentrates on cash transmission and banking, but also includes some discussion of credit in recognition of the importance of this to the modern bank, and the consumer.[55]

ENSURING ACCESS AND LIMITING EXCLUSION

Cash Transmission and Banking

Creating New Products: The Basic Bank Account

An important element in the battle against social exclusion is the basic bank account.[56] It has already been noted that lack of access to money transmission presents significant difficulties for consumers. As cash transactions can sometimes be more expensive than others, for example in relation to the paying of bills, those without access to a bank account may be classic examples of the poor who pay more.[57] Gas consumers who settled their bills by direct debit were found to have paid on average 12 per cent less than those who used pre-payment meters and 7 per cent less that those who paid by quarterly bill.[58] Furthermore, automated payments facilitate spreading payments and so budgeting, something of particular importance to the less affluent. As Cruickshank noted, even the cashing of a personal cheque may be difficult and expensive without a bank account. There are also some products that cannot be purchased by cash. The Joseph Rowntree Foundation Study *Kept Out or Opted Out?* identified day to day money management as one of the main areas of unmet need for financial services.[59]

The Cruickshank Report suggested that to participate fully in the economy, a consumer would need access to banking services which are able to: receive electronic credits; make electronic payments; deposit cash or cheques; and obtain cash from automated teller machines (ATMs) or use retail cash back facilities.[60] Prior to this The Director General's Inquiry into *Vulnerable Consumers and Financial Services* had argued that there was

---

[55] Insurance and investments are excluded as falling outside what can generally be described as banking products, although it is recognised that even here, banks may play a part.
[56] Also known as the introductory or starter account. In the United States, some states have introduced legislation to require banks to offer what are known as 'first', 'basic' or 'lifeline' accounts. These share many characteristics with basic bank accounts in the UK. See Financial Services Authority, *In or Out?* above n 1 para 6.42.
[57] See D Caplovitz, *The Poor Pay More: Consumer Practices of Low Income Families* (New York, Free Press, 1963).
[58] Above n 4 para 305.
[59] E Kempson and C Whyley, above n 10 at 41.
[60] Cruickshank, above n 5 para 7.6.

'a need for an account which would help consumers to manage modest resources on a tight budget'.[61] It recommended that banks and building societies offer access to a basic, on-line, low cost current account on which it is not possible to incur high charges for unauthorised credit. This would involve bank accounts being 'unbundled' from credit facilities.[62] These should be offered through post offices and other retailers.[63] The Report also suggested that 'the potential for post office automation, including any developments to enable electronic payment of social security, to provide on line, low cost current accounts be examined'.[64] Of course there have been developments since then, not least in the area of technology. According to the Banking Code Standards Board, a basic bank account will usually have the following features: employers can pay income directly into the account; the Government can pay pensions, tax credits and benefits directly into the account; cheques and cash can be paid into the account; bills can be paid by direct debit, by transferring money to another account or by payment to a linked account; cash can be withdrawn at ATMs; there is no overdraft facility, and the last penny in the account can be withdrawn.[65]

It appears that the major banks have made some limited inroads into addressing the needs of the more vulnerable by the creation of basic bank accounts.[66] However, the four largest clearing banks have 14 per cent of the market share for basic accounts, compared with 68 per cent of the market for current accounts. It seems likely that they are not making enormous efforts to improve their market share. One matter of some concern is that the major banks are failing to market their basic bank accounts with the enthusiasm with which they market their other products, and doing little even to alert consumers to their availability. Section 3.1 of the Banking Code states: 'before you become a customer, we will…give you information on a basic bank account if we offer one and it would appear to meet your needs'. The Financial Services Consumer Panel commissioned research to discover whether those for whom basic bank accounts were intended were able to open them and whether those who expressed an interest in opening an account were offered information about basic bank accounts. The Panel found that when the consumer expressed concerns at the risk of debt or becoming overdrawn only one bank referred to information about basic bank accounts. That was also the only bank

---

[61] Above n 4 para 703.

[62] Quoted in M Hewitt 'Left Out in the Cold' (1999) 22 *Fair Trading* 12 at 14.

[63] There has been some scepticism about whether allowing retailers such as supermarkets to provide bank accounts would assist inclusion. See *In or Out?* above n 1 at para 7.8.

[64] *Vulnerable Consumers*, n 4 para 705.

[65] Banking Code Standards Board, *Survey of Subscriber Institutions on Basic Bank Accounts* (July 2003) at 8.

[66] Above n 60, ch 7.

whose leaflets contained prominent information about basic bank accounts.[67] When consumers tried to open accounts none was told about basic bank accounts, despite the fact that in several cases the consumer had expressed concern about becoming overdrawn. The House of Commons Treasury Committee concluded that 'banks need to engage in more proactive and innovative marketing if they are to be taken seriously on their expressed commitment to overcome financial exclusion'.[68] The BBA has questioned the accuracy of the Panel's research because of its small sample size.[69] It has also restated its commitment to tackling financial exclusion. At the same time, the BBA has made it clear that there will be difficulties in making the basic bank account cost effective. Data that the BBA received from banks in 1998 suggested that it could cost up to £80 per customer to set up a basic bank account and around £70 a year to maintain it.[70]

It should be noted that steps have been taken to make basic bank accounts more visible and that progress appears to have been made since the Financial Services Consumer Panel published the results of its research. Research for the Banking Code Standards Board found that banks had improved in relation to the information that they made available on basic bank accounts. Awareness of the product increased between 2002 and 2003 both for staff and potential customers. However, significant concerns remain. In particular, market research conducted through mystery shopping found that the correct basic bank account was only recommended in 50 per cent of cases.[71]

The basic bank account is connected with the creation of 'Universal Banking'. 'The Universal Bank' was conceived to provide banking services to those who find it difficult to access traditional bank accounts because of their poor credit history. In May 2001 the Government stated that it had reached agreement on the provision of universal banking services with the UK's leading banks and building societies. Customers will now be able to take advantage of the Post Office's 17,000 branches either through a new post office card account or one of the contributing institutions basic bank accounts. The creation of such a facility is particularly important as the Government has announced its determination that welfare payments should be made electronically wherever possible, something that it is estimated will save the taxpayer £600 million

---

[67] Financial Services Consumer Panel, *Basic Banking Research: Summary of Key Findings* (Spring, 2002). The Report was prepared for the FSCP by Saville Rossiter Base.
[68] House of Commons Treasury Select Committee, *Banking, Consumers, and Small Businesses,* 5th Report of Session 2001–02, *Hansard* HC 818–I 30 July 2002, **para 8.**
[69] British Bankers, Association Press Notice, 'Response to the Financial Services Consumer Panel Mystery Shopping Survey' 23 April 2002.
[70] I Mullen, 'Promoting Financial Inclusion', 14 December 2002 (BBA) available at <http://www.bba.org.uk>.
[71] Above n 65 at 6.

per year.[72] The changes to the way that benefits, state pensions and war pensions are paid will mean that the post office remains important.[73] All recipients of such payments will need a bank or building society account, a basic bank account or a post office card account.[74] The Treasury Committee was less than wholehearted in its support of the concept of the Universal Bank, arguing that it is 'primarily an attempt to bolster post office business and to preserve access to pensions and benefits where such access would be lost by Post Office closures'.[75] There is no doubt that this is an important part of the Government's strategy for the Post Office. Patricia Hewitt, the Secretary of State for Trade and Industry, said that the initiative 'brings us a step closer to our aim of creating modern, vibrant post offices at the heart of local communities'.[76] Many of the main financial services providers signed contracts with Post Office Ltd to provide access to basic bank accounts through the post office.[77] The relationship between basic bank accounts and the Universal Bank is clearly very close.

Creating Duties to take into Account the Needs of Communities

An alternative approach, for which there has been some support in the UK, is to create legal duties similar to those found in the Community Reinvestment Act (CRA) in the USA.[78] The Act obliges financial institutions to show that their deposit facilities serve the convenience and needs of the community in which they are chartered to do business. This includes the need for credit as well as the need for deposit services.[79] This

---

[72] The US experience of such matters has not been an entirely happy one. Although the US Treasury designed the Electronic Transfer Account, (ETA) a low cost account designed to facilitate the payment of electronic benefits, it was forced by public pressure to allow consumers to receive benefits in more traditional ways. See J Lee, 'The Poor in the Financial Market: Changes in the Use of Financial Products, Institutions and Services' (2002) *Journal of Consumer Policy* 203 at 212.

[73] A similar idea had been put forward by the No.10 Efficiency Unit established by Margaret Thatcher under Sir Derek Rayner, but failed to find support. See Sir Peter Kemp, 'Why Don't the Banks Like the Universal Bank?' above n 17.

[74] The Post Office Card Account is a new account that is operated by the post office for the purpose of receiving the state payments mentioned above. It does not allow direct debit or standing orders and will not receive other payments such as wages although it does, of course, allow withdrawal of cash via card and PIN.

[75] Treasury Committee, above n 68 para 11.

[76] 'New Post Office Banking Contracts Another Step Forward for Customers' (DWP Press Release 11 December 2002).

[77] In May 2003 the institutions associated with the scheme were: Abbey National, Alliance and Leicester, Bank of Ireland, Bank of Scotland, Barclays, Clydesdale Bank, Co-operative Bank, First Trust Bank, Halifax, HSBC, Lloyds TSB, Nationwide, NatWest, Northern Bank, Royal Bank of Scotland, Ulster Bank, Woolwich and Yorkshire Bank.

[78] 1997 12 USC 2901. See I Ramsay and T Williams, 'Racial and Gender Equality in Markets for Financial Services' in P Cartwright (ed) *Consumer Protection in Financial Services* (London, Kluwer Law International, 1999) 265.

[79] See J Lee, above n 72 at 207–08.

is subject to the requirement that the bank's actions must be consistent
with the sound and safe operation of the bank. Each institution's record is
regularly evaluated.

Although the lack of sanctions for non-compliance is frequently
viewed as something of a weakness, there are some powers available that
should give banks cause for concern. Examinations are carried out by the
federal agency responsible for the institution in question. The appropriate
agency then produces an evaluation of the institution, which includes a
rating and a statement describing the basis of the rating. This is made
public.[80] The Act could be seen primarily as an information-based measure, acting to shame the banks into action, and highlighting possible
forms of invidious discrimination.[81] For example, the bank must maintain a file which it makes available to the public for inspection. This
includes, inter alia, all written comments received from the public about
the bank's performance in meeting community credit needs, and the
bank's response, a copy of the public section of the bank's most recent
CRA Performance Evaluation prepared by the Federal Deposit Insurance
Corporation (FDIC), and a list of services generally offered at the bank's
branches and descriptions of material differences in the availability or
cost of services at particular branches, if any. There is clear value in having this information in the public domain, and it appears that banks take
the information seriously.

Despite the criticisms that can be made of the CRA for lacking 'bite',
the performance of an institution under the CRA is taken into account by
the agency. For example, the FDIC takes performance into account in considering an application for approval of: the establishment of a domestic
branch or other facility with the ability to accept deposits; the relocation
of the bank's main office or a branch; the merger, consolidation, acquisition of assets or assumption of liabilities; and deposit insurance for a
newly chartered financial institution. In relation to new financial institutions, a newly chartered institution must submit a description of how it
plans to meet CRA objectives with its application for deposit insurance.
When considering the application the FDIC will take this description into
account, and may deny approval on that basis. There does seem to be evidence that banks make great efforts to ensure that they receive a
favourable CRA rating. It has been argued that banks do maintain
branches in low-income areas that they would close purely on economic
grounds to this end, although it is difficult to quantify the effect that the
CRA has had on branch closures.[82] In relation to the provision of credit, in

[80] Community Reinvestment Act, above n 78 s 2906.
[81] Ramsay and Williams, above n 78 at 276–77.
[82] See R Avery *et al*, 'Changes in the Distribution of Banking Offices' (1997) *Federal Reserve Bulletin* 707; Financial Services Authority, *In or Out?* above n 1, paras 6.41–6.42.

particular mortgages, it has been argued that the CRA 'has led many banks to initiate strong outreach efforts to identify low-income and minority households with acceptable credit risk profiles who are interested in becoming homeowners'.[83]

There is no equivalent of the CRA in the UK. However, the Company Law White Paper's concept of an 'Operating and Financial Review' (hereafter, OFR) has some similar elements. The introduction of such a review can be justified in part on the basis of the need for further information to assess the position of major companies and their future prospects. However, it has been suggested that a further justification concerns

> the need to provide a check of the discharge by directors of their inclusive duty to the members to promote the success of the company on the basis of taking into account the company's need to foster its relationships with stakeholders, its impact upon communities affected and the environmental and reputational concern.[84]

How the OFR will work in practice is still unclear. The Operating and Financial Review Working Group, which was set up in December 2002, published a Consultation Document in June 2003 to examine elements of the topic. The Company Law Review (CLR) argued that there were some items that should always be covered by an OFR. These were, the company's business and business objectives, strategy and principal drivers of performance; a fair review of the development of the business over the year and position at the end of it; and the dynamics of the business.[85] There were also items that should be included whenever the directors judge them to be material. These included matters such as corporate governance, values and structures, key relationships with employees, customers, suppliers and others, and policies and performance on environmental, community, social, ethical and reputational issues. Directors are to decide what is material for their particular business. It seems likely that companies will feel obliged to publish information on these matters. As Davies observes: 'it is difficult to believe that the directors of any major company could make a nil return under all these heads on the grounds that these matters were not relevant to an understanding of their company'.[86] But what effect in practice will this have? The CLR states that the purpose of the OFR is 'to show, in the director's own terms, what matters about the business as regards performance and direction'.[87]

---

[83] Financial Services Authority, *In or Out?* above n 1, para 6.48.
[84] Davies, above n 24, at 549.
[85] Department of Trade and Industry, *Modern Company Law for a Competitive Economy: Final Report* (DTI) June 2001, para 8.40 available at <http://www.dti.gov.uk>.
[86] Davies, above n 12 at 549–50.
[87] *Modern Company Law*, above n 85 para 8.33.

The White Paper opines that companies which fail to provide adequate information 'will risk adverse comparisons and questions from shareholders and others'.[88] To the extent that the OFR raises questions about whether the company's approach is in touch with consumer expectations it may have some benefit. In the context of banks, it may be that on the basis of information contained in the OFR, consumers feel that inadequate attention has been paid to a bank's moral obligation to the communities it serves and take their business elsewhere. Withdrawal of business can be seen as the ultimate sanction. But it must be questioned how far disclosure of this type will provide an incentive for banks to fulfil some the social responsibilities that we have identified.

Creating New Modes of Delivery: Sharing Branches

Much of the negative publicity that banks have received in recent years has centred on decisions taken to close branches. It was mentioned above that by the end of 1998 there were 14,904 branches of banks and building societies in Britain, 5679 fewer than 10 years previously. There is little doubt that many consumers value personal contact via a branch.[89] Research on retailing has found that consumers frequently go shopping looking for social contact, and branch banking plays a part in that.[90] However, there is little doubt that branch banking is costly for financial services providers. The Cruickshank report found that using a branch counter for a transaction costs about £1. The operating costs of British banks in the 1980s were estimated to amount to 65 per cent of their gross income.[91] The cost of operating a telephone banking service, by contrast, has been estimated at less than 50 per cent of a branch-based service.[92]

Given the importance attached to branch banking by consumers, but the huge cost disincentives to providing them, it might not be surprising that efforts have been taken to provide a middle way. One such approach has been the sharing of branches. Research by Kempson and Jones examined the extent to which individuals and small businesses faced difficulties because of the distance they lived from bank branches.[93] The authors looked at a number of ways by which these needs could be met, such as by cash machines, agency banking arrangements through the post office

---

[88] *Modernising Company Law*, above n 22 para 4.33.
[89] This is particularly strong among less affluent consumers. See KPMG, *Distribution in Retail Banking* (London, KPMG, 1998), cited in *Vulnerable Consumers and Financial Services*, above n 4 para 317.
[90] AM Forman and V Sriram, 'The Depersonalization of Retailing' (1991) 67(2) *Journal of Retailing* 226.
[91] Organisation for Economic Co-operation and Development, *Banks Under Stress* (OECD 1992), cited in *Vulnerable Consumers and Financial Services*, above n 4 para 312.
[92] Above n 4 para 312.
[93] E Kempson and T Jones, *Banking without Branches* (London, BBA, 2000).

network, and shared banking services. In January 2002 the British Bankers' Association started the Shared Banking Services (SBS) pilot scheme with support from Barclays, HSBC, Lloyds TSB and NatWest. The Scheme allowed personal and small business customers at 10 sites across England and Wales, to undertake simple banking services through the branch of another participating bank.

The pilot does not appear to have been as successful as might have been hoped, or expected. An independent review of the service found that overall, the SBS attracted an additional nine visits a day at each branch. Although it provided 'a really valuable service to the minority of people who chose to use it', the Report felt that the needs of customers could be met in other ways. In the case of personal customers the obvious way would be through Post Office bank agency agreements. The Report concluded that 'it is difficult to see how [the SBS agreement's] continuation could be justified by the banks'.[94]

Other Modes of Delivery

The Post Office has been seen by many as the solution for delivering financial services to less affluent consumers. But other solutions are possible, and it may be that innovation on the part of financial services providers means that a variety of alternatives will emerge. Access to cash is clearly of concern to many consumers, and the most obvious means of access is via automated teller machines (ATMs). Although bank branch closures have meant that certain channels have been cut off, there is no need for ATMs to be placed at, or even near, banks. The number of ATMs has increased dramatically in recent years, with some being placed in areas that may be helpful to communities who are poorly served by banks.[95] Transactions can, of course, be conducted without branches via telephone and internet banking, but even with increasing numbers of households having access to these facilities, it seems unlikely that they will be appropriate for the least affluent consumers. Other possibilities include the use of supermarkets, or not for profit organisations such as credit unions and community banks.

Facilitating the Opening of Accounts

Research suggests that the majority of those who do not have a bank account choose not to have one. According to the Office of National Statistics, of those identified without an account, only three per cent had

---

[94] E Kempson, *Evaluation of a Pilot Service* (Personal Finance Research Centre, April 2003) at 50.
[95] PAT 14 gives the example of Bank of Scotland placing ATMs in convenience stores on council housing estates, above n 3 para 4.45.

either been refused one or had their accounts closed by their banks.[96] However, it is generally thought that opening an account is more difficult than it needs to be because of the identification requirements that have been put in place to counter money laundering. The law requires banks to ensure that potential customers provide evidence of their identity and address before opening an account. The British Bankers' Association (BBA) website suggests that if consumers do not have a passport, driving licence, utility bill or council tax bill then they should ask the banks what other documentation they accept. The BBA suggests that banks might accept a letter from a 'responsible person' who knows the consumer and can confirm their name and address.[97]

Consumer Credit

The Office of Fair Trading identified short-term consumer credit as an essential financial service. Although borrowing is often seen as worsening the position of more vulnerable consumers, it has been argued that it is frequently unavoidable.[98] For example, less affluent consumers may need to borrow to purchase essentials.

From the point of view of access, credit raises particular issues. Most fundamentally, credit subjects consumers to harmful risks in a way that many other financial services do not. Any discussion of credit needs to take into account the problems created by indebtedness, which is frequently the result of credit being too easily accessed, rather than too difficult to access.[99] There is little evidence of consumers not having any access to credit. The problem is that where consumers cannot access credit from mainstream suppliers, they are forced instead to look to alternative sources of credit, and this creates further problems. Put simply: 'being excluded from credit has come to mean being unable to access *mainstream* credit facilities'.[100] Any examination of access to credit must be viewed in this context.

The two main groups who are likely to be denied access to mainstream credit have been identified as those with poor credit records or a history of bad debt, and those living on low incomes.[101] The first group will frequently look to the non-status lending market. This market encompasses

---

[96] E Kempson and C Whyley, *Access to Current Accounts* (BBA, August 1998) at 17.
[97] British, Bankers' Association, 'Advice on Account Opening Documentation' available at <http://www.bba.org.uk/public/consumers>.
[98] E Kempson and C Whyley, *kept out or opted out* above n 10 at 25.
[99] In the year to March 2002, Citizens Advice Bureaux dealt with nearly 650,000 debt enquiries. (National Consumer Council, *Rating Credit*, January, 2003).
[100] *In or Out?* above n 1 para 3.120.
[101] *Ibid.*

firms that specialise in offering credit to higher risk customers at higher than usual rates of interest. Loans will frequently be secured on the borrower's property, and may well be for the purpose of repaying existing debts. The borrowers are overwhelmingly likely to be in social classes C, D or E. Although many firms are reputable, there is evidence that others engage in predatory sales practices and, where the loan is secured, have little regard to the ability of the borrower to repay. The second group, those on low incomes, will generally look to the alternative credit market such as money lenders, pawnbrokers, and mail order catalogues. The most vulnerable may be forced to deal with unlicensed moneylenders.[102] Although those using the alternative credit market will generally do so because they will be unable to secure credit from other sources, it has been pointed out that some borrowers choose this market. Reasons given for this have been identified as:[103]

> easy simple and non-bureaucratic access; simple, straightforward and transparent products; manageable repayments made on a weekly basis, that do not require banking facilities; no hidden charges or penalties for default; and a flexible and sympathetic approach to repayments.

It is important that these factors are borne in mind. If consumers understand that they are paying more for credit, but are content to do this because of the flexibility and other characteristics of the transaction then such arrangements may not be as problematic as they appear at first. Regulatory efforts should perhaps be concentrated upon increasing transparency and promoting competition, while, of course, taking enforcement action against those in contravention of the law. Rowlingson concludes that 'by and large, customers of moneylenders are happy with the service they receive and are not exploited by the companies'.[104] But this picture may not reveal the full story. In many cases, customers may not be aware of the availability of other forms of credit, and how costs compare. Indeed, Rowlingson accepts that 'there is … evidence that customers do not fully understand and compare the costs of credit through using the APR'.[105] A recent campaign by 'Debt on Your Doorstep' has targeted Provident Financial, one of the best known firms, criticising its interest rates (and its profits).[106] The NCC is also campaigning for tougher action against non-status lending, including better policing of lenders, paid for by an

---

[102] *Ibid* para 3.121.
[103] *Ibid*, para 3.145.
[104] K Rowlingson, *Money Lenders and their Customers* (London, Policy Studies Institute, 1994) at 151.
[105] *Ibid* at 155–56.
[106] See E Mayo, 'Credit and Debt: Key Questions' speech to the Trading Standards Institute (TST) Conference, 25 June 2003.

increased licence fee, and more emphasis on responsible lending. These arguments appear to have had some influence on the Government's White Paper, which is considered below.[107]

One possible solution to issues of access to credit would be for mainstream banks and other financial institutions to become more involved. It would be possible for banks to take greater account of the individual circumstances of the consumer through risk-based pricing. It appears that the majority of mainstream lenders would prefer not to lend than to lend to high-risk borrowers at a level that reflects that risk. Furthermore, the difficulty is sometimes one of inadequate information on the part of the provider. As the Cruickshank Report noted: '[b]anks ration credit through the use of automatic scoring techniques. So having no transaction or credit history often means no loan from mainstream providers, at any price'.[108] A very different approach is taken by those companies that specialise in providing credit in the sub-prime market. Whereas major mainstream lenders charge high penalties to those who default, those dealing with the sub-prime market build the risk of default into the price of the loan. The result is that defaulting consumers subsidise good consumers in the former case, but good consumers subsidise defaulting consumers in the latter.[109] It appears unlikely that pressing mainstream lenders to provide credit to less affluent consumers will be a viable solution without some degree of compulsion. As we have already seen, the Government has been willing to put some pressure on banks to provide access to basic bank accounts, but it is highly unlikely to pressurise them into providing cheaper loans.

The Government has stated its commitment to reforming the Consumer Credit Act 1974, and its latest thinking being found in the Consumer Credit White Paper. The White Paper is in large part concerned to deal with lending practices that relate to poorer consumers. It is beyond the scope of this article to go into detail on the proposals, but it is important to flag up some of the likely changes. First, action will be taken to try to improve the information that consumers receive both before and after they enter a contract.[110] Secondly, efforts will be made to tackle unfair practices, for example by making it easier for consumers to secure redress, and reforming the provisions for dealing with unfair credit bargains.[111] In addition, the licensing regime, which is widely considered to be ineffective,

---

[107] Department of Trade and Industry, *Fair, Clear and Competitive: The Consumer Credit Market in the 21st Century* (Cm 6040, December 2003) (hereafter 'the White Paper').
[108] Cruickshank Report, above n 5 para 7.3.
[109] A Leyshon, D Burton, D Knights, C Alferoff and P Signoretta ,'Towards an Ecology of Retail Financial Services: Understanding the Persistence of Door-to-Door Credit and Insurance Providers' (forthcoming in *Environment and Planning A*).
[110] Above n 107 para 2.22.
[111] *Ibid* para 3.3.

will be reformed.[112] Thirdly, illegal money lenders (loan sharks) will be tackled, with the aims of bringing illegal money lenders to court more frequently, and 'creating a climate where victims can come forward—confident that prosecutions will be undertaken, and convictions obtained, without fear of reprisals.'[113] Finally, the Government is keen to tackle overindebtedness.[114] Some of the initiatives mentioned above should help in this regard. In addition improving financial literacy through better education and awareness, which is discussed below, will also be central to reducing overindebtedness. But one additional factor should be mentioned. The Consumer Credit White Paper makes reference to a recently much used term: 'responsible lending'. It looks as though the concept of responsible lending may become increasingly important as a means of protecting consumers. The proposed Consumer Credit Directive, has recommended introducing 'know your client' rules, with a view to making lending more responsible. The borrower would be required to disclose all relevant information to the lender when asked, and in return, the lender would be subject to know your client obligations. This would mean that lenders would have to advise on the most appropriate product in its product range and assess the ability of the borrower to repay before granting credit.[115] The White Paper emphasises the role of self-regulation in encouraging responsible lending, noting the role of the Office of Fair Trading in encouraging trade associations to develop codes of practices to deal, in particular, with firms' dealings with vulnerable consumers.[116] The White Paper also notes that the FSA's mortgage regime covers responsible lending practices and aims to ensure that lenders take closer account of the consumer's ability to pay. The White Paper states that the Government will support the inclusion of a duty on creditors to lend responsibly in the forthcoming Consumer Credit Directive. How precisely this is likely to be implemented is unclear, and the White paper states merely that 'Government, industry and the voluntary sector will look at how to deliver the requirements of the Directive'.[117]

Although it is impossible to disagree with the desirability of taking action against those lenders that adopt clearly objectionable tactics, there is a risk that increased regulation could have an undesirable exclusionary effect. Martin Hall, Director General of the Finance and Leasing Association has argued that some of the changes 'could easily backfire, increasing the cost of credit and creating credit deserts for consumers

---

[112] *Ibid.*
[113] *Ibid* para 5.59.
[114] The DTI has, for example, established a Taskforce on Tackling Overindebtedness.
[115] Art 9.
[116] Above n 107 para 5.63.
[117] White Paper, above n 107 para 5.67.

with little or no access to the mainstream market'.[118] Keith Mather, the Director General of the Consumer Credit Trade Association was more encouraging, arguing that 'if the government is sensible and balanced about the way this is implemented, I don't think lenders will retrench or be more cautious about providing credit.'[119] It seems unlikely that the UK Government's proposals will have a significant exclusionary effect and some initiatives, which could have this result to a limited extent, appear to be more than justified on the basis of the benefits that they bring for less affluent consumers. However, it is clear that some Member States are pressing for more interventionist measures in the new Directive, including the imposition of interest rate ceilings, which, however well-intentioned, might not bring the benefits hoped for.[120] In particular, unless banks (and other lenders) are placed under an obligation to provide loans to less affluent consumers at a particular rate of interest, they are likely to respond to interest rate ceilings by withdrawing loans to those they deem too great a risk.[121]

The risk that increased regulation will remove an important source of credit for some less affluent consumers raises difficult questions about the role of consumer credit law and the consequences of regulation. The Crowther Committee argued that 'there is a level of cost above which it becomes socially harmful to make loans available at all, even if the cost is not disproportionate to the risk and expense incurred by the lender'.[122] Although this may appear to be an admirable approach, the risk is one of regulatory backfiring, where the result of the regulation is to push the consumer into an even more perilous situation. In such circumstances, it is vital that alternative modes of borrowing are provided.

There is considerable support among commentators for credit unions to take on an increasing role as providers of credit for less affluent consumers. One characteristic of credit unions is that they require their members to save before they can borrow, with the amount of credit linked to the amount saved. The Government appears to regard credit unions as playing a central role in the provision of credit, particularly for poorer consumers. In the words of the Economic Secretary to the Treasury '[t]here is plenty of scope for credit unions to develop their role in the UK and the Government is keen to see them succeed'.[123] There is particular

---

[118] J Croft, 'Shake-Up May Harm Poor's Attempts to Borrow Money' *Financial Times* (9 December 2003).
[119] *Ibid.*
[120] See D Cayne and M Trebilcock, 'Market Considerations in the Formulation of Consumer Protection Policy' (1973) 23 *University of Toronto Law Journal* 396.
[121] *Ibid* at 414–18.
[122] HM Treasury, *Report of the Committee on Consumer Credit* (the Crowther Committee) (1971, Cmnd 4596) para 6.6.6.
[123] R Kelly MP, 'Tackling Financial Exclusion as Part of the Social Exclusion Agenda', 5 July 2001.

support for the development of US-style Community Development Credit Unions, of which there are currently about 460 in the UK. There is considerable literature on credit unions and their role will not be tackled in detail here.[124] Suffice it to say that recent indications are that the Government still sees credit unions at the heart of the provision of banking services. In the Consumer Credit White Paper, the Government argues that '[t]he credit union ethos of thrift, financial planning and self-help, together with their ability to offer access to affordable loans, means they are well placed to make an important contribution to tackling financial exclusion'.[125]

A final point concerns the role of the Government in providing credit to consumers. The Social Fund operates a system of interest free 'budgeting loans' which provide help for important day to day costs that are difficult to budget for.[126] In addition, the Fund provides 'crisis loans' which are designed to help in an emergency or disaster which puts the applicant and/or his or her family at a risk to their health and safety. Loans are discretionary and are aimed at those receiving income support or income-based job-seeker's allowance. The Chancellor of the Exchequer has described the Fund as providing 'a safety net of grants and interest free loans for the most vulnerable in times of crisis'.[127] In 2002–03 the Social Fund made £4.5 million awards with a gross expenditure of over £820 million. There have been strong arguments for reform or abolition of the Social Fund.[128] In its 3rd Report for 2000–01, the Select Committee on Social Security argued that while those on the lowest incomes struggle to repay even interest free loans from their weekly benefit 'there does appear to be the potential for the role of the Social Fund to be expanded to a wider group of people, offering interest free loans to people excluded from normal credit markets'.[129] In the 2003 Budget the Chancellor of the Exchequer announced an additional £90 million for the Fund over the three years to 2005–06, so there is some evidence of a commitment to the Fund's expansion. The Government has also stated its commitment to reforming the Fund, although it is unclear precisely what that will entail. The Consumer Credit White Paper states that the Department for Work and Pensions is 'looking to see what further improvements can be made

---

[124] See for example M Brown, P Conaty and E Mayo, *Life Saving: Community Development Credit Unions* (2003, NEF/ NACUW/ NCC).

[125] The White Paper, above n 107 para 5.49.

[126] For details of the Social Fund see <http://www.dfwp.gov.uk>.

[127] HM Treasury, *Pre Budget Report 2003*, 10 December 2003, available at <http://www.hm-treasury.gov.uk/pre_budget_report/prebud_index.cfm> at para 5.77.

[128] For an interesting account of the rationales behind the introduction of the Social Fund see G Craig, 'Classification and Control: The Role of Social Fund Loans' in G Howells, I Crow and M Moroney (eds), *Aspects of Credit and Debt* (London, Sweet and Maxwell, 1993) 109.

[129] HM Treasury, Select Committee on Social Security 3rd Report HC 2000–01 (27 March 2001), para 123.

to enhance the ability of the social fund to help those on low incomes manage their finances'.[130]

CONCLUSIONS

If it is accepted that it is desirable that consumers have access to appropriate banking services, and that the free market will not provide that access, it is important to think of how it may be delivered. As is generally recognised, this is not a problem for which there is a single simple solution. Banks can be encouraged, or perhaps compelled, to develop products that better serve the needs of the less affluent, and there is likely to remain a role for the state in relation to certain types of provision. As Wilhelmsson argues, it is possible to find justifications for placing duties on banks to take account of the needs of the less affluent, and this can be done on a number of bases. However, the arguments are not as strong as those justifying the placing of such duties on privatised utility companies for the reasons explained above. Perhaps the strongest argument in favour of expecting banks to fulfil some 'social justice' obligations is that (at least in relation to larger banks) the state provides an implicit guarantee to their continuance. While the Financial Services Authority has argued that no bank should *expect* to be bailed out automatically, it is clear that the FSA's objective of ensuring market confidence will mean that some banks will be regarded as too big to fail. The *quid pro quo* for this safety net might be seen to be the taking on of business in the name of social justice and financial inclusion. In addition, new suppliers and modes of supply can be encouraged, and the Government's commitment to the expansion of credit unions and the use of the post office network for banking suggest that this will be a significant factor in the battle to improve access.

It is important to remember that while there will be occasions where consumers have no access to a particular product or service, in many cases the problem will be lack of access to an appropriate product or service. This is particularly apparent where credit is concerned. The White Paper contains some details of the Government's approach to consumer credit reform, and, as explained above, the initiatives are to be welcomed. Although there is some risk that the reforms might have a limited exclusionary effect, it is submitted that this is a price worth paying for the increased protection that consumers will receive. It does reveal, however, the importance of thinking about how credit might be provided through alternative sources.

For all forms of financial services, improving supply can provide a partial solution, but it is also important that consumers are helped to make

---

[130] The White Paper, above n 107 para 5.48.

appropriate choices from the forms of supply available. It is therefore important that the discussion in this chapter is viewed in conjunction with that in the rest of the book, and in particular, chapter three. Improving public understanding of the financial system through information, advice and education lies at the heart of this. The FSA has the objective of improving public understanding of the financial system, and this relates closely with its objective of providing the appropriate degree of protection for consumers. Whatever changes are introduced to the substantive law, it is important that sufficient attention is paid to tackling financial exclusion through improving financial education. The Cruickshank Report's observation that: '[t]he strongest curb against the mis-selling of financial products is to equip customers with the knowledge and confidence to ask the right questions and to seek out the best products or the ones which suit them best' remains a central message for those concerned to tackle financial exclusion effectively.[131]

---

[131] Cruickshank Report, above n 5 para 4.127.

9

Conclusions

INTRODUCTION

T HIS BOOK EXAMINES the role of the law in regulating banks in the interests of the consumer. Banking is one of the most closely regulated industries and in the UK, that regulation has become more transparent, visible and focused since the passing of the Financial Services and Markets Act 2000 (FSMA). This chapter draws together some of the books themes, and sets out its principal conclusions.

REASONS AND OBJECTIVES

Section 2(2) of FSMA sets out the regulatory objectives of the Financial Services Authority (FSA) and s 2(3) sets out the principles of regulation that the FSA is obliged to consider. How effective they are as a method of accountability is a matter for debate, but there is no doubt that they provide a helpful focus for the FSA, as well as a useful benchmark by which to judge its actions. To some extent, all the objectives and principles have implications for consumer protection, although those of most direct and obvious relevance to this are the consumer protection and public awareness objectives. However, it has been pointed out that the market confidence objective also links closely with them. Consumers are unlikely to be adequately protected where market confidence is lacking, and market confidence depends to some extent on consumer confidence. This confidence is provided in part by an adequate regime for consumer protection. Chapter two has emphasised that prudential regulation—regulation to minimise the risk of firms failing with adverse consequences for consumers—is an important element of consumer protection.[1] As the FSA has recently accepted, however, the extent to which a regulator can be expected to prevent the failure of banks is a topic not clearly understood by consumers.[2]

---

[1] See also D Llewellyn, *The Economic Rationale for Financial Regulation* (FSA Occasional Paper 1, April 1999) at 18.

[2] Financial Services Authority, *Reasonable Expectations: Regulation in a Non-Zero Failure World* (FSA, September 2003) para 2.10.

Chapter two explained that regulation (including intervention to save failing banks) can be justified from an economic perspective. The principal economic justifications for the regulation of banking are the threat of systemic risk and the existence of information asymmetry, both of which are examples of market failure.[3] There is a close connection between the threat of systemic risk and the need to maintain market confidence. Indeed, perhaps the main reason that maintaining market confidence is important is that it minimises the chance of systemic risk. Market confidence is maintained, and systemic risk avoided, in a variety of ways. These include imposing minimum standards through the prior approval process, ensuring those standards are maintained by continuous supervision, providing incentives not to withdraw deposits and so initiate bank runs through depositor protection schemes, and providing the possibility of emergency assistance, for example through a lender of last resort.[4] As explained in chapter two, the nature of fractional reserve banking means that such measures are necessary. In relation to information asymmetry, it is argued that the informational disparity between parties, in particular banks and consumers, justifies regulation to address it. This is considered in more detail in chapter three, and is considered below. However, the existence of market failure does not automatically justify regulation to correct it. As Howard Davies has argued, 'regulation, or any form of official intervention, is only justified ... where the cure is not worse than the original disease'.[5] It is therefore important to undertake some form of cost–benefit analysis before deciding whether, and if so how, to proceed.

Despite the centrality of market failure to justifying regulation, it is also possible to find justification on non-economic or social grounds. We might, for example, seek to justify regulation because of the redistributive benefits it brings, and the values it protects. The main examples were identified in chapter two as distributive justice, paternalism and community values.[6] The essence of these rationales is that regulation is justified on the basis of what is fair and decent, rather than solely on the basis of what is economically efficient.[7] Throughout the book, reference is made to the redistributive effects of regulation. In short, regulation imposes costs and produces benefits, and how that regulation is designed determines who pays (and how much) and who benefits (and how much). The key, of course, is to try to design regulation that produces the desired results. For the FSA, this means the results that accord most

---

[3] See H Davies, 'Why Regulate?' Henry Thornton Lecture, City University Business School, 4 November 1998.
[4] See eg C Goodhart, *The Central Bank and the Financial System* (Basingstoke, MacMillan, 1995) ch 17.
[5] Above n 3.
[6] See also A Ogus, *Regulation: Legal Form and Economic Theory* (Oxford, Clarendon Press, 1994) ch 3; I Ramsay, *Consumer Protection: Text and Materials* (London, Weidenfeld and Nicolson, 1989) ch 2.
[7] A Ogus, *ibid* at 46.

closely with its regulatory objectives. Where the consumer protection and public awareness objectives are concerned, there might appear to be relatively little room for the FSA to seek social justice-based outcomes.[8] However, while there is no doubt that FSMA does not include some objectives that would have given the FSA more of a social justice focus (particularly in terms of providing access to financial services), there is room within the objectives to ensure that socially just results are achieved. In particular, the public awareness objective has led to the FSA playing an important role in encouraging financial capability, and tacking financial illiteracy. This raises an issue to which we will briefly return later—that regulation does not fall neatly into specific categories when we try to justify the theoretical basis for its use. It should also be remembered that the FSA is not the only body with responsibility for banking regulation. Consumer credit law, for example, falls within the responsibility of the DTI, and is enforced largely at a local level by trading standards officers. As will be seen below, much conduct of business regulation in banking is performed through the *Banking Code*. Within each of these areas, there is room for social justice objectives to be met.

TOPICS AND TECHNIQUES

It has already been mentioned that one of the principal economic justifications for banking regulation is the existence of information asymmetry. The most relevant example of this informational disparity for our purposes is that between consumers and their banks. Despite arguments that banks, like other producers, are under sufficient incentives to ensure that consumers are appropriately informed about their products, and that where they are not the market will provide a solution, there are good reasons to believe that this will not always be so.[9] Chapter three argues that it is important to think about the various types of information that consumers need in order for them to be able to make informed choices in the marketplace. The chapter divides them into the following rough groupings: financial education; product information; institutional information; and rights and redress. It is accepted that there will be overlaps here—the division is provided merely as a framework for analysis rather than as a rigid taxonomy. What this division reveals is that consumers have needs for very different types of information, and that different consumers will have very different needs at different times.

---

[8] Taylor comments that with the exception of the public awareness role of the FSA there has been little extension of regulation to promote social objectives. See M Taylor, 'Accountability and Objectives of the FSA' in M Blair *et al*, *Blackstone's Guide to the Financial Services and Markets Act 2000* (London, Blackstone Press, 2001) 17 at 34.
[9] See Office of Fair Trading, *Consumer Detriment Under Conditions of Imperfect Information* (OFT Research Paper 11, prepared by London Economics, August 1997) para 3.2.

There has been a tendency for the consumer protection law of many jurisdictions to see the correction of information asymmetry or deficits as the principal justification for consumer protection. Hadfield, Howse and Trebilcock argue that information deficits provided 'the key analytical basis for early consumer protection law', and many commentators have emphasised the supremacy of information remedies.[10] Correcting information asymmetry is a means of helping the market to function, and can be justified both on the basis of efficiency and ideology. In terms of efficiency, better information facilitates shopping around, which provides incentives for suppliers to improve quality and lower prices. In relation to ideology, information helps consumers to make choices consistent with their preferences, and so protects the integrity of individual decision-making. Focusing upon information remedies frequently reflects the idea that consumers are, and should be encouraged to be, sovereign rational maximisers of their own utility. To some extent, this view is reflected by the consumer protection objective in FSMA, which refers to 'the general principle that consumers should take responsibility for their decisions'.[11] Information remedies can play some role in improving the ability of the consumer to take such responsibility.

Despite the undoubted value of improving the supply of information to the consumer, a key concern with relying on information remedies is that they may have unintended distributive consequences. Wilhelmsson has drawn attention to what he calls the information paradigm.[12] He argues that as information measures are neutral as to their recipients this produces 'an advantage for the consumers who are well-equipped to use the information'. He therefore concludes that 'measures based on the information paradigm may reproduce and even strengthen social injustice'.[13] There is evidence that where consumer protection law focuses on disclosure, its benefits may be mainly to those consumers already better-placed to protect themselves.[14]

However, it may be that rather than move to alternative forms of regulation, we should concentrate on addressing information asymmetry in a more constructive way. The FSA's public awareness objective may show the way forward. By focusing on issues such as financial literacy and capability, and looking in detail at how consumers are likely to

---

[10] H Hadfield, R Howse and M Trebilcock, 'Information-Based Principles for Rethinking Consumer Protection Policy' (1998) 21 *Journal of Consumer Policy* 131. See also H Beales, R Craswell and S Salop 'The Efficient Regulation of Consumer Information' (1981) 24 *Journal of Law and Economics* 491.
[11] FSMA s 5(2)(d).
[12] T Wilhelmsson 'Consumer Law and Social Justice' in I Ramsay (ed), *Consumer Law in the Global Economy* (Aldershot, Dartmouth, 1997) 217 at 223.
[13] *Ibid* at 224.
[14] See eg WC Whitford, 'The Functions of Disclosure Regulation in Consumer Transactions' (1973) *Wisconsin Law Review* 400 at 414.

engage with information provided, the FSA is able to overcome some of the obstacles to consumers' ability to deal with information provided. It has been suggested, for example, that '[t]he strongest curb against the mis-selling of financial products is to equip customers with the knowledge and confidence to ask the right questions and to seek out the best products or the ones which suit them best'.[15] The National Consumer Council has similarly commented that consumer education 'empowers people so they can interpret information, negotiate, make judgements and choices, enquiries and complaints'.[16] By adopting a close understanding, and a broad interpretation, of the information that consumers need, we may more effectively be able to rely on information remedies as a consumer protection tool. The FSA's establishing of a strategy for financial capability is likely to play an important role in addressing these issues and further details of the strategy are awaited with interest.[17] This is considered further below.

Improving the provision of information (broadly interpreted) to consumers is therefore an important technique within the regime for regulating banks in the interests of the consumer. However, perhaps the main technique that has been used to regulate banking is prior approval, otherwise known as screening, licensing or authorisation.[18] Prior approval gives a regulator the power to screen out institutions which fail to meet minimum standards. Continued supervision ensures that once authorised, banks continue to meet those standards. Although it might in theory be possible for consumers continually to monitor the performance of banks, in practice this is unrealistic. It has been argued that, 'in effect, consumers delegate the task of monitoring to a regulatory agency'.[19]

There seems little doubt that prior approval will be central to any regime for regulating banks. It gives a significant degree of authority to the regulator to determine who operates within the banking system, and the standards upon which they operate. As the FSA has argued, it is more likely to meet its regulatory objectives by setting and enforcing standards for entry, than by addressing problems later.[20] The degree of power vested in the regulator represents both the strength and the weakness of this form of regulation. The first difficulty concerns the effect that prior approval is liable to have on competition. It is likely to reduce the number

---

[15] *Competition in UK Banking* (the Cruickshank Report) (March 2000 para 4.127).
[16] National Consumer Council, *Consumer Education: Beyond Consumer Information* (NCC, 2001).
[17] See Financial Services Authority, *Towards a National Strategy for Financial Capability* (FSA, 2003).
[18] See A Ogus, above n 6 ch 10.
[19] D Llewellyn, above n 1 at 25.
[20] Financial Services Authority, *A New Regulator for the New Millenium* (FSA, January 2000) para 50.

of banks in the market, and might have the effect of protecting incumbents at the expense of potentially beneficial competition.[21] This could reduce efficiency as well as consumer choice. It might also lead to regulators being 'captured' by the regulated.[22] Prior approval schemes are also expensive to operate compared with other forms of regulation. Moreover, as with most other forms of regulation, these costs are largely hidden, leading potentially to over-demand by consumers.[23] A final risk to consider here is that prior approval may lead to consumers being under a false sense of security. Taylor has identified the risk that 'a regulatory regime might result in a shifting of responsibility from the firms' management to the supervisory authorities'.[24] Even if regulators do not take on that responsibility, there is still the risk that consumers believe that they have. In the context of consumer credit it has been argued that consumers will see the holding of a licence as a guarantee of competence and legitimacy.[25] This takes us back to a central issue, already mentioned, of the divergence between consumer expectations and the reality of what regulation can be expected to deliver. It could be argued that the more visible and intensive the regulation, the more consumers are liable to reply upon it, rather than on their own judgment. However, despite these concerns, there is little doubt that prior approval, as perhaps the clearest example of preventive regulation, is of enormous importance in protecting the consumer of banking services.

The prior approval regime under FSMA ensures, as far as possible, that banks meet the minimum standards set out in the *FSA Handbook*. In many areas of retail banking legislation plays relatively little part, self-regulation being the regulatory technique of choice. The UK has relied heavily upon the *Banking Code* to control the relationship between banks and their customers.[26] The *Code* was created following the recommendations of the Jack Committee and has been through various manifestations.[27] Aiming to set standards of good banking practice for institutions to follow when dealing with consumers in the UK, the *Code* now covers a wide variety of

---

[21] It has been noted that prior approval generally has the support of the occupation in question. See W Gelhorn 'The Abuse of Occupational Licensing' (1976) 44 *University of Chicago Law Review* 6 at 11.

[22] See MH Bernstein, *Regulating Business by Independent Commission* (Princeton, Princeton University Press, 1955).

[23] '[T]he potential benefits of extra regulation/supervision are patent, and the costs are nearly indiscernible'. C Goodhart *et al*, *Financial Regulation: Why, How and Where Now?* (London, Routledge 1998) at 63.

[24] M Taylor, 'Accountability and Objectives of the FSA' in M Blair *et al*, *Blackstones Guide to the Financial Services and Markets Act 2000* (London, Blackstone Press, 2001) at 35.

[25] See Department of Trade and Industry, *A Consultation Document on the Licensing Regime under the Consumer Credit Act 1974* (DTI, 2002) para 2.4.1.

[26] The *Banking Code* (March, 2003).

[27] See *Banking Services Law and Practice: Report by the Review Committee* (the Jack Report) (Cm 622, February 1989) ch 16.

products including accounts, card products and services and loans and overdrafts.[28]

The *Code* has certainly brought benefits for consumers. In some cases it merely reflects existing law, but even this can be beneficial. As already noted, an important element in consumer protection is improving consumer awareness of the way the banking system operates, and their rights within that. Provided the *Code* is properly advertised, it can play a valuable role here. Furthermore, in some cases the *Code* goes further than the law requires, for example in the protection it offers to consumers whose cards are misused.[29] Chapter five notes that one of the advantages of codes of practice is that they can contain provisions that would be more difficult to incorporate into legislation. Codes are, after all, designed to go beyond the legal minima. The *Banking Code*'s first independent reviewer concluded that the *Code* should continue to be 'principle-based', with its Guidance for Subscribers setting out how those principles should be interpreted in practice.[30] The main concerns with the *Code* are those of self-regulation more generally. Banks have to decide whether to subscribe to the *Code*, so its coverage is not universal, although in practice it is substantial. Perhaps more significant is the issue of compliance. The task of ensuring compliance with the *Code* is undertaken by the *Banking Code* Standards Board (BCSB) through a combination of compliance inspections and market research activities such as mystery shopper visits. This system is a step forward from that undertaken by the *Code*'s former Independent Review Body, and is cited by the National Consumer Council (NCC) as an example of best practice.[31] When it comes to enforcing the *Code* by disciplining breaches, there is a question mark over the effectiveness of the BCSB's powers. The NCC has emphasised the needs for 'adequate, meaningful and commercially significant sanctions for non-compliance', and it is not certain that this is satisfied.[32] The BCSB's Board has a variety of sanctions at its disposal, including publishing details of the bank and the breach in the Annual Report, issuing directions as to future conduct, issuing recommendations on the remedy of past conduct, issuing a warning or reprimand, cancelling or suspending a bank's registration, or publicly censuring the subscriber.[33] There has been some support for these powers. The *Banking Code* Review Group, for example, argued that the power to fine was not necessary on the basis that 'reputational risk via "naming and shaming" presents a powerful

---

[28] In some cases it operates alongside legislation such as the Consumer Credit Act 1974.
[29] *Banking Code* s 12.
[30] E Kempson, *Independent Review of the Banking and Business Codes* (November 2002) para 2.3.
[31] National Consumer Council, *Better Business Practice* (January 2001) at 12.
[32] *Ibid.*
[33] *Banking Code* Standards Board, *Compliance Policy*, cl 3.2 (available at <http://www.banking-code.org.uk>).

sanction for ... [the BCSB's] members'.[34] However, this absence of a power to impose fines remains perhaps the principal concern. As chapter five explains, adverse publicity can potentially have a significant impact upon banks, but it does mean that the sanction is determined by 'the capricious jury of public opinion'.[35] Despite these concerns, it is concluded that the *Banking Code* has brought benefits for consumers, and with some development can continue to do so alongside more interventionist forms of regulation.

In a perfect market there is little need for regulation. As outlined above, consumers in such a market are perceived to be sovereign rational maximisers of their own utility, with suppliers responding to their demands. Where problems do occur, they are resolved by consumers switching or suing. Suppliers are thus incentivised to comply with consumers' demands if they are to remain in the market. In practice, markets are imperfect, and consumers are unable to play the roles ascribed to them by economic theory. The limitations posed by information asymmetry and systemic risk have already been identified. But even where information is accurate and helpful, and externalities such as systemic risk are not present, consumers may still be unable to control the market in the ways outlined. For the market to function effectively, consumers need to be able to implement their rights effectively under the private law. The traditional method for so doing might be seen as litigation under the law of contract. However, consumers face transaction costs when trying to establish private law rights, with the result that many wrongs go uncorrected. Litigation is time consuming, expensive and unpredictable, and consumers are classic examples of 'one shotters' dealing with the banking industry's 'repeat players'.[36]

These difficulties can be addressed in a number of ways. Where there is a strong regulatory system in place, with minimum standards enforced, occasions for individual redress should be less frequent. Furthermore, the regulatory framework may allow for enforcement action to be taken against banks, in some cases resulting in redress for consumers.[37] Secondly, there may be intervention in the private law to expand consumers' rights, for example by creating a regime for the control of unfair terms in consumer contracts, or allowing consumers to challenge a credit

---

[34] Banking Services Codes Review Group, *Cracking the Codes for Banking Customers* (May, 2001) para 3.14.
[35] B Fisse and J Braithwaite, *The Impact of Publicity on Corporate Offenders* (Albany, State University of New York Press, 1983) at 310.
[36] M Galanter 'Why the 'Haves' Come Out Ahead: Speculations on the Limits of Legal Change' (1974) 9 *Law and Society Review* 95.
[37] This might include, for example, trading standards officers prosecuting banks under the Consumer Credit Act 1974 or the FSA applying for an order for restitution under s 382 of FSMA.

agreement on the grounds of it being extortionate.[38] However, perhaps the most important way of addressing the difficulties identified is to introduce an effective form of alternative dispute resolution (ADR). The form of ADR favoured in the UK for dealing with consumers' complaints about financial services has been the ombudsman, and this has now been put on a statutory footing with the creation of the Financial Ombudsman Service (FOS). Chapter six looks in some detail at the role of the FOS. It concludes that financial ombudsman schemes have brought considerable benefits to consumers, and that they are a vital means of overcoming some of the transaction costs (in particular enforcement costs) that consumers face in obtaining redress. They still involve the individual taking action, and so reflect what Wilhelmsson refers to as the 'individual claims paradigm'. He concludes that where consumer protection law rules 'require some form of reaction on the part of individual consumer in order to become effective', they will tend to benefit only more affluent and better informed consumers.[39] However, these problems are considerably reduced where redress is available through an ombudsman scheme rather than merely a court.

In some cases, consumers' claims for redress are for compensation where the banks with which they deal have become insolvent. The avenue for redress here is provided by deposit protection schemes. Deposit protection schemes play two vital roles in banking regulation. First, they provide a payout to consumers in the event of a bank being unable to meet its liabilities to depositors. Secondly, by providing the guarantee of such a payout, they reduce the incentive for depositors to initiate a run on the bank should rumours develop about the bank's solvency. Given the speed with which rumour can spread, and the difficulties faced by consumers in distinguishing between those banks that are adversely affected and those that are not, deposit protection schemes therefore play an important role in maintaining market confidence and minimising the chance of systemic risk. This demonstrates again the close relationship between market confidence and consumer protection.

Despite the importance of deposit protection schemes, it is possible to criticise the UK scheme, and some of the assumptions upon which it is based. First, although the scheme protects 100 per cent of the consumer's first £2,000, it protects only 90 per cent of the next £33,000 and nothing thereafter. The 10 per cent loss that the consumer must bear is referred to as 'co-insurance'. The justification for it is that moral hazard would arise were consumers to be more fully protected. It is sometimes suggested that

---

[38] See the Unfair Terms in Consumer Contracts Regulations 1999 (SI 1999 no 2083), and the Consumer Credit Act 1974 ss 137–40.
[39] Above n 12 at 224.

where consumers are subject to co-insurance, they have strong incentives to choose banks carefully and monitor them closely.[40] Were a higher degree of protection to be provided, the suggestion is that consumers would act irresponsibly.[41] However, it is doubtful that consumers are able effectively to perform these functions. In most cases they lack the information and expertise to choose carefully, and monitor closely, the banks with which they deal. Indeed, in many cases consumers choose bank deposits ahead of other investments because they are perceived as low risk. It is therefore questionable whether the risk of moral hazard is as great as is sometimes suggested. Secondly, the idea that consumers will be under an incentive to monitor their banks is based on the assumption that they know that they are subject to limited protection. Research suggests that consumers lack this basic knowledge.[42] It is possible that many consumers believe that their deposits are fully protected. It is also possible that they believe that their deposits are not protected at all. If they believe the former, then they are under incentives to take little care when choosing a deposit, and to leave their deposit where it is if the bank is rumoured to be in trouble. If the latter, then while they are under an incentive to take care (even though, as has been argued, most will be unable to carry this out) they will also be under an incentive to withdraw their deposits at the first hint of difficulty. This would be likely to raise the spectre of systemic risk. There is no easy solution to this problem. Attempts by states such as New Zealand to improve information and market incentives, and to forego reliance on deposit protection schemes have some supporters, but it is questionable whether consumers can really play the role envisaged for them.[43] What is important is to take steps to raise awareness of the consequences of particular actions and so to try to encourage those who are able to make informed choices to do so, while providing an appropriate degree of protection to those who are not. This will not be easy, but can in part be addressed through the financial capability initiatives mentioned above.

Consumer protection law tends to focus on how consumers are protected in their dealings with business. However, a number of important studies have focused on the rights of those who do not have the same access to mainstream products or services as the majority. The debate on how to tackle financial exclusion forms an important part of this

---

[40] See Financial Stability Forum, *Guidance for Developing Effective Deposit Insurance Systems* (FSF, September 2001).

[41] *Ibid* at 8.

[42] Research for the FSA indicates that consumers are confused as to the level of protection they receive from the regulatory system. See Financial Services Authority, above n 2 para 2.12.

[43] See D Mayes, *A More Market Based Approach to Maintaining Systemic Stability* (FSA Occasional Paper 10, August 2000).

discussion. Chapter eight examines whether it is appropriate to require banks to provide certain banking services to consumers where they would not, on a simply economic basis, do so. There are difficult policy arguments here, and the solution is not clear. Perhaps the most appropriate conclusion is that multi-pronged action is necessary to address some of the most concerning elements of financial exclusion. Banks appear to have made some steps forward in the provision of basic bank accounts. While it looks as though considerably more could be done to bring these products to the attention of those consumers who would benefit most from them, the willingness of banks to develop the products is an important start. In relation to loans, it is important that attention is paid to the suppliers of credit to less affluent households. As has been emphasised 'being excluded from credit has come to mean being unable to access mainstream credit facilities'.[44] The best solutions here may be to encourage alternative forms of supply, for example from credit unions, while trying to take action against illegal money lenders. Unfortunately, one possible effect of initiatives requiring lenders to engage in responsible lending is that they may be less inclined to deal with less affluent consumers. The Director General of the Finance and Leasing Association has warned the risk of creating 'credit deserts for consumers with little or no access to the mainstream market'.[45] Although this may be going too far, it does reveal the risk of 'regulatory backfiring', where regulation creates unintended and counter-productive consequences.[46] Perhaps the best conclusion is provided by the words of the Crowther Committee, that, 'there is a level of cost above which it becomes socially harmful to make loans available at all, even if the cost is not disproportionate to the risk and expense incurred by the lender'.[47] This returns us to the issue of paternalism, which is considered below.

CONCLUDING THOUGHTS AND THEMES

Several themes run through this book, and it seems appropriate to identify three here. The first is that there is an important role for the law in regulating banks and banking, and that such regulation can be justified on both economic and social grounds. The most obvious justification for

---

[44] Financial Services Authority, *In or Out? Financial Exclusion: A Literature and Research Review* (FSA, July 2000) para 3.120.

[45] J Croft, 'Shake-up May Harm Poor's Attempts to Borrow Money' *Financial Times* (9 December 2003).

[46] See C Sunstein, *Free Markets and Social Justice* (New York, Oxford University Press, 1997) ch 11.

[47] Report of the Committee on Consumer Credit (the Crowther Committee Report) (Cmnd 4596, 1971) para 6.6.6.

regulation is market failure (the FSA has recently argued that market failure provides *the reason* [author's itallics] for regulation), although the question whether correcting the market failure is cost-effective will still have to be asked.[48] However, there are non-economic or social rationales for regulation too. These recognise that by focusing on the economic rationales for regulation, we pay little attention to issues of distribution. As has been argued, '[r]egulation may be inspired by a desire, which is quite distinct from efficiency aims, to achieve a "fair" or "just" distribution of resources'.[49] Likewise, and as indicated above, paternalism may provide a justification for intervention. There is a growing acceptance that consumers are not the rational maximisers of their own utility that they are sometimes thought to be, and that regulation should reflect this.[50] One way of so doing is by accepting that, on occasions, the choice of some consumers will need to be limited. In some cases this will be on the grounds of practicality. As Ogus recognises, paternalistic regulation 'has to proceed by applying uniform controls on certain activities where it is assumed that many individuals make unwise decisions'.[51] Furthermore, it is important to recognise that when it comes to examining specific examples of regulation, they will frequently defy neat categorisation on the basis of the rationales that justify them. Many of the provisions considered in this book can be justified on economic and non-economic grounds.[52] Indeed, it is worth noting the observation of Ramsay that 'it is often very difficult to distinguish between situations where governments are responding to problems that prevent individuals from reaching a rational judgment and those where government is overruling preferences and substituting its own judgment'.[53]

A second argument is that there are many different available regulatory techniques and that an effective system of banking regulation is likely to utilise a variety of them. Despite the risks of prior approval mentioned in chapter four, it remains a hugely important technique where banks are concerned. The Basel Committee's *Core Principles for Effective Banking Supervision* emphasise the need for states to have a

---

[48] Financial Services Authority, above n 2.

[49] Ogus, above n 6 at 46.

[50] See the growing body of literature on behavioural approaches to law and economics. Eg, see C Jolls, C Sunstein and R Thaler 'A Behavioural Approach to Law and Economics' (1998) 50 *Stanford Law Review* 1471. For an alternative approach see R Posner 'Rational Choice, Behavioural Economics and the Law' (1998) 50 *Stanford Law Review* 1551.

[51] Ogus, above n 6 at 53.

[52] A good example is that of deposit protection schemes which can be justified on grounds of the existence of information asymmetry and systemic risk, or on grounds of paternalism or distributive justice. See ch 7.

[53] I Ramsay, 'Consumer Redress and Access to Justice' in C Rickett and T Telfer (eds), *International Perspectives on Consumers' Access to Justice* (Cambridge, Cambridge University Press, 2003) 17 at 21.

licensing authority that can set criteria and reject applications that fall short of them.[54] What is important is that the risks of prior approval are taken into account, and that regulators are sensitive to some of the possible adverse results from such an interventionist form of regulation. Likewise, information remedies and self-regulatory standards can be beneficial and address some consumer interests that the unregulated market might not address. What may be necessary is a re-focussing of effort to better identify why consumers may suffer detriment and why they find it difficult to take responsibility for their decisions, as is expected of them by the FSA. Whether this be through ignorance, lack of financial capability, lack of appropriate financial products or the absence of effective avenues for redress, the regulatory system, broadly understood, can play an important role.

The final point concerns the relationship between what consumers are entitled to expect of regulation, and what regulation is entitled to expect of consumers. The importance of financial education, and the raising of both public awareness and financial capability have been emphasised as fundamental to an effective consumer protection regime. The FSA has made important steps forward in this regard, and its 2003 publication *Towards a National Strategy for Financial Capability* is indicative of the seriousness with which this will be addressed in the future.[55] In short, the strategy is about 'providing consumers with the education, information and generic advice to make their financial decisions with confidence'.[56] The success of this will be measured on the basis of how well target groups have been reached, how well awareness, understanding and confidence have been changed, and how well changes in specific behaviour have been achieved.[57] The strategy is extremely welcome. It shows the FSA's determination to encourage consumers to reach the levels which, as noted above, were championed by the Cruickshank Report.[58] It should be read alongside another important FSA initiative—that relating to consumer understanding of the regulatory regime. The FSA has for some time stated that it runs a non-zero failure regime. The FSA does not guarantee that firms (including banks) will not fail, and consumers should not necessarily expect it to. But it is clear that this message is not always being received. The report of the Parliamentary Ombudsman into Equitable Life identified 'the fundamental mismatch between the nature and expectations of the prudential regulatory regime ... and the understanding and

---

[54] Basel Committee, *Core Principles for Effective Banking Supervision*, Principle 3.
[55] Financial Services Authority, *Towards a National Strategy for Financial Capability* (London, FSA, 2003).
[56] *Ibid* at 3.
[57] *Ibid* at 16.
[58] Above n 15.

expectations that policyholders and others appear to have had of that regulatory system'.[59] This is backed up by empirical research.[60]

This book is, of course, concerned primarily with regulating banks (rather than other financial services firms) in the interests of the consumer. It seems likely that if consumers expect the regulatory regime to guarantee the survival of insurance companies, then they are equally likely to expect such a guarantee in relation to banks. Indeed, some consumers will be aware of the arguments that some banks will be saved at all costs, as they are 'too big to fail'.[61] There might even be some implicit support for that approach in the FSA's literature. The regime, the FSA has stated, seeks to ensure

> as low an incidence of failure of regulated firms and markets (especially failures which would have a material impact on public confidence and market soundness) as is consistent with the maintenance of competition and innovation in the markets.[62]

As one of the FSA's statutory objectives is maintaining market confidence, failures of banks that might impact significantly upon that confidence will have to be treated seriously. As indicated by the quotation, the FSA has to take competition and innovation into account, but these are merely the principles of regulation, not the objectives of regulation. It is market confidence that represents a statutory objective. While the FSA recognises the importance of encouraging competition, it can be seen as subordinate to maintaining market confidence. Where market confidence is likely to be adversely affected to such an extent that systemic risk may arise, swift and decisive intervention can be expected. In the UK, this will involve close liaison between the FSA, the Bank of England and HM Treasury.[63] What this means is that it is legitimate for consumers to expect intervention where statutory objectives (such as market confidence) can be met proportionately. The difficulty for the consumer (and the regulator) is to know when the failure of a firm is likely to have such an impact upon objectives such as market confidence that action to save it is justified. It has been argued that the FSA is likely to regard some banks as too big to fail, because of the effect that such failure would have on market confidence, but it will not always be clear which banks fall into this category.[64]

---

[59] The Parliamentary Ombudsman, *The Prudential Regulation of Equitable Life*, cited in *Reasonable Expectations*, above n 2 para 1.3.
[60] Financial Services Authority, above n 17 paras 2.10–2.13.
[61] See Goodhart, above n 4 ch 17.
[62] Financial Services Authority, above n 20 para 4.
[63] On the basis of a Memorandum of Understanding agreed between them.
[64] Indeed, this 'constructive ambiguity', where regulators deliberately make it difficult to predict how they will react in given situations, can be justified on the basis of the need to reduce the risk of moral hazard. However, it risks reducing market confidence. See A

One of the arguments against bailing out failing firms, or indeed fully compensating consumers following a bank failure, is that it provides undesirable incentives.[65] Consumers, as we have seen, should be expected to take responsibility for their decisions where they can. Where they are immune from such responsibility economic theory tells us that moral hazard emerges. The FSA describes moral hazard as 'the danger that providing protection or insurance against an event occurring may increase the probability of that event occurring by changing behaviour in a more risk-seeking manner'.[66] But as our discussion of deposit protection suggests, moral hazard is only generated by regulation where consumers are aware of the protection they are likely to receive and act on this. It seems likely that many consumers are unaware of the protection they receive from the regulatory system. There is therefore likely to be a mismatch between consumers' expectations of what regulation can deliver, and the reality of what it is designed to deliver. In theory, this can be addressed through improving public awareness. But this does not address the fundamental problem of improving consumers' ability to make informed choices. Even if consumers are aware of their protection there is a question over how much care than can be expected to take. Efforts to bring more effective market discipline into the regulatory system may be well-intentioned, but consumers are frequently ill-placed to play a significant part in that discipline. If consumers are unable to exert market discipline then moral hazard may not pose the threat that is sometimes suggested. Improving public awareness and financial capability are unquestionably important, but it should be remembered that there will always be a vital role for regulation where consumers cannot meet the high standards that economic theory expects of them.

Campbell and P Cartwright, *Banks in Crisis: The Legal Response* (Aldershot, Ashgate, 2002) at 69–70.

[65] It should be remembered that there are many ways for the regulatory system to deal with a failing bank. See T Asser, *Legal Aspects of Regulatory Treatment of Banks in Distress* (Washington, IMF, 2001); A Campbell and P Cartwright, *ibid*; and E Hupkes, *The Legal Aspects of Bank Insolvency: A Comparative Analysis of Western Europe, The United States and Canada* (The Hague, Kluwer Law International, 2000).
[66] Above n 2 para 4.27.

Index

Printed in the United Kingdom
by Lightning Source UK Ltd.
134285UK00002B/31-33/A